IRAN AND AMERICA

Re-kinding a Love Lost

By

Badi Badiozamani, Ph.D.
Ghazal Badiozamani

PUBLISHED BY EAST-WEST UNDERSTANDING PRESS

Badi@Badi.net or www.Badi.net

In affiliation with the
**Center for East-West
Understanding**

Library of Congress Control Number: 2005903817

ISBN: 0-9742172-0-4

Cover and Text Design by John Cole, Santa Fe, NM

Printed in the United States of America

To the memory of Professor Abdolhamid Badiozamani,

To Mehrangiz (Nasreen), Ghazal & Ghazalle,

To all those whom I love,

To those who promote Human Rights and freedom,

To those who strive to bring peace and harmony to the world,

To the Center for East-West Understanding,

To Iran & America

CONTENTS

PART 1

PART II

PART III

ACKNOWLEDGEMENTS

To acknowledge those who graciously gave the benefit of their time, insight, knowledge, and expertise is an impossible task. This work would not have been possible without their valuable contributions.

A particular debt of gratitude goes to the late Professor Yahya Armajani who was the inspiration, the guiding light and the major source of information for this book. The tapes of the lectures given by him at the authors' residence as well as his library and personal notes and writings that were inherited by the authors, provided an ocean of information and intellectual wealth. I must thank M.R. Kargar and Ahmad Chaychi, Director and Deputy Director of the National Iranian Museum, for their assistance in providing information as well as many photographs. Further, I would like to express my gratitude to Mrs. Roohangiz (Parvaneh) Mohammadi, Dr. Tajalli Saghaie and Sepehr Irandoost for the invaluable support they provided me in Iran.

PROLOGUE

"You look around the world at potential trouble spots, (and) Iran is right at the top of the list...." U.S. Vice President Dick Cheney made it clear during an interview with MSNBC on President Bush's inaugural day that Iran will be the focal point of United States foreign policy in President Bush's second term. Indeed, Iran's recent efforts to acquire advanced nuclear technology highlight the urgency of the need to devote attention to this ancient country.

The question of how best to engage Iran to ensure peaceful disarmament is at the top of the world's diplomatic agenda. Hassan Rowhani, Iran's equivalent of national security adviser and the nation's chief negotiator on the nuclear issue the best way to guarantee that Iran would not build bombs was if it could develop "a close and comprehensive relationship" with the West. "The tone of their remarks has been unsuitable," he said, "We are not seeking tension with the United States. We are seeking to resolve our problems with America but it's the Americans who don't want the problems to be resolved. There is no problem in today's world that can't be resolved."

It seems that the United States has taken this advice to heart; the Bush Administration recently joined the European Union in the effort to engage Iran through diplomacy. This marked difference in strategy, as compared with other interventions in the Middle East, reflects the vast difference between the people, history and potential force of Iran and its neighbors.

Moreover, other developments in the Middle East such as the nuclear testing by Pakistan, the war in Afghanistan against fanatic Moslems and Al Qaeda terrorists, the toppling of the regime of Saddam Hussein in Iraq and the continuing pursuit of Middle East peace have once again put the spotlight on Iran as a potential force whose power must be reckoned with and utilized as a stabilizer. As Karim Sadjadpour, an analyst in Tehran for the International Crisis Group recently stated, "The paradox of Iran is that it just might be the most pro-American - or, perhaps, least anti-American - populace in the Muslim world." In a recent survey, nearly three-fourths of the Iranians polled said they would like their government to restore dialogue with the United States. This potential for partnership is the motivating factor in pursuing a diplomatic path, and as I will argue with this book, should be informed by the long and turbulent history of engagement between Iran and the United States.

In the light of these developments, it is appropriate for Americans –businesspeople, tourists, scientists, diplomats, and the general public as well as young Iranians all over the world- to be offered a fresh set of information on this ancient nation by someone who is both Iranian and American by the virtue of having spent half of his life in both countries. In the following work, the reader will find answers to many questions such as: who are Iranians? Where do they come from? Why are Iranian and Persian used interchangeably? Why do many of them consider their country a super power? Is Iran as new as Iraq and Pakistan-its neighboring countries whose boundaries came to existence only a few decades ago - or as ancient as the Greek and Roman empires? How long has America known Iran? Who were the first Americans who went to Iran? What has America done for and to Iran? What contributions have the Iranians made to the world and to the United States? And above all, how can peace, friendship and economic relations be re-established between Iran and America?

Finally, the epilogue encompasses the notion of Iran as a superpower, its major role and its unique geophysical presence in the Caspian region as well as in the Persian Gulf, why relations between Iran and the U.S. should be resumed and on what terms, and similarities between the two nations. Also in this section, a published article by two prominent professors on the reasons why resumption of diplomatic and scientific relations is of utmost significance for world safety in relation to nuclear energy is quoted in its entirety.

INTRODUCTION

One characteristic that Iran has displayed through the years has been an astonishing continuity. Home of one of the most ancient civilizations of the Old World, Iran has seen its civilization continuously renewed for over 100 centuries. Various evidences, especially those from the Archeological Museum of Tehran, prove that since the fourth millennium before Christ, the civilization of Susa, or rather the civilization of which Susa was one of the most brilliant examples, extended as far as the Caspian. Many excavated objects establish that pure Iranian art was already established in Azerbaijan during the 8th century B.C. Yet another evidence, the paintings found in a cave in the southwestern part of Iran, date back to 40,000 years before Christ.

The torch thus lit upon the Iranian plateau at the dawn of history has never been extinguished. The arrival of the Macedonians in 331 B.C. did not even amount to an interlude. Alexander not only failed to Hellenize Iran; he Iranianized himself by proclaiming that he was the successor of Dariush-King of Kings- and Xerxes. Soon the Parthian Arsacids (who we know today were pure Iranian) in 238 B.C. and then the Persian Sassanids in 224 A.D. restored the beautiful continuity of the Empire of the King of Kings. Even Eslam did not break this tradition as Mazdean spiritualism found its ultimate consummation in Eslam, in the same way that Platonic spiritualism found its ultimate expression in Christianity.

What Eslam caused (637 A.D.) was a brief visible rupture not a breakdown of real continuity. Iran embraced Eslam with faith and in doing so found itself once again. Even more, Iran found in Eslam new means for action, a new radiance, because the coming of Eslam to Iran had to a large extent the reverse effect of carrying the Iranian spirit to vast areas of the Moslem world. History is unwavering in its recognition of the leading role

that Iranian scholars, thinkers, and artisans, as well as Persian administrators, played in Abbasid civilization, as much with the Arab caliphs as
at the Turkish court.

The impact of Iranian civilization was so powerful that it assimilated
the foreigners established on its soil with great facility. After only a few
number of years Saljooghs (Saljuqs)-a Turkish speaking tribe of Irano-Turkish stock in mid 11th century-, Mongols (13th century) and Turkamans had
become as completely Iranian as the Scandinavians became French in Nor-
mandy. Each time, through the same radiance of its civilization, Iranian-
ism has reappeared with renewed vitality, continuing to yet another renaissance.... Clear examples are the Samanid and Buyid renaissance of the
10th century and the Safavid renaissance of the 16th and 17th centuries.

This continuity, unbroken through so many centuries, has enabled Iran
to develop a civilization which is profoundly humane and which has displayed this quality ever since its first appearance in history. According
to the Greeks as well as the Bible, the Achaemenian Empire distinguished
itself by its tolerance towards all religions and all the races as well as by
the comprehensive and beneficial character of its administration. The Sassanians, although very pious Mazdeans, showed no less tolerance towards
the Christian Nestorian Church (which became a second national church),
in the West than to Buddhism in the East, to which they lent their painters
and sculptors.

Inspired by this broadly humane ideal, by this persistent life of the
spirit, Persian literature has given birth to a classicism of merit as universal as Greco-Roman classicism in the West, and to a humanism equally rich
in spiritual treasures as that of the western Renaissance. The influence of
Persian poets like Sa'adi, Hafez and Mowlavi (Rumi) and Omar Khayyam
has been felt not only by everyone in Persia; throughout the Eslamic world,
in all of Turkish and Arab Asia, but by all who in the Occident taste the
pure lyricism of inspiration in complete perfection of the form.

Iran has the privilege of being both Orient and Occident at the same
time. Its grammar and vocabulary remain clearly Indo-European, thus
keeping its mind frame very close to that of the Western nations. And yet
it holds all the values of Moslem civilization to which it itself has contributed so much.

The richness of the Iranian tradition has enabled it to welcome the
most diverse influences without ever renouncing its own identity. Hellenis-
tic influence, Arab influence, Sino-Mongol influence have each in their turn
been accepted, assimilated, and Iranianized. Plato and Aristotle, carried
on by the Avicennas, the Ghazalis, and the Sohrevardis, received their nat-

uralization papers in Persia, while Chinese art on numerous occasions has been welcomed there with interest.

A true Central Empire at the heart of the ancient world, Iran, without losing any of its own originality, served as a link between East and West. Its language became the literary language in part of Moslem India. Its art, in the Sassanian era, coincided with the development of the Byzantine art, and in the Safavid period, with the formation of the Indo-Mongol art. Its architecture and its miniatures spread as far as Golconda and Bengal. In the late Middle Ages, Buddhism had introduced the Iranian schools of painting into China, and it was missionaries coming from Iran, who, in the Sassanid and Abbasid periods, carried Christianity to the heart of the Chinese Empire.

Research shows that at the time of Marco Polo it was Persian that served as the commercial language, the language of civilization throughout Central Asia-from Bokhara to Peking.

As history records, Iran has served mankind well because it made the powerful and refined culture which it developed over the centuries into an instrument of peace and harmony among the nations. The most diverse races communed and continue to commune through Iranian thought and poetry. Persian poets, as we have noted, have attained universality. The sentiments that they express directly affect an American just as they do an Indian, a Turk or a Russian. The Persian mystics, while profoundly Moslem, speak no less to the heart of a Christian, a Jew or a Brahman. They too belong to humanity as a whole.

The major problem of the present time is perhaps that of reconciling East and West. Iran's cultural capabilities and resources can be best utilized so that an accord is realized. Through the genius of its language and thought, and through the example of all its history, Iran can once again become a place where East and West are harmoniously reconciled.

GEOGRAPHY

Iran is a land of great contrasts: a land of snowy mountains and luxuriant valleys, of deserts and jungle. Three mountain ranges form a triangle around the land. The smaller, volcanic Sabalan and Talesh ranges in the northwestern provinces of Azarbaijan provide fertile pastures. The very long, Jurassic-era Zagross range stretches from northwestern province of Kordestan to Bandar-e Abbas in the southeast. Alborz range stretches from the Caucus and Azarbaijan in the northwest towards northeast passing south of the Caspian Sea. Within the mountain ranges are valleys, some as much as sixty miles long and twelve miles wide. There are two vast deserts at the heart of Iran, the Dasht-e Kavir (more than 200,000 sq. km in size) and the Kavir-e Lut or Dasht-e Lut (more than 166,000 sq. km). Rainfall varies from sixty inches in the dense jungle bordering the Caspian Sea in the North to zero in some parts. Iran is 4.5 times the size of California, twice as populous (65 million) and rich in minerals and oil and stands as the world's second largest gas resource.

PART I

CHAPTER ONE

LOVE AT FIRST SIGHT

As they stepped foot onto the fertile soil of the Azarbaijan province, the young couple stared in amazement at the breathtaking range of snow-clad mountains and the pristine lake that welcomed them. Sent by the American Board of Commissioners for Foreign Missions in Boston to visit the Assyrians (otherwise knows as Nestorians) in northwestern Iran, Harrison Gray Otis Dwight and Eli Smith settled into the town of Oroomieh (Rezaiyeh) in 1830 as the first two Americans ever to visit Iran. Four years later, the Rev. Justin Perkins, D.D. tutor at Amherst College, and his wife arrived in Tabriz to shepherd the Christians in Oroomieh. Asahel Grant, M.D. and his wife joined the Mission the next year and they all set out together on a journey from Tabriz for Oroomieh. Arthur Judson Brown, Secretary Emeritus of the American Board of Commissioners For Foreign Affairs writes in One Hundred Years, A History of the Foreign Missionary Work of the Presbyterian Church in the United States of America that they "were warmly received by crowds of Assyrians who came out to meet them beating drums and timbales on November 20, 1835."[1] Both Americans and Persians were exalted by the possibility of mutual cooperation. During their time in Persia, several of the missionaries wrote extensively of their adventures. The first American book ever published about this country was in all likelihood by Dr. Grant.[2] Perkins also wrote a narrative of his eight years in Iran[3] and another on Missionary Life in Persia. Later, his son wrote about the life of that pioneer group.[4]

As Missionaries, the goal of the group was not only to spread the faith of Christianity, but to aid the community in its development. In 1834 Mohammad Shah Ghajar (Qajar Dynasty) granted Rev. Justin Perkins the authority to start the first American school in Oroomieh to educate the youth in history, geography, arithmetic and geometry.[5] It did not take the spirited mission long to lay the foundations of a new edifice for knowledge and there came into existence at Oroomieh not only a school but a large hospital as well. Gradually more than forty village schools and secondary schools were built in that area. Similar institutions were created in Tabriz, Hamadan, Kermanshah, Rasht, Mashhad and Tehran.[6]

The first girl's school in Iran was the American Girl's School opened in Tehran on April 24,1874. It was initially called Iran Bethel and later Noorbakhsh. In 1889 Nasser-e-din Shah showed interest in the American Girl's School. He issued orders for payment of the sum of 100 Toomans annual subsidy to the school. The student body of 77 included a Moslem and a Jew.

When Nasser-e-din Shah received reports that both American as well as Moslem girls attended the school his interest was further peaked. On the morning of Nov. 4, 1890, sixteen years after its establishment, the Shah and his courtiers paid a visit to the school. He was curious to know what the girls had learned. He ordered one of the girls to the board and asked her to write something. The nervous girl was totally unable to write anything. The Shah took the chalk from the girl's hand and wrote a few words in Latin and Persian.

The Shah then inspected the school. He was even interested to inspect the sleeping quarters, but was dissuaded from doing so. Two years later, when he received a report stating that the Moslem girls were wearing high-heel shoes and getting dressed in the fashion of American girls, he barred Moslem girls from attending the American School. The restriction, however, was lifted after the fasting month of Ramazan.[7]

The Start of Political Relations

On December 13, 1856, during the administration of President Buchanan and the reign of Nasser-e-Din Shah, the relationship was formalized in the Treaty of Friendship and Commerce in Constantinople (Istanbul). The agreement, containing eight Articles, and was signed on behalf of Iran by Iran's Ambassadors Farrokh Khan Ghaffary Amin-ol-Molk and the United States Minister Carroll Spence.[8] This treaty was the first formal relation between the two countries and set a precedent for further American participation in Iran. Although the missionaries had initiated the interchange of cultures, it was the government that would have to establish a political exchange.

Among the Missionaries who gradually traveled to Iran were a sister and brother-in-law of Congressman Dawes. The presence of the couple and their link with the House of Representatives undoubtedly helped to accelerate and promote the establishment of an official interchange. The Bill for the Establishment of a Legation in Tehran was introduced and put through by Congressman Dawes. Representative Dawes, with the help of his wife, eventually wrote a history of this effort based of official documents and notes exchanged between the two governments[9], thus further contributing to the publicity of formal relations.

Throughout the 1880s, Dawes repeatedly appealed to the Secretary of State in connection with events in Oroomieh, such as sectarian disputes, and urged for immediate action to protect American lives. Throughout the nineteenth century Britain and Russia intrigued in Iran, jealously sought to draw Iran into its sphere of influence. Pursuing its basic policy of isolation and non-entanglement, the United States carefully avoided entering this field of European confrontation. Furthermore, the American people knew nothing about Iran and were not interested. There was no public opinion to back up legislative measures relative to this situation. Dawes started an intensive campaign from the very platform of the House. On February 6, 1882, he called for the file of difficulties, confronted American citizens and stressed the need to establish diplomatic relations between the youngest yet strongest government in the world and the oldest nation of Yore, which wielded the greatest power as a torchbearer of civilization. His claims were echoed by many of the American Foreign Service.

On May 2, 1887, American Minister John W. Foster reported from St. Petersburg to the State Department that there was a strong desire by the Iranians for an American post in Iran. Having stopped in London on his way to his post in St. Petersburg, Foster met Iran's Minister to the Court of St. James who expressed the wish that the United States Government assigned a representative to Iran. The same impression had been left by the Shah himself when speaking to the American Consul General on his visit to Russia several years before. In St. Petersburg, Iranian Ambassador Mirza Hossain Khan Sepahsalar, on his mission to offer congratulations to the Czar on the occasion of the latter's accession to the throne, expressed regret that the United States Government had no official relations with Iran even though the existence of a Treaty of Friendship and Commerce between the two countries made such relations a necessity. The Ambassador argued for creating a formal post by pointing out that American vessels visited Iranian ports and American citizens lived in Iran. Since the cost of living in Tehran was very low, the United States could have a

Charge d' Affaires without incurring too much expense.

There was no doubt in Foster's mind that his government's representative would be welcome in Iran. His report proved successful in its aim.

On August 3, 1882, the Foreign Relations Committee submitted a bill to the House requesting an appropriation of five thousand dollars to cover the salary of a Charge d'Affaires and Consul General in Tehran. One of the representatives did not see why, in the absence of sufficient trade relations, the United States should have a consul General in Iran. Representative Williams of Wisconsin, who was defending the bill, pointed to the fact that the bill was submitted to the House Committee on behalf of two Secretaries of State at the request of the United States Minister to St. Petersburg, representatives Curtin from Pennsylvania and Mr. Kasson, former American Minister to Australia.

To prove that there was indeed extensive trade with Iran, Mr. Kasson wrote to the State Department that Iran's annual trade was between 18 to 20 million dollars, 12 million representing imports and 7 million exports. He argued that American cotton might find its way to Iranian markets and American kerosene was already on sale in Iran.

Curtin argued that Iran' s sheer size as well as its historical and geographical importance merited increased attention. He stated:

> Iran has a population of approximately eight million. Its territory is three times as France. Large and rich cities are numerous: Tabriz has the population of 120,000, Tehran 85,000, Mashhad 70,000, Esfahan 60,000, Yazd 40,000.... During last year alone 40 million dollars worth of cotton was absorbed by the city of Tabriz. A major part of it was American cotton that came from England as piece goods. It has recently been held that Iran will never again rule the world as she did during the reign of Cyrus, but as time goes by and history repeats itself a day will come when a commercial and religious influence will engulf hundreds of millions of human beings. Her geographical position is highly important.

Because Iran was so unknown to the United States, the Foreign Relations Committee, when submitting the bill to Congress, did not venture to ask for a Minister Resident lest it might be voted down. The most it expected was a Charge d'Affaires and Consul General. However, an amendment was later introduced to provide for the title of Minister Resident. On August 5, 1882, 48 years after the American Presbyterian Mission settled in Iran to set up schools and hospitals, Congress ratified the Act on the Establishment of a Legation in Iran.

The first man nominated to assume the duties of a Charge d'Affaires and Consul General was Dr. Henry Jessup, an American Missionary in Syria. He turned down the offer for he thought it unwise and unsuitable for a Minister of the Church to serve in a diplomatic capacity. Of the list of names proposed to Congress by the Secretary of State, Fredrick T. Frelinghuysen, the chances were in favor of a New Yorker who had been in the Orient for about 24 years. He spoke Greek, Turkish, and French and had written a book on the Turks and the Greeks. On January 29, 1883, President Chester A. Arthur assigned S.G.W. Benjamin as Minister Resident to put up a Legation in Tehran. Benjamin accepted his commission on February 27, 1883.

Benjamin arrived in Tehran on June 9, 1883, having passed through Bordeaux, Marseilles, Constantinople, and Baku. At Anzali the royal steam yacht, courteously placed at the disposal of his party, carried them to the summer pavilion of the Shah. After an elaborate breakfast, the party left by steamer for Pir-Bazaar, where they were received by the Governor of Guilan and a group of dignitaries.

Benjamin then rode to Rasht with a cavalcade of some 50 other people. On his way to Rasht he was greeted by 6 sub-Governors of neighboring towns with their attendance all on horseback. Some 200 men came up to meet and join the procession to the Governor's office. There a Guard of Honor presented arms, and a magnificent reception was offered.

The party had scarcely had the chance to enjoy the numerous festivities in Rasht when Benjamin received a telegram stating that the Shah would leave Tehran on June 11. According to etiquette, any foreign envoy who reached his post when the Shah was away had to remain outside the city gate until his return. Therefore, in order to avoid the possibility of being forced to remain out of the city for numerous months, he asked his interpreter and secretary to take care of the family while he was to go back to Tehran more expeditiously by "Chapar" (mail pony express).

He soon realized that his journey would require a great deal of hard work and endurance. Some 220 miles were made on horseback with his "Mehamandar" (official host), galloping the first twelve farsangs past breath-taking views of the Alborz mountain range (some 6,300 feet above sea level) and the gigantic peak of Damavand that towered above Tehran at a height of 20,000 feet.

While still on the road, word came that in order to show his good will towards the United States, His Majesty intended to receive him with all the honors normally awarded to the highest rank of envoys. Benjamin requested that a public reception be called off, as he had traveling clothes on, and after some 300 miles horse riding he would be too tired for lengthy ceremonies.

He wanted to keep at his former speed to the city gates, yet was informed that the Russian Minister was traveling ahead with 96 horses loaded with luggage and was moving very slowly. International etiquette and rules of protocol practiced in Iran would not allow his entering the city of Tehran either before the Russian envoy or on the same day. Thus he was even further delayed just outside Tehran. Benjamin was told to stop at a station a few miles from the capital until further instructions. He found the Iranians in ceremony amazingly punctilious and acting with meticulous scrutiny. Outside the city nearing one of the royal pavilions, a messenger hastily came up with a gift box of sugarplums (cherry drops). Tea and Ghalyan (water pipe) were served while the Russian Minister rode a richly caparisoned royal stallion to meet Benjamin. Others, also on horseback, were escorted by not less than a thousand royal guards. As the procession approached the beautifully tiled city gate, the Cossacks started horse racing, firing in the air, and demonstrating equestrian acrobatic feats. Huge crowds gathered on both sides of the road to watch the spectacle and policemen and soldiers lined up at intervals to hold back the onlookers.

On June 10th the chief of protocol called and informed Benjamin that His Majesty would receive him in audience at 1:00 p.m. June 11, and would immediately leave on his summer vacation. The Russian Minister had been received the previous day.

A serious concern to the unceremonious American was his formal dress which looked too plain and unpretentious for official visits and audiences of the court which seemed so fastidious in the observance of the least punctilio of a social code and matters of the protocol. Yet his appearance was easily improved by the accompaniment of his cavalcade. A royal coach driven by 6 horses, a horseman on each horse, twenty footmen dressed in velvet garments and glamorous feathered hats and twenty others on horseback parading in procession, formed the diplomatic cavalcade, accompanied by the Foreign Office representative acting as host. As soon as the party entered the court, a thunderous canon boomed through the city in honor of the United States.

Once inside the palace, a magnificent flight of stairs with walls decorated with sumptuous paintings of European masters leading to a large saloon faced Benjamin. The Shah was standing at the end of the hall wearing an elegant royal garment embellished with ten diamond buttons, each of the size of a pigeon's egg. Benjamin read his address to the Throne in French. The Shah, who also spoke French, listened attentively, yet stood with an interpreter by his side. He expressed pleasure and replied that close diplomatic relations between the two countries would be to the advantage of both nations. He then inquired whether the America Legation in Tehran would be temporary or permanent. Benjamin answered that there was every reason to believe the Legation would be permanently maintained. The Shah emphatically stated his desire that the Legation be permanently established at the capital. His attitude was quite natural and Majestic; perhaps a little nervous, as every now and then he pulled up his golden glasses to his crown. The Mayor of Ghazvin came out at Aghababa with boxes of confectionery which were laid on the floor as part of the ceremony.

All went smoothly for Benjamin and his family while in Tehran. It was only when they left the city that there was a clash based on mistaken identity. On June 12, 1884, Benjamin and his daughter were going out to their summer retreat in a coach. Two horsemen were riding ahead of the vehicle. Arriving at the teashop midway on the road to Shemiran, they found several coaches parked in the shade of the trees along the roadside. Cabs or carriages used to stop at this point for refreshments, tea and Ghalyan (waterpipe). There seemed to be no special reason why he should be cautious.

Suddenly, about twenty soldiers dashed out, attacking Benjamin's horsemen.

Benjamin quickly realized that the soldiers were royal guards and that the Shah's harem was stopping there. In such cases only Foreign Ministers and their families had the right of way, which meant that Benjamin should have been free to go, but the soldiers paid no attention to who was in the coach and inflicted heavy blows on his driver. Quickly and boldly the driver pulled the Minister and his daughter to safety. One of the Court ladies ordered her eunuch to rush to their rescue, but he arrived on the scene only after the arm of one of Benjamin's men was fractured.

The next day Benjamin sent a note of protest to the Minister of Foreign Affairs with a message that he would lower the Legation flag unless amends were made in thirty-six hours. On the third day of the incident at 11 A.M. Sani-od-Dowleh, one of the outstanding Ministers, called and conveyed an official regret. A letter was received in the afternoon from the Ministry of Foreign Affairs requesting the Legation to have its Iranian Secretary together with the driver and the horsemen call the next day at the royal summer resort in Saltanatabad. There the Grand Master of Ceremonies ordered the assailants to be flogged. The Secretary interceded with success to stop corporal punishment. A commanding captain of the battalion called the Legation in the afternoon of the same day and apologized for the rough conduct of his guards.

Two days later, Benjamin called at the Ministry of Foreign Affairs to express his gratitude, and thus the first conflict between Iran and the United States was quickly and peacefully resolved.

During his stay in Iran, Benjamin wrote a voluminous book entitled *Persia and the Persians* that was published in London in 1887. In this book he describes his journey, the physical aspects of Persia, the city of Tehran, country seats in Shemiran, the different peoples of Persia, conditions of service, and the Shah and the Royal Family. He also gives sketches of several leading officers of the Persian government, mountaineering, a glance at the arts, religious and philosophical sects, the passion play, resources, products and trade, sectarian and secular institutions, laws, faiths, and the political situation. In another book[10] he stated that the scope of his new work was entirely different from that of *Persia and the Persians*. The latter work was intended to provide a description of Persia as it was; while *The Story of Persia* was the history of the country and offered a narrative of the most noteworthy characters and events of this ancient empire from its foundation in pre-historic times.

This work differs from other histories of Persia in providing more proportionate attention to the legendary period of her history than is usual with those who have dealt with this subject. Moreover, it devotes a special portion to the great carrier of the house of Sassan, which in Benjamin's opinion, had never received full justice from Christian historians. Benjamin's long stays in the East, including several years in Persia, along with his enthusiasm for understanding and grasping the true life of the people in this area of the world, led him to form a higher and more just opinion and estimate of the Middle East than many European writers were willing to concede.[11]

In 1885, when the Democrat Party took over the administration, Benjamin resigned his post in conformity with diplomatic practice. On November 20, 1885, President Grover Cleveland appointed Fredrick H. Winston to succeed Benjamin. After Spencer Pratt of Alabama was appointed as the third U.S. Minister and Consul General on August 3, 1886, Iran decided to open its own legation in Washington. Iran's Consul General to India, career diplomat Haji Hossain Gholi Khan Mo'tamed-ol-Vezareh the seventh son of Premier Mirza Agha Khan Noori, was assigned as Minister Plenipotentiary and Envoy Extraordinary to Washington. He had previously served as Assistant Minister of Foreign Affairs.

It took him and his staff of ten English-speaking members of the Iranian Foreign Service nearly two months to make a very hard journey to the United States. This envoy was later nicknamed Haji Washington after the treacherous pilgrimage made to Haj by devout Moslems. The Iranian ambassador's friendly attitude, his sociable nature and his peculiarities of character won him easy access to wide circles. His reports in general were positive and quite illuminating.[12] These writings soon sparked an interest in Iran among American academia, and a number of Iranologists began to appear at the start of the twentieth century. The first of which was Abraham Valentine Williams Jackson.

Jackson can truly be considered a tireless American Iranologist. He not only possessed detailed first hand knowledge of the land of Iran, but was consumed by an unprecedented passion for the study of Iranian literature and Persian religions. From 1903 through 1926, he visited Iran five times. He wrote travel books and published scholarly works. He also combined the two when he wrote *Book of Travel and Research,* published in 1906. In order to write this book, Jackson conducted an extensive study of various works from that of Zoroaster the Persian Prophet, Herodotus the Greek historian, Arab writers, to the writings of Edward Browne and Lord Curzon. By doing so, he shed light on certain historical points that had not been clear or even known before.

Encouraged by the wide reception that his book had received, Jackson published another one entitled *From Constantinople to the Home of Omar Khayyam* in which he described his journeys in 1907 and 1908 from Constantinople through northern Iran into Turkestan. Jackson's pilgrimage-like visit to Omar Khayyam's home contributed to the latter's growing fame in Europe and America.

For forty-two years Jackson was Professor of Indo-Iranian Languages at Columbia University until his death in 1937. During this period he wrote many books and articles of which three require more notice. The first of which is *Zoroaster, the Prophet of Ancient Iran.* This book deals with the life of Zoroaster, the Master whose teachings are still followed by present day Parsis. It is a biographical study based on tradition that tries to present Zoroaster in a true historical light. The book grew out of the author's lectures at Columbia and assembled all that was generally known until 1898, either from history or from tradition about Zoroaster. By compiling this book, Jackson hoped "that others may discern some sparks of the true flame amid the cloud, and that in some measure it may contribute to a more general knowledge of this Sage of the Past, the Persian Prophet of Old, the forerunner of those Wise Men of the East who came and bowed before the majesty of the newborn light of the world".

In the first chapter of this book Jackson links the classic Greek philosophers with their contemporary Persian thinkers:

The classical tradition that Pythagoras studied under these masters (the Persian Magi) in Babylon may not be altogether without foundation. Plato we know was anxious to visit the Orient and study with the Magi, but the Persian wars with Greece prevented him. The followers of the Sophist Prodicus, a contemporary of Socrates, are reported to have boasted of their possession of secret writings of Zoroaster; and even a Magian teacher, one Gobryas, is claimed as the instructor of Socrates. Aristotle, Deinon, Eudoxus of Cindus, and especially Theopompus were familiar with the Zoroastrian tenets. A work bearing the name of Zoroaster by Heraclides Pontiacus, a pupil of Plato and of Aristotle, is mentioned in Plutarch....

Early Persian Poetry is another book that truly shows Jackson's genius. This scholarly work provides an account of Persian poetry down to the tenth century poet, Abolghasem Ferdosi, and contains many examples of the poet's craft translated by the writer from Pahlavi or the later Persian. It is an extraordinary introduction to a literature that is unfortunately too little known, and captures the poetic nature of the people themselves. Jackson states: "Persia has always been a land of poetry, nor has lyric quality ever been lost from the voice of her people. The guide who leads the traveler's cavalcade across the mountains, and the master of the caravan...can each troll snatches of verse from poets centuries old."

Research in Manichaeism is the last book that Jackson wrote. This was the culmination of his many years of work and lectures on this religion and the important position that it had as a rival of Zoroastrianism and of Christianity. Manichaeism was the more important of the two schismatic movements in Zoroastrianism that arose early in the third Christian century within the Persian Empire. (The other, Mazdakism, came into existence considerably later.) It was combated and execrated as violently by orthodox Zoroastrianism as it was by orthodox Christianity when it spread westward into the imperial domains of Rome. Mani endeavored, by making a synthesis of elements from various existing religions, to form a new religion, electric in character and inspired by the fervor of his own idealistic enthusiasm, one that should not be confined by national borders, but be universally adopted. In other words, Mani's aspiration was to bring the world, Orient and Occident, into closer union through a combined faith, based on the creeds known in his time. Similarly, through his tireless study and teachings of Iranian history and literature, Jackson too created a closer link between East and West. Jackson did a great deal to further the study of the Iranian culture.

No person, be he Iranian, European, or American, has done so much to spread and popularize throughout the world information regarding the high qualities of Iranian culture and art as has Professor Arthur Pope. In the years from 1925 until 1939 Professor Arthur Upham Pope made at least 10 trips of study and research within Iran. In 1930 he founded the American Institute for Persian Art and Archeology, which was known as the Iranian Institute, with its headquarters in New York. In addition to his major publications described below, he wrote almost innumerable articles on Persian art, and was a leading spirit in organizing the great exhibitions of Iranian art held at London, Moscow, Leningrad, and New York.

In 1930 Professor Pope published *An Introduction to Persian Art Since the Seventh century A.D.* that was prepared to appear in connection with the exhibition of Persian art held at London. The book is well described in the publisher's introduction:

This is the first substantial volume in any language dealing with the arts and crafts of Persia as a whole. The text which presents much valuable new information, the result of personal research in Persia and in the principal museums of the world, is refreshingly unpedantic and illuminating. The illustrations embrace architecture, sculpture, bronzes, carpets, textiles, ceramics, calligraphy, miniatures, landscapes, and-not the least important-gardens; in the a word, no branch of the arts and crafts is neglected...perhaps the chief feature of the volume is the wonderful series of photographs taken by Mr. Pope himself in the course of his travels in Persia, where by reason of his position as Honorary Advisor in Art to the Persian Government, he was granted access to the places and buildings from which foreigners would have hitherto been vigorously excluded.

At the same time Professor Pope pondered the idea of preparing a comprehensive work that would deal in an authoritative fashion with every phase of Iranian art. At the time, there was no complete study nor was any single man able or qualified to undertake such a monumental task. Leading scholars were called upon to contribute sections dealing with their special field. Under the direction of Professor Pope and the associate editor, Dr. Phyllis Ackerman, a great mass of material was welded into a homogenous account. Finally, *A Survey of Persian Art* appeared in 1938.

This text consists of three volumes of text, three volumes of plates and another volume containing indices and bibliographies. The text volumes include some 400 line drawings while the plate volumes have 1300 large collotype plates made by the Oxford University Press and some 200 color plates executed by such noted printers as Jaffe of Vienna, Stone of Bombay and Albert Levy of Paris. The text runs to some 2817 pages, consists of 69 chapters and 56 sub-chapters, and is the work of 70 eminent scholars from 12 countries. In describing the art as a whole Professor Pope writes:

Art seems to have been the most fundamental and characteristic activity of the Iranian peoples, the most adequate record of their life, their most valuable contribution to world civilization.... It was an essential element in that first of all civilizations, which emerged on the Iranian Plateau more than 6,000 years ago and it played a vital role in all subsequent ages, maintaining throughout a well-defined individuality.

The peculiar genius of Persia found its most adequate embodiment in the so-called arts of decoration, those that depend for their effect upon beauty of pattern and expressive design. In these Iran attained a mastery that scarcely faltered through the unequaled duration of her cultural history.... There is no term in Western languages that is quite satisfactory for such an art as that of Iran. Words like 'ornamental' or decorative' suggest something derivative and of secondary importance.

The arts of many lands are partly unintelligible, without reference to Persian contributions. Europe is the heir of a medieval culture on which Persian influences, direct and indirect, had a profound effect; and even earlier the Iranian contributions to classical culture, though as yet imperfectly determined, were definite and perhaps fundamental. Iran is one of the central facts in the artistic life of Asia and the fountain source of much that was finest and most enduring in Eslamic culture, which disseminated Iran's influence across both Asia and Africa.

Furthermore, Iranian culture is of vital interest as an historical phenomenon. All the cultural processes are exemplified here, and all can be illuminated by knowledge of their course in Iran. The inhabitants of the Iranian plateau were endowed with unique aesthetic gifts. ...Art in the Iranian plateau has the longest continuous history. Notable objects appear there in the fourth millennium B.C., and there are reasons for thinking that a sophisticated civilization in which art plays a definite role first emerged here. In addition to this immense time span, the art of Iran, despite it's traditional characters assumed a baffling complexity, due not merely to the multiplicity of its relations and the range of its sources, but also variety of its own arts: for in a very real sense art in the great periods in Iran was almost co-extensive with life itself. It was out of such a background that issued some of the most beautiful things that have been created.

...The survey offers an organized and critical summary of what is at present known concerning the course of Persian art, and thus in a sense it may be thought to close a period of preliminary work in such studies. But the survey by no means presumes to be a definite work or to diminish the urgent necessity for further exploration and investigation....

Not only did Professor Pope contribute a great deal to the study of Iran, but he played an active role in joining East and West as well. The idea of creating the first bi-national cultural center was proposed by Professor Pope on April 23, 1924 while presenting a lecture in the presence of Prime Minister Sardar Sepah (later Reza Shah). The goal of such an entity would be:

To make known to the people of both countries their social, scientific, literary, cultural, educational, commercial and industrial lives; to promote relations between the two peoples; to guide and assist students who want to go to the United States to study, and vice versa.

Hossain Ala, who had served with distinction as Iran's Minister Plenipotentiary and Envoy Extraordinary in Washington and who had laid the foundation of Iran's Society in that country, with similar aims and objectives, also suggested the creation of such a center, later called Iran-America Relations Society. A great number of eminent statesmen and scholars served in this entity. Thus Professor Pope was highly regarded among both American and Iranian circles as one of the most learned and productive scholars of Iran. Other followed in his footsteps.

Professor Erich Schmidt, of the Oriental Institute of the University of Chicago is credited as the first American who undertook the most extensive archeological excavation in Iran. In 1931 he headed excavations at Persepolis, Ray, Damghan and the mountains of Lorestan. Professor Schmidt's extensive work at Persepolis lasted from 1935 until 1939. A preliminary study of the results of this expedition appeared in *The Treasury of Persepolis and Other Discoveries in the Homeland of the Achaemenids*. It contains subjects such as trial excavations in the Persepolis plain, the uncovering of the treasury at Persepolis, and miscellaneous finds including foundation documents of Xerxes and clay tablets, the defense system of Persepolis, and about 97 illustrations. The clay tablets included thousands of documents of the Achaemenid period written in the Elamite language that have since been studied and translated extensively.

A generous contribution by his wife, Mary Helen Warden Schmidt, enabled Dr. Schmidt to undertake an aerial survey of Iran. The principal object was to conduct an exploration of archeologically unknown parts of Iran with pictorial documentation of all the important sites. This fascinating undertaking started in the fall of 1935 and continued through spring of 1936. The end result of this massive undertaking was *Flights over Ancient Cities*, published in 1940. To show the enormity of this task, one has only to cite the fact that in the plains of Persepolis alone, more than 400 ancient sites were mapped.

Although all of the above scholars contributed greatly to the advancement of academia in Iran, none was more active in actually advancing education than Dr. Samuel Jordan. Without any doubt, he is considered the most respected American among Iranians. Dr. Jordan, whose own education had begun in one of the one-room schools of the time in rural Pennsylvania, devoted 43 years of his life to education in Iran and became the Father of Modern Education in this country. Dr. Jordan was first of a long series of Lafayette College graduates who went as Missionaries to Iran, many of whom were supported by other Lafayette students through the "Lafayette in Persia" project. Upon his arrival in Iran with his wife Mary, in November of 1898, Jordan started learning Persian. According to Dr. Arthur C. Boyce, a close colleague who served as Jordan's Assistant-Principal in High School and Vice–President in college, the conditions for the development of the American School in Iran were particularly favorable from about the time of Jordan's arrival in Tehran. The Persian people had been greatly stirred by the success of the Japanese in their war against Iran's ancient and supposedly all-powerful enemy, Russia. Persians had ambitions to do something themselves.

Education of girls was almost altogether neglected. Some progressive families gave their daughters a limited education by bringing tutors into the home. Many Moslems thought it dangerous to teach girls to read and write. Men who studied abroad had studied mostly in France, Germany or Belgium. Very few went to England and almost none to America. The French Government was very active in promoting the use of the French language in Iran and study in France. French became the foreign language taught in Persian schools. However, many people saw the growing importance of English and expressed a desire to learn English instead of French. Thus the American schools became very attractive to thoughtful Persians because of its English as well as its method. The American curriculum and spirit made learning an adventure instead of just a mass of material to be memorized and repeated. The American School For Boys in Tehran increased rapidly in numbers and prestige. In spite of its phenomenal success in elementary and high school classes, Dr. Jordan held persistently to his ideal and purpose to bring into being a full-fledged college.

In his appeals for men and money, Dr. Jordan argued that " The Persian boy is fully the equal of his American brother in his native ability and aptitude to learn. With only the training our American High School has been able to give, our graduates are found in all parts of the country in positions of honor and trust. A high school training is not sufficient for the needs or the demands of the situation." His quest was soon fulfilled.

The American School For Boys in Tehran, originally opened in 1873 as a very small primary school for Armenian and Jewish students, advanced to a full twelve-year elementary and high school in 1913, and finally evolved into a full college in 1925. The purpose of the college, as stated in the college catalogue, was as follows:

It is the purpose of the Alborz College of Tehran to prepare young men to enter every phase of life in Iran with an intelligent understanding of the new world conditions as well as the new problems in all sections of the country.... The changing conditions brought about by the new day in Iran demand more than ever the young men to be trained to meet the needs of just, strong, enlightened and patriotic citizens. The College has a rare opportunity to cooperate in a unique way in meeting this great educational need by bringing the best from the west to supplement the great good in Iranian culture.

In 1926, the Presbyterian Board of Foreign Missions appointed a Board of Trustees to act for the Board in all necessary matters. One of the first duties of the Board of Trustees was to make application for a charter under the Board of Regents of the University of the State of New York, making it possible for the college to confer B. A. Degrees with recognized authority. Faculty members were highly regarded graduates of Lafayette College, Yale, Princeton, University of Chicago, Syracuse and Indiana University. A number of highly regarded Persian scholars including Dr. Rezazadeh Shafagh, a Ph.D. from Berlin University and Dr. Yahya Armajani, a Ph.D. from Princeton and many more also served as faculty. In 1940 the school was purchased by the Iranian government and incorporated into the national school system.

During Mr. And Mrs. Jordan's tenure in Iran, many great changes and developments came into existence: a Boarding School was established in 1910, Summer Camps and Boy Scouts were formed in 1911, a school paper was established in half Persian and half English in 1921, a famine relief group was formed, and an International Relations Club in affiliation with Carnegie Endowment For International Peace was established. The college became a demonstration of the success of diversity for the student body contained representatives of all racial and religious groups including Moslems, Armenians, Jews, Zoroastrians, rich students as well as poor. They worked and played together and made their friendship without regard to distinction.

When Iran brought American advisors for the Ministry of Finance beginning with Morgan Shuster in 1911 and during two administrations of Dr. Millspaugh in 1922-7 and 1943-5, English-speaking assistants were found for them among former American School students. Many of the Persian young men were trained and placed in responsible positions that continued to hold after the Americans left. Dr. Jordan liked to think that the change brought about in the lives of Persians and their society were revolutions that were building better lives and better social order for all Iran. So distinguished was Dr. Jordan's service to the Iranian people in every area of life that he was described by Justice William O. Douglas in his book *Strange Lands and Friendly People* as "The man who did more to create goodwill between Persia and America than any other man". Before leaving Iran, Dr. and Mrs. Jordan received the Iranian decoration of the First Scientific Medal - the highest honor in education that the government could bestow.

Another great American inspired by the spirit of Iran and its people was Howard C. Baskerville, born in Nebraska on April 10, 1885 and a graduate of Princeton University Theological School. When he finished his studies in 1907, he was invited by the Presbyterian Mission to go to Iran and teach in their Memorial School in Tabriz. He proved himself to be a prodigy of valor when he took up arms with his students and revolutionaries in support of the Iranian Constitutional Movement - in spite of admonitions by the Mission and Consular authorities—and gave his life on the battlefield

on April 21, 1909. Because of his heroism and actions, many Iranians refer to him as the American Lafayette in Iran.

Professor Rezazadeh Shafagh, who was a student of Baskerville's at the time, documented this American hero's story in the Tehran Journal, December, 14, 1959. According to Professor Shafagh, Baskerville began to show increasing concern with the revolution in the city where he was teaching. He became interested in Iranian politics. He was an active witness in the struggle of the people for freedom, justice, and a constitution. He was bitterly critical of Sir Edward Grey's agreement with Russia in 1907 for he felt it betrayed the cause of the liberal movement in Iran. He became more and more moved by Iran's plight. He repeatedly said that he could not watch calmly from a classroom window the starving inhabitants of the city who were fighting for their rights. He soon established relations with some leading nationalists. The story is given below from the perspective of one of the students in Tabriz:

A number of students, including myself, met and formed a committee for the organization of schoolboy volunteers. Baskerville was very much interested in this organization. Hundreds of boys joined the demonstrations in favor of our national movement. I was elected to go to Sattar Khan (the leader of the revolutionaries) and ask for arms. For the first time I met that fiery man with rather small but fascinating eyes. The courtyard was crowded with armed men, all talking about an attack which had just been made by government troops on the western flank of the city. The fighting was going on and Sattar Khan was just about to leave for the front. Near him sat the old and respected educational leader, Sayyed Hossain Khan Adalat.

Sattar Khan hearing my plea replied sternly, saying that we should rather go back to our school and study. "We are fighting for you", he chided me, "instead of being armed with weapons, better you get armed with knowledge which is so vital for carrying a real constitutional government."

The venerable Sayyed Hossain Khan supported him firmly, urging me to give up the idea. I left in despair and Sattar Khan rode for the front. I continued sharing the activities of my friends and schoolmates and even began making public speeches in the name of the schoolboys. My parents, although proud of my role as a patriot, were nevertheless concerned. All that comforted them was the knowledge that I was pursuing a noble cause.

Soon Baskerville joined us in fact. He proposed to train us for military service. Soon we were gathering on the campus, training daily under his command. Meanwhile, Baskerville continued his classes and we pursued our lessons as far as possible.

Finally, arrangements were made to provide us with the short German rifles that happened to be comparatively abundant in the city arsenal. Within a short time many outsiders asked to join our party and were taken in by our American teacher and commander.

Not surprisingly the school authorities viewed Baskerville's undertaking with alarm since in their view, it was not compatible with the policy of the school. But Baskerville was firm, despite Dr. Wilson's advice to him and us, his students, not to meddle in politics before we finished our education.

It was the 13th day of the Persian New Year that our young American teacher officially threw his lot with us. The 13th day of Norooz, then, as now, was celebrated as a day of public excursion. There was little chance for a besieged city to deserve this national tradition, but Sattar Khan had called for a general gathering of volunteers to take place on the "Maydan-e-Mashgh" or the drill field.

Thousands of volunteers were present and even before the parade began, many were shouting and shooting in the air while others were galloping around the drill field.

Our school group, headed by Baskerville, was placed on the northern flank where Sattar Khan was watching the activities. Suddenly, word came to Sattar Khan that the American consul (William F. Doty) would like to see him. Orders were given to let the consul in. ...He shook hands with the consul and then called me to act as an interpreter.

"You, Young Man," he addressed me " tell the consul he is very welcome to our campus. I am sure the American nation has full sympathy with us in our struggle."

The consul, who appeared pale and nervous, thanked Sattar Khan, saying that he admired the sacrifices of the Iranian nation. He said, however, that he was here to ask Baskerville for an explanation. Sattar Khan addressing himself to me, said that I should explain to consul that "we are very proud to have Mr. Baskerville take active part in our national striving against despotism and foreign infiltration, but, on the other hand, this is a dangerous undertaking which may lead to fatal consequences. We would regret this very much. I would rather advise that this young American continue with his teaching, which we need badly, and leave the fighting to us. If however, he insists, he is very welcome although we can not take any responsibility for what may happen."

Then the American consul addressed himself directly to Baskerville and warned him in a trembling voice: "As an official representative of the United States of America I am compelled to remind you that you as an American citizen have no right to interfere with the internal politics of this country and that you are here to act as a teacher and not as a revolutionary; further the enterprise may prove fatal to you. Therefore, in my capacity as an American and as a consul I advise you to give up this idea and join the school which is your vocation".

Baskerville who had been listening with brimming emotion, replied: "I thank you for your kindness, but I can not remain calm and watch indifferently the sufferings of a people fighting for their right. I am an American citizen and am proud of it, but I am also a human being and cannot help feeling deep sympathy with the people of this city. I am not able to go on teaching calmly and quietly while tragic events happen daily around me. I assure you I am not afraid of any fatal consequence and I am determined to serve the national cause of Persia."

The consul was visibly agitated and reiterated his warning, but Baskerville remained firm. At last the consul said Sattar Khan farewell and rode on. Sattar Khan, who had listened attentively, asked me to tell him all that was said. He then shook Baskerville's hand admiringly. "Our way of fighting is different from that of these Westerners", he warned, "may God help you!".

The siege of the city was nearing a climax. Some of the inhabitants were actually starving. Food and money were being collected by the national committee to support the needy. Some houses had been transformed into local shops since stores lay in the war zone. The government was urging the "insurgents" to surrender and the Russian consul had just started threatening to bring in Russian soldiers upon the pretext of opening the way for provisions.

All these factors made it necessary that the besiege break out of Tabriz in order to let food come in. Many consultations took place under Sattar Khan to plan for such an attempt. It was on this occasion that Baskerville became imbued with the idea of helping with his little group of young men.

In our last class meeting in April, he spoke to us about our duty to serve our country and he related episodes from the American Revolution. He added that in spite of the fact that the Great Britain had abandoned the policy of encouraging Persian Nationalism since the treaty of 1907 with Russia, Sir Edward Grey, the British Foreign Secretary, still opposed the idea of Russia's advancing on Iran. We left the class pledging to follow our teacher who was ready to give his life for our country.

On the 18th of April it was confidentially announced that a sortie would take place at dawn from Sham-Ghazan, the most western part of the city, half of which was in the hands of the enemy. Baskerville told us to be ready and gather in a place assigned, before dawn. That evening I left home telling my parents I was going to spend the night wit my cousin. I went there but later I joined a few friends at the home of a relative from where we were supposed to leave to Sham-Ghazan area. Late in the night we were told that the attempt was postponed. Meanwhile my parents had heard about our plan. I still remember the deep concern written across the face of my father when he finally found me in our relative's house after having searched for me on foot for hours without food.

The following day was April 19. This time the sortie was to take place. We all made the necessary preparations. All the needed divisions were ordered by Sattar Khan to take up their posts at dawn. Our party of some 40 or 50 men, student and other volunteers, were ordered by Baskerville to advance toward Sham-Ghazan.

We marched about an hour until we approached the trenches. We then were ordered to be very quite, for we were supposed to take over the enemy by surprise in the dark. We advanced in small, scattered groups, passing through some gardens apprehensively, for we were not sure whether the enemy had taken positions there.

Emerging from a garden into a lane, Baskerville paused for a moment. No shooting had taken place here. Many of us thought that perhaps the enemy was unaware of our approach. Baskerville then gave the order for attack, not seemingly caring how many of us were with him. All of a sudden bullets began to fly above us. Fortunately, none of us was hit. Baskerville ordered us to throw ourselves down behind a pile of dirt that happened to be right where we most needed it. He stretched himself ahead of us. Unknown to us, he began crawling along a bed of a small waterway leading into one of the gardens on the left of us. He inched his way through the hole in the garden wall.

According to a later eyewitness account, at this moment he suddenly began firing at the invisible enemy hidden in the trenches. He was struck down by a bullet. Soon our troops from the adjacent trenches were shouting, "the American is hit." Our men began attacking the enemy's flank, thereby giving us the time to cut across the wall with pick axes. We all pulled as one man until the wall was broken through. To our regret, we saw Baskerville had been hit. He tried to rise, bleeding from a neck wound. We managed to crawl back through the hole in the wall, taking our wounded friend to a place of shelter. Baskerville was still alive and some of us had hoped that he might survive.

I held the body of my teacher against my breast. The others helping to hold him up but the blood was gushing from beneath his necktie. In a few moments Baskerville gave out his last breath.

Our fighters delivered Baskerville's body to the school authorities. Two of the great national leaders took me in their company and went to Wilson's home to express condolences on the part of Sattar Khan and the people. I still carried my short rifle on my shoulder. I was still stained by the blood of my teacher, my commander, and my friend.

The whole city was stunned by the news of the death of the "young American". Arriving home, I found mother in a state of indescribable affliction. For years after, she used to remember " the young American" and grieved for the mother who had lost such a son in a foreign land far from home.

The following day, thousands crowded the streets along the passage to watch Baskerville's funeral. Men and women, young and old, seemed afflicted and grieved. The bier was being escorted by the school community, soldier-students with inverted weapons, dignitaries and leaders of revolution and ranks of the volunteers. The body was taken to the American graveyard on the southern skirts of the city where Dr. Wilson said the prayers in a trembling and moving voice. Mr. Taghizadeh, one of the leaders of the revolution, made a short impressive speech: "young America in the body of young Baskerville", he said, "gave the sacrifice for the young constitution of Iran."

Only seven years later, in 1916, Dr. Samuel Graham Wilson followed Baskerville by giving his life while doing relief work in our country. He is buried next to Baskerville.

Baskerville has had a permanent place in the memory of the Iranian public ever since 1909. The first formal tribute paid to his memory was in the opening session of the second parliament or National Assembly (Majless) November 15, 1909. Taghizadeh, the famous deputy from Azarbaijan, made a memorial speech mentioning the self-sacrifice of Baskerville for the cause of the Iranian constitution. The speech found emotional response on the part of the members and spectators. Since those days stories and articles have been published about Baskerville both in Tehran and Tabriz the latest of which is a movie script written in 1998 by M. J. Jozani and published in English and Persian. His pictures became popular all over the country. A fine rug was woven in Tabriz under the care of the nationalists with Baskerville's portrait in natural size and with his name on it. But that valuable rug never got to Baskerville's family, for which it was meant, because of the out- break of World War I.

Papers, books, and pamphlets have treated the Baskerville episode on various occasions. A few include:

1. *History of the Iranian Constitution* by S. A. Kasravi (4th ed. first published in 1938), pages 891-897 states:

    In the opening years of the Constitutional Movement the memorial school was of great significance for our country, especially after Baskerville joined the staff and later gave his life for the freedom of

our country. This noble young American after having arrived in
Tabriz and noticing the struggle in which the citizens were engaged
to save their country, entered in negotiation with a number of his
students and volunteered to cooperate with them, forming a group
to train them for military service. He refused to follow the admonitions of the school authorities and of the American consul and
joined the national volunteers. One cannot help admiring the lofty
spirit of this young man who sincerely offered himself for our
national cause. The death of this sincere young American caused a
general grief and meant a great loss for the Nationalists.

2. The late Senator M. Malekzadeh, the son of the renowned orator of
    the revolution, writes in his book *History Of The Constitutional
    Revolution Of Iran* (V.5 Tehran 1955, page 237):

    An American school had been established in Tabriz for many
    years for the education of our young men. A young American not
    older than 25 years came to teach there and, while educating our
    young students, established relations with the liberal and cultural
    personalities in Tabriz. In a time when the inhabitants of the city
    were struggling for freedom, he took a vivid interest in the move-
    ment, gathered around himself a number of liberal young men and
    gave military training. Then came the fighting and the young
    American who was leading his group with great enthusiasm was
    shot and fell. His glorious name will live forever in the revolution-
    ary history of Iran.

3. Another book entitled, *Azarbaijan in Revolution* by K. T. Behzad
    (Tehran, 1954) says:

    Baskerville, a young American who had spent his young years
    up to 25 in a free country like America, was startled to see the cruel
    life in Iran full of suffering. It is, therefore, no wonder to find him
    having developed intense emotional sympathy with the revolution-
    ary movement around him after he came to Tabriz.... This emotion
    it was that induced him to take part together with his group, which
    consisted mainly of rather un-experienced young men.... He shed
    his blood on the soil of Iran, in fact with that blood he inscribed
    the "Truth on the Ground".

In 1950 a grave tablet in metal was prepared by a group of patriots in
Tabriz which with the approval of the American officials was laid on the
grave during a ceremony. A poem from the late National Poet of Iran, a

poet of the revolution, Aref Ghazvini, about Baskerville, is a part of the inscription on the tablet. A translation is as follows:

> O, thou, the revered defender of the freedom of men,
> Brave leader and supporter of the justice and equity.
> Thou hast given thy life for the felicity of Iran.
> O, may thy name be eternal, may thy soul be blessed!

Further American Involvement

A couples of years later, as an aftermath of the Persian Revolution and the defeat of the despots' counter-revolution, the first American financial mission was employed to create order out of chaos and corruption.

In 1911 hopeful Iranians saw an energetic young attorney from Washington heading a staff of assistants arrive in their country to put a disorganized and disrupted finance into good shape. There again, was a truly American manifestation of courage and devotion displayed in what may be termed a tragic but symbolic pageantry of Persian trials and tribulations.

Qualified by reason of his profound sincerity and sympathy, with a proper background in Cuban and Philippine Customs Services, 1897-1905, and as Philippine Secretary of Public Instruction, 1906-1908, W. Morgan Shuster appeared on the Persian scene in 1911 as Treasurer-General with plenary powers. He promised to espouse Iran's liberal ideals for radical reforms and infuse new life into its financial and economic institutions.[13] Although he went to Iran with the blessing of both the British and the Russian governments, Shuster literally interpreted the Anglo-Russian convention of 1907 whereunder two powers had speciously pledged themselves to uphold a sovereignty they had deliberately violated and dishonored by the substance and sprit of that infamous document. Gallantly and zealously Shuster assumed leadership of the historical reform movement that was doomed at its inception to incur Russian and British displeasure and dissent.

Firm in his purpose, he joined hands with Iranian nationalists and patriotic parliamentarians. In his book, *The Strangling of Persia*, he explains:

> It was for the purpose of educating the Persian people to have a respect for the law that, as soon as the excitement and confusion of the civil war last summer began to abate, I demanded the payment of taxes by

a number of ...grandies like Alaao'd-Dowleh, Prince Farman Farma and the Sepahdar. When Prince Farman Farma at last saw that I was in earnest about his actually paying taxes, he went before the Council of Ministers, recounted his valiant services to the constitutional government, both as a General of the Army and as Minister of War, and finished by sobbing on the Premier's shoulder. The members of the Council were so overcome that they wrote me a polite letter stating that the Prince would not have to pay any taxes until they could look into the question. Farman Farma brought the letter in person, and I told him that he could take his choice between continuing his valiant services to the constitution by paying all his overdue taxes the next day, and having me cease his grain warehouses and save him the trouble. I wrote the Council that if they would kindly attend to the rest of the government, I would endeavor to look after the taxes. The Prince paid most of his taxes the following day.[14]

Shuster fervently fought the infernal forces of corruption on all internal and external fronts. His ill-fated tenure came to a premature close with his forced departure on January 11, 1912, following a brutal Russian ultimatum at a bayonet's point to set their troops on the march to Tehran. With that ominous attitude, the Northern and Southern powers formally tore up the deceptive guarantees of Persian independence.

Utterly helpless and absolutely hopeless in this heart-rending catastrophe, an ardent admirer, the renowned Aref of Ghazvin, lamented Shuster's expulsion in a moving piece of poetry written in the temper and mood of the moment, which begins as follows in translation:

Shame on the host whose guest unfed doth from the table rise!
Rather than this should happen, make thy life his sacrifice!
Should Shuster fare from Persian forth, Persia is lost in sooth!
O let not Persia thus be lost, if ye be men in truth[15]

Shortly after his departure, Shuster wrote his book entitled *Strangling of Persia* and dedicated it " To The Persian People in the endeavor to repay in some slight measure the debt towards them and by their unwavering belief, under difficult and forbidding circumstances, in my desire to serve them for the regeneration of their nation". The work is a detailed account of the remarkable series of events which culminated in the writer's expulsion from the post of Treasurer-General of Persia in January, 1912. In the belief that the real interest of humanity and the betterment of international relations demand that the truth be told in cases of this kind, Morgan Shuster wrote down the facts with a bluntness that, perhaps under other circumstances, would be subject to criticism.

In Dr. Millspaugh's book, which will be discussed later, he sums up the Shuster episode in the following words:

In 1911, Mr. W. Morgan Shuster, with a group of American assistants, came to

Persia on the invitation of the Imperial Government, to reorganize and administer the finances of the country. Within a month after his arrival, the Majless (parliament) passed a law conferring upon him comprehensive powers as Treasurer- General. He was supported by a majority of the Majless and a large body of public opinion; and, since the unfortunate termination of his work by reason of international complications, Persians have never ceased to respect him as an incarnation of their own highest aspirations.

Ten years after the forced departure of Shuster, Dr. Arthur C. Millspaugh was employed by the Iranian government for the purpose of reforming the Iranian public finance system. In 1925 Dr. Millspaugh wrote of his experiences in Iran in *The American Task in Persia*. His purpose in this book was to tell the story of the American financial mission in Iran since the beginning of his work in 1922. The problem of Persia, he says, should be a vital interest to any other people which desire to see the stabilization of the world and the achievement everywhere of efficient government based on the will of the governed.

Historically, Persia was a world empire long before Rome extended its powers beyond Italy; and the Persians were one of the few people who defied and defeated the Roman armies. Little attention has been given to the contributions of Persia itself to civilization. Persia either created or appropriated and improved much of the best in the science and art of the ancient world.

The continuous existence of Persia as a nation, from remote antiquity to the present time, the architectural grandeur exemplified by the ruins of Susa and Persepolis and by many other monuments and antiquities, as well as the poetry of Ferdosi, Sa'adi, Hafez, Omar Khayyam, the persistence through the centuries of beautiful and artistic work in textiles, silver, brass, and pottery, and the persistent progressive moment with the maintenance of nationality all illustrate the extraordinary vitality and power of recuperation possessed by the Persian people.

Standing between the East and the West, invaded by East and West and invading both, the Persians have always had a rare capacity for drawing on the special gifts of other peoples without losing their own characteristics and integrity...[16]

In his book, Dr. Millspaugh acknowledges the support he received from the strong man in the government. He said "the collection of taxes was vital to our success; but I am certain that we should have failed in this regard, - in-spite of the energy, tact, and resourcefulness of Colonel McCormack's direction of the Internal Revenue Administration, -had it not been for the existence of a strong army and the willingness of Reza Khan Pahlavi to cooperate with us...."[17]

Dr. Millspaugh was once again employed by the Iranian government from 1943 to 1945. It was under disastrous war conditions that he returned in 1943 to serve both a wartime and peacetime purpose. His second mission collapsed as a result of vehement opposition and lack of support. This was partly because the Persians could not understand why the United States had joined forces with the Russians and British in World War II. This was a great blow to the American prestige in Iran. The Iranians now were classifying the Americans with their enemies. In 1944 the criticism of Dr. Millspaugh and other Americans in the service of Iran grew more severe. In the meantime fuel was added to the fire by communist propaganda both in and out of the so-called Toodeh or People's Party.

Lover's Quarrels

Between 1830 when the first Americans set foot in Iran through 1940, hundreds of Americans had established through their good and impressive activities a vast ocean of good will between Iran and the United States. These activities had established a reputation for America that was positive and warm. As the Persians sought to free themselves from the crushing embrace of the British and the Russians, they beckoned to America, which they saw as a powerful potential ally. The many Americans who had lived in their midst had given them good reason to place their hope and trust in the United States.

Reza Shah Pahlavi, a pragmatic nationalist, who reigned between 1925 and 1941, applied the time honored Persian technique of protecting Iran's national integrity by balancing such powerful predatory countries as Britain and the Soviet Union with a third party alliance. In the case of Reza

Shah, this third force was Germany, a country whose ideology greatly impressed him. By 1941, over 1,000 German advisors, businessmen, and officials were stationed in Tehran alone. The Allies, who considered Iran's role in the coming confrontation with Germany to be of a crucial geostrategic importance, were deeply disturbed. Britain and the Soviet Union invaded and occupied Iran on August 25, 1941, driving the proud Shah into exile. The United States joined the USSR and Britain in occupying the country. During World War II, Iran served as an important supply bridge (The Bridge of Victory) to the beleaguered Soviet Union, which was under German attack from the west.

Reza Shah was succeeded by his 22-year-old son, Mohammad Reza Pahlavi. The young Shah found himself in a tenuous political position. In January of 1942, a Tripartite Treaty that guaranteed the territorial sovereignty and political independence of Iran in line with the Atlantic Charter, was signed with Iran. This treaty, however, did not diminish the fears of the new Shah or his advisors, who saw the real possibility of their country's dismemberment. In this context, the experienced Iranian aristocrats and statesmen decided to put forth a heavy American presence and influence in the country. American policy makers agreed that the United States should become involved in Iran as part of the Allied war effort.

On March 10, 1942, Iran was declared eligible for lend-lease aide. American decision-makers realized immediately that Iranian independence was in accordance with the long-term interests of the United States. In January of 1943, the State Department issued a memorandum analyzing America's developing role in Iran in which the British and Soviet interventionism in Iran was decried:

Although Russian policy has been fundamentally aggressive and British policy fundamentally defensive in character, the result in both cases has been interference with the internal affairs of Iran, amounting at times to a virtually complete negation of Iranian sovereignty and independence.[18]

The document further stated "the United States alone, is in the position to build up Iran to the point at which it will stand in need of neither British nor Russian assistance to maintain order in its own house." Eight months later the Secretary of State, in a communication to President Franklin D. Roosevelt, discussed the moral and humanitarian reasons for an American presence in Iran to offset British and Soviet ambitions. He added: "From a more directly selfish point of view, it is to our interest that no great power be established on the Persian Gulf opposite the important American petroleum development in Saudi Arabia."[19]

The American presence in Iran in the early 1940's included many missions, advisory teams and other individuals. During this era, the major focus of attention was the diplomatic legation headed by Minister Louis G. Dreyfus, Jr., who served as the American Minister Plenipotentiary to Iran during the difficult war torn years of 1940 to 1944. Despite the resentment existing in Iran because of the Allied occupation of this country, Dreyfus and his wife, Grace, remained popular in the Iranian society, for they touched the lives of many Iranians including the lower classes. Grace Dreyfus, who had been a volunteer nurse in World War I, opened both a clinic and an orphanage in the poor districts of south Tehran. It is said that it was Minister Dreyfus whose intervention with the Soviet Embassy saved the Capital of Iran from an air raid on the night of Anglo-Soviet occupation. Arthur Millspaugh, the financial advisor at the time, writes in his second book called *Americans in Persia*:

Mr. Louis G. Dreyfus, who presided over the legation at the time of my arrival, was generally considered the best as he was the most popular and effective of the men who had represented the United States in Tehran. The Minister's wife had captured the hearts of the Persians, not only as a charming hostess, but also as a sympathetic and tireless worker in the slums of Tehran. Daily, she took medical care to hundreds of the poor people.... No publicity agent, aiming to dramatize and popularize America in the Persian mind, could have improved on Mrs. Dreyfus' spontaneous, simple and sincere technique. The department instructed the Minister to give the mission cooperation and support; and this he did with consistency, sympathy, friendliness and good effect.[20]

Aside from the diplomatic mission, three military missions were sent to Iran during this period. The first was headed by General Clarence Ridley, who was sent to Iran as intendant general to the Iranian Armed Forces from 1942 to 1947. Ridley attempted to strengthen the organization and forces of the badly weakened Iranian army. Another military mission was the Persian Gulf Service Command (PGSC) that was headed by General Donald Connolly and consisted of nearly 30,000 noncombatant American troops who aided the Allied cause by providing the USSR with badly needed wartime supplies over the Iranian land bridge. The Persian Gulf Service Command personnel, who began arriving in Iran in December of 1943, played a vital role in supplying the Soviet Union with more than five and a half million tons of goods during the war.[21] The third military mission to Iran was the team headed by Colonel H. Norman Schwarzkopf (father of General Norman Schwarzkopf, who headed the American military forces against the Iraqis in the Persian Gulf War of 1991) and staffed by 24 police experts who served as advisors to the Iranian gendarmerie (rural police force). Schwarzkopf's mission, called GENMISH, was extended three times within 1942 and 1948, and American advisory missions to the gendarmerie continued until the late 1970's.

The United States also established two small, but significant intelligence gathering organizations in Iran. Office of Strategic Services (OSS) employees were stationed in Tehran along with a new military intelligence team directed by Colonel Baker, the United States Military attaché, affiliated with the embassy in Tehran. The latter group had individuals resident in crucial rural areas of Kordestan, Azarbaijan and in the Ghashgha'i area between Esfahan and Shiraz. By the end of the war, an Office of War Information and a press and information office attached to the embassy had also been established.

Many American Generals, diplomats and even presidential envoys traveled to Iran on numerous occasions. Unfortunately, rivalry, lack of cooperation and lack of coordination became very apparent among these Americans. The seriousness of the situation can be seen in the words of a February of 1944 OSS Report, which states that "the apparent clumsiness and lack of unified policy among the American group is leading an increasing number of thoughtful Iranians to believe that they eventually will have to look to the Soviet Union for aid".[22]

This intense lack of unity among Americans was taking place in the area of the Iranian Volcano of Internal Politics. It was during this time that political parties and publications representing all shades of the ideological spectrum were proliferating, spreading their social ideas and political messages. A large and vocal group of extreme nationalists decried external and imperial intervention in the affairs of their country. Within this coalition were committed groups who demanded the destruction of the old aristocracy and an end to internal corruption and exploitation. On the other hand, strongly entrenched landed and bazaar interests sought to protect their power and privilege. Some of these forces were willing to cooperate with external forces in order to protect the domestic status quo in which they thrived. It was under these circumstances that Arthur Millspaugh, who had returned to Iran for his second term of mission, found himself trapped between these powerful Iranian millstones.

The wealthy classes and the profiteers were horrified by Millspaugh's attempts to impose progressive income taxes and to introduce reforms that directly threatened their personal wealth. His proposals to cut back on military expenditures also alienated entrenched interest. On the other hand, the nationalists resented Millspaugh's interventionary powers in Iran's internal affairs. They were also suspicious about his alliance with personalities such as Sayyed Ziaeddin Tabataba'i, who were considered by many to be British sympathizers. Furthermore, they disliked the high-handed manner in which he seemed to operate. All forces were combined in the figure of a Nationalist Aristocrat, Dr. Mohammad Mosaddegh, who took it upon himself to lead the attack against the Millspaugh mission.

Sayyed Zia and his followers argued that Iranians should support the Millspaugh mission in order to guarantee a strong and certain American presence in Iran, which would in turn promote reform while protecting Iran from a takeover by either the British or the Soviets. The Soviets, of course, were fueling the anti-Millspaugh fervor.

Dr. Mossadegh argued that Millspaugh's team of Americans was composed of third-raters whose performance was poor and unguaranteed by the United States government. He expressed that this external mission was, in any case, in no position to dictate Iran's best interest. He added that Millspaugh's drive for extraordinary power violated the letter of the Iranian constitution and the authority of the Iranian parliament (Majless). Being a nationalist, Dr. Mossadegh believed that America's increasing influence would only reinforce the British position, thereby tipping the delicate political balance that had traditionally marked British-Russian relations within Iran. He was convinced that the Soviets were being increasingly alienated and could easily be goaded into a direct intervention into Northern Iran because of the growing American- British nexus. Dr. Mossadegh was clearly not anti-American, but he did not want an American presence to become overwhelming to the point of destroying the protected balance that he referred to as "negative equilibrium."

Dr. Mossadegh's careful differentiation between the Dreyfus mission and the Millspaugh venture is apparent in his statement to the Majless on August 12, 1944 :

> I am sure that the Americans do not want one of their citizens who is employed and paid by this country to treat us the way he does. Iranians will never forget that America defended Iran in 1919, and they will always appreciate that help. The popularity of Mr. Dreyfus and his respected wife within the Iranian community is an indicator of the warm feeling that Iranians have for Americans. There is no hard feeling, therefore, between me and the American advisors, but Dr. Millspaugh does not want anyone to discover what he is doing. He wants to act always in secret.[23]

On January 8, 1945, the Majless stripped Millspaugh of all his economic powers. Thirty-eight days later, he submitted his resignation.

The Problem of Oil

The events surrounding World War I brought the realization that oil was a critical resource for any nation that sought to maintain power. Thus, special attention was placed on the oil producing nations of the Middle East, especially Iran. The British had already been enjoying a huge oil concession in Iran since 1909. In 1920 the Standard Oil Company of New Jersey (today's Exxon) began to negotiate for an oil concession in northern Iran. Two years later, Sinclair Oil made the same attempt. Further efforts were made by American Oil, a subsidiary of the Sea Board Oil Company, in 1937 and by Standard-Vacuum Oil (today's Mobil) in 1940. During this twenty year period the opposition of the British to giving such concessions was a huge factor in the failure of American oil companies to gain access to Iran.

In 1943, with the encouragement of the Iranian government and the Department of State, the Standard-Vacuum Oil Company (Mobil) actively renewed their quest for a concession in Iran. The British nervously monitored this American initiative. In November Royal Dutch Shell sent two London representatives to Iran to seek the same concession that Standard was after. The rush for concessions in Iran was complicated in early 1944 when Sinclair joined the race. These activities alarmed many Iranian nationalists as well as the Soviets. In September 1944, the Soviets dispatched their influential vice commissar for foreign affairs to Iran in order to obtain an oil concession in the north. This action, coming on the heels of the strong American and British representatives, placed Iran, already an occupied country, under enormous pressure. Iranian leaders were horrified at the struggle of the powerful occupying forces who fought over their life-blood.

Iranian domestic forces now began to play a determining role in the political and economic struggle. Dr. Mossadegh took the initiative and criticized Iranian Prime Misters Ali Soheili and Mohammad Sa'ed for encouraging the United States in its search for oil concessions in Iran. On October 8, 1944, the Iranian cabinet voted to postpone all oil concessions. This action infuriated the Soviet Union and its proxy political organization in Iran, the Toodeh party. The Toodeh party organized wild demonstrations inside Iran while the Soviet Union applied pressure from without. Iranian nationalists like Mosaddegh were concerned that a new Prime Minister or cabinet might yield to pressure and grant further concessions. On

December 2, 1944, Dr. Mossadegh suddenly and masterfully presented an oil bill in the Majless that would forbid the government from granting any oil concessions without legislative approval. This proposal caught the Toodeh party's members off guard and passed overwhelmingly. In effect, it guaranteed that no more oil concessions would be granted as long as Iran was an occupied country.

The Soviets were infuriated by this proposal and argued that the moratorium on concessions only favored the British, who already possessed a petroleum position in Iran. They argued that if Dr. Mossadegh sought equilibrium, the only way to balance the British influence in the south was to grant the Soviet Union a concession in the north. This notion, of course, was rejected by Dr. Mossadegh. Despite the fact that the Soviet Union labeled Dr. Mossadegh pro-British, and the Toodeh party launched a major propaganda attack against him, the actions taken by the Iranian government effectively terminated the American and Soviet drive for oil concessions.

The resolution of the economic and political rivalry that dominated great power relationships in Iran was ultimately crafted by intelligent Iranian statesmen. They shrewdly shaped a policy that deprived the Soviets from gaining oil concessions by temporarily blocking the Americans from getting into Iranian oil fields. In accomplishing their goal, they were aided by American inexperience, and the dislike of the British for an American oil presence.

The United States policy makers misunderstood the internal political forces of Iran and clearly underestimated the role that these forces played in determining events. This point is eloquently made by Mark Hamilton Lytle in his book *The Origins of the Iranian-American Alliance, 1941, 1953.* Lytle states:

> The failure of American diplomats to recognize the Iranian contribution was symptomatic. The Americans frequently assumed that all Allied actions determined the results, both for good or ill, of events in Iran. With their big power bias, the Americans ignored the vital role Iranians played for themselves.[24]

For many years Iranians complained and protested the treatment they received from the Anglo-Iranian Oil Company. In 1948 the government of Iran provided the AIOC a document listing twenty-five points of dissatisfaction and calls for improvement. Among them were:

1. The status of the Iranian employees of the company

2. The need to have access to the accounts and ledgers of the company since these figures affected Iran

3. The demand that Iran receive its share of the profits from the company's operations outside of Iran

4. The amount of revenues accruing to the government of Iran. In 1951, an Iranian representative told the United Nations Security Council that in 1950 the Anglo-Iranian Oil Company had earned a profit close to 200 million British Pounds from its oil enterprises in Iran. Of this, Iran had only received 16 million Pounds as royalties, share of profits, and taxes. The company's profits that year alone, after deducting the share paid to Iran, amounted to more than the sum of 114 million Pounds paid to Iran during the entire past half a century.[25] The Iranians stressed the fact that Iran received considerably less in royalties than the sums paid in taxes to the British government.

On March 15, 1951, the Iranian Majless passed a bill to nationalize the oil industry. Five days later, the bill was ratified by the Senate. In response to the bill, U.S. Secretary of State, Acheson stated, "we recognize the right of sovereign states to nationalize, provided there is just compensation."[26] In a meeting between British and American officials in Washington in April 1951, the Americans again made it clear that they recognized the Iranian right to nationalize. On the other hand, the British seriously considered a military response.

President Truman's policy was to attempt to placate the British while trying to convince Dr. Mossadegh, the Iranian Prime Minister, to agree on a compromise. American leaders were convinced that any British military attack was not only unwarranted but also might serve as a pretext for Soviet intervention. As Secretary of State Dean Acheson stated, "only [in the case of]an invitation of the Iranian government, or Soviet military intervention, or a communist coup d'etat in Tehran, or to evacuate British nationals in danger of attack could we support the use of military force."[27]

The British Foreign Minister, Anthony Eden later admitted that "the temptation to intervene…must have been strong, but pressure from the United States was vigorous against any such action."[28]

Though Americans supported the Iranian government in its decision to nationalize oil, concern about the precedent set for other oil exporting countries was tremendous. This is documented in Arthur Krock's memories when he reveals a conversation he had with President Truman:

The President said he thought Mexico's nationalization of oil was 'right', even thought so at the time; but it was regarded as 'treason' to say so. If, however, the Iranians carry out their plans as stated, Venezuela and other countries on whose supply we depend will follow suit. That is the great danger in the Iranian controversy with the British.[29]

In spite of the initial support, the United States soon joined the British in opposition to Iran's Prime Minister. According to professor James Bill, "Mossadegh himself unwittingly adopted a political tactic that only reinforced U.S. decisions."[30] In order to encourage desperately needed moral and financial assistance from the United States, he began to raise the specter of a communist threat to his country. He argued that American assistance was essential if Iran were to stay out of the communist camp. This approach had exactly the opposite effects form the one designed by the elderly Prime Minister. Rather than attracting aid, it provided further justification for those U.S. policy makers who agreed with the British that intervention and overthrow were the only realistic alternatives. In August of 1953, Dr. Mossadegh's government was overthrown.[31]

The First U.S. President in Iran

The first United States President to visit Iran was Franklin Delano Roosevelt, who traveled to Tehran in November 1943 for the famous Tehran Conference also attended by Winston Churchill of England and Joseph Stalin, the head of the Soviet Union. This took place in a critical period of time for Iran, in the midst of World War II, when Iran was occupied by the Allied forces. Unfortunately, President Roosevelt managed to insult the Shah and the Iranian people when he refused to return a visit from the Shah. This contrasted sharply with a special effort made by Stalin, who called on the Shah for a lengthy meeting. Iranians were baffled and upset by this diplomatic omission which was probably because of American ignorance and misunderstanding of the situation in Iran.

The American mistake was perhaps due to the fact that American officials were not greatly knowledgeable and well informed in the Iranian culture, history, society and politics. This was not the case with the British. For instance, the British Minister - and later Ambassador - Sir Reader Bullard, who served in Iran for five years (1939-1944), had many years of experience in the Middle East and had studied Persian, Arabic, and Turkish. His understanding of Iran was greatly furthered by his studies with one of the greatest Western scholars of Iran, Edward G. Browne. In Tehran, Bullard was assisted by another eminent western Iranologist, Ann Lampton, then press attaché to the British legation. Another example is Colonel G.D. Pybus, assistant military attaché in Iran and head of British intelligence, who was a scholar of Iran who wrote and recited Persian poetry. Bullard's opinion about the first American Ambassador to Iran, Leland B. Morris, which is quoted in Mark Lytle's *"American-Iranian Relations"* is very revealing: "The fact that the State Department is so ill-informed about the situation here confirms my impression that the United States Ambassador, though honest, frank and ready to help, is himself ill-informed as well as inert." Leland B. Morris served as the first American Ambassador when the American legation was upgraded to the status of embassy in 1944 in Iran. Thus while the British made extensive efforts to understand the environment in which they worked, the American diplomats remained ignorant of the local culture. This was a cause of continued offense to the Iranian people.

Further Roots of Resentment

In spite of all the help and support that the United States provided to Iran, America's behavior and the policies it adopted in this country, caused a great deal of long lasting resentment among Iranians. This bitterness is a direct result of two inter-related actions: America's interference in internal affairs of Iran (which was similar to the actions of the Russians and the British), and more importantly, the disregard for Iran's constitutional establishment. This disregard was exemplified in America's cooperation with the British on two specific occasions that ultimately led to the establishment of an autocracy. The first occurred in the mid-1940's when the Shah was advised to oust Prime Minister Ghavam. The second event was in 1953 when a coup d'etat was enacted against Prime Minister Mossadegh.

The first incident, which is probably less publicized, is extensively studied by Iranian scholar Professor Habib Lajevardi of Harvard University in his article published in the *International Journal of Middle East Studies*. Due to it's detailed account of the events, it is reproduced as an appendix to this chapter in its entirety with the hope that the new policy makers in both countries shall take lessons and refrain from making the same detrimental mistakes.

Continued Cooperation

Although the seeds of resentment had been planted by the actions of the United States, cooperation continued. During the 1940s, Iran signed a number of important contracts with either the U.S. government or American firms that tightly bound the two nations. The first important economic contract was signed on December 17, 1946 between the government of Iran and Morrison-Knudsen International. The purpose of this contract was for Morrison-Knudsen International to prepare a study of Iran's economic potential. On October 6, 1947, General Ridley's small advisory mission was expanded into a major United States Army mission, hereafter known in Iran as ARMISH. On October 8, 1948, Iran signed a contract with Overseas Consultants Inc. (OCI) to survey Iran's economic capabilities in line with the establishment of a seven-year development program. In 1949, the United States Air Force became part of the ARMISH arrangement. In 1950 the Military Assistance Advisory Group (MAAG) further expanded the ARMISH. The ARMISH-MAAG mission was one of the pillars of Iran-American relations until1979.

In 1949, Senator J.W. Fulbright introduced a resolution for the establishment of the United States Commission for Cultural Exchange with Iran. Its purpose was to promote further understanding between the two nations by a wider exchange of knowledge and professional talents through educational contacts. Consequently, an agreement was signed in Tehran between Iran's Prime Minister, Asghar Hekmat and the United States Ambassador, John C. Wiley, on September 1, 1949. Tehran University's Chancellor, two other professors, the American cultural attaché and two other Americans served on a commission that was subsequently formed. Under this agreement, funds were made available by the government of the United States to finance studies, research, instruction and other educational studies of the citizens of the United States and nationals of Iran in both countries. Later, amendments were signed on November 25, 1957, June 20, 1961, and October 24, 1963, to improve and expand this program.

In November 1949, the Shah of Iran made his first visit to the United States. In October 1950, an important technical aid agreement was signed between Iran and the United States under the Point 4 Program. Point 4 was a term applied to the continuing technical cooperation program of the United States from 1950 to 1965. In his inaugural address, in January 1940, President Truman had announced the United States would extend technical assistance designed to help the free people of the world to help themselves by producing more food, clothing, more material for housing and more mechanical power. This was to be one of the four major pillars of the United States Foreign Policy.

In 1951, William E. Warne was asked to become Point 4 director for technical cooperation with Iran. As Assistant Secretary of the Interior, he had specialized in resource development programs much like those he faced in Iran.

"I am sorry this isn't a more important street." Mayor of Tehran said without introduction. "But it is the one beside your most important building." The formal gathering was a pleasant surprise for Warne. The Mayor pulled out a paper and read out loudly the city's official expression of "appreciation and gratitude for the mission's valuable contributions to the municipality of Tehran". The street had been named "Khiaban-e Asl-e Chahar,"[32] Point 4 Street. In the same spirit other avenues were named after presidents Roosevelt, Eisenhower, and Kennedy, as well as Dr. Samuel Jordan.

Warne detailed his service in Iran from 1952-1957 in his book *Mission for Peace*. Another account of the Point 4 mission in Iran was provided by Dr. Carence Hendershot, the Point 4's Chief of Education Division from 1961 to 1965, in his book entitled *Politics, Polemics and Pedagogues*. Point 4 focused on technical aid, agriculture, health, and education, and its activities were spread through the Iranian countryside.

In 1955 Great Britain put together an economic and political alliance named the Baghdad Pact that was signed by Iran, Great Britain, Iraq, Pakistan and Turkey. The United States did not become a formal member of the pact, but it supported it by financial contribution and assistance. At the time, John Foster Dulles, the United States Secretary of State, encouraged, supported and even pressured as many countries as possible to sign alliance treaties and defense pacts that would be pro-Western and anti-Soviet. Due to strategic and military reasons, Washington policy-makers wanted Iran as a central member of the Baghdad pact. The American government's view is evident in a memorandum prepared by the Joint Chief's of Staff Joint Intelligence Committee on April 13, 1955:

> The natural defensive barrier provided by the Zagross Mountains must be retained under Allied control indefinitely. Because western Iran includes the Zagross Mountain barrier, geographically, Iran is the most important country in the Middle East, excluding Turkey. Iranian participation in a regional defense organization would permit the member countries to take full advantage collectively of the natural defense barrier in Western Iran and would permit utilization of logistical facilities of the area. The relative importance of Iran in relation to other

countries of the Middle East would be significantly increased if she became a partner in a regional defense organization which included Turkey, Iraq, Pakistan.

In the same year, a six-member delegation of the House of Representatives on a special study mission to the Middle East traveled to Iran, and as a result, urged increased U. S. military assistance to Iran.

In 1957, under the auspices of Dwight D. Eisnehower, a policy was designed by the United States to protect the territorial integrity and independence of nations requesting aid when threatened either by armed communist invasion from without or by subversion from within. This policy was called the Eisenhower Doctrine. To reinforce support of this doctrine, a delegation of American Congressional Members traveled to the Middle East. In return for its enthusiasm, Iran was promised increased economic and military assistance.

On July 14, 1958, a brutal revolution swept Iraq during which the entire Royal Court, including the Crown Prince, was beheaded and decapitated. The revolution accelerated the American Aid Program to Iran, and military considerations became the focal point of U.S. thinking on Iran. In October 1958, the Secretaries of Treasury and Defense visited Tehran, and on March 5, 1959, the United States and Iran signed a bilateral defense agreement that strongly guaranteed an American military commitment to Iran. The agreement stated:

In case of aggression against Iran, the government of the United States of America, in accordance with the constitution of the United States of America, will take such appropriate action, including the use of armed forces, as may be mutually agreed upon and as is envisaged in the joint resolution to promote peace and stability in the Middle East, in order to assist the government of Iran at its request.[33]

This agreement angered the Soviets, especially in light of the fact that the Shah, pursing the traditional Persian policy of equilibrium and trying to create bargaining power with the West so that his support would not be taken for granted, had warmed up Iran's relation with the Soviet Union throughout 1956 to 1959. His visit to Moscow in 1956 had resulted in considerable economic and diplomatic interaction including signing of many trade agreements between the two nations. The Soviets, on their part, had been actively courting Iran, trying to sign a fifty-year non-aggression pact in order to neutralize the Baghdad pact.

On December 14, 1959, President Eisenhower paid a six-hour official visit to Iran during which he addressed the Iranian parliament. In his message, he stressed the special partnership and togetherness with Iran and emphasized that: "military strength alone will not bring about peace and justice."[34] This was a culmination of the emphasis that the American leaders had put on the need for economic planning and rational administration. It was based on this idea that private and public economic and aide missions to Iran flourished during the 1950's. Apart from previously stated economic aide through missions and foundations, public and private projects included the Ford Foundation/Harvard University Advisory Group attached to the Plan Organization; expanded activities of the Near East Foundation; the American Friends of the Middle East; the Iran Foundation, which funded the Shiraz Medical Center; and the Lafayette College consortium, which was charged with the development of a technical college in Abadan. Investment firms and banks also entered the Iranian financial market.

A project signed in 1957 between the Development and Resources Corporation of New York and the Plan Organization in Iran was the biggest private venture to date. It entailed a huge plan to develop Khoozestan Province through the construction of a series of dams and a complex new irrigation system. In 1958 Chase Manhattan bank and Lazard Brothers became partners in a development bank (Bank Omran).

U.S. involvement in Iran deepened with the rise of the Kennedy Administration. President John F. Kennedy's policies towards Iran were based on reform from above. His advisors made many suggestions to the Shah of Iran in this regard. Included were: opening the Pahlavi Foundation to public inspection; appointing respected Mossadeghist nationalists to important government posts; sending to exile or exerting control over many royal family members; cultivating the middle class and the public; undertaking reforms in the judiciary, the civil service, planning, land tenure, education, taxation, etc.

In May 1961, the Shah, with a strong U.S. encouragement, appointed Dr. Ali Amini as the Prime Minister. According to former U.S. ambassador Armin Meyer:

> The Kennedy administration was very concerned about Iran and immediately set up a task force.... The result of that task force was to instruct our ambassador that we would provide $35 million in aid to Iran in return for which we would expect from Iranians various steps which we considered necessary for progress, including even a suggestion as

to the prime ministerial candidate we considered best qualified to administer the proposed reforms.[35]

In February 1962, President Kennedy's special envoy, Chester Bowels, visited Iran recommending land reform and economic planning. In a long visit with the Shah, he stressed repeatedly the primary importance of economic and social progress over military considerations.[36]

In August 1962, Vice President Lyndon B. Johnson paid an official visit to Iran. During his stay, Johnson, aside from meeting the Iranian leaders, went to the streets of Tehran, talking, hugging and shaking hands with Iranians. According to the then United States Ambassador to Iran, Richard Holmes, at his formal state dinner on August 25, 1962, Johnson laid great stress on the proposition that the ultimate strength, prosperity and independence of Iran would lie in the progress made in the fields of economic well being of the population and in social justice.

In his departure speech, Lyndon Johnson stated: "We all agree on the necessity for programs of responsible change. We all have seen that the status quo alone provides no safeguard for freedom." Johnson then quoted from John Kennedy's Inaugural Address: "If a free society cannot help the many who are poor, it cannot save the few who are rich."[37] Indeed, the entire Kennedy administration consistently advocated greater social justice and development of the rural sector. This ideology was best shown in the creation of the Peace Corps.

On October 14, 1960, Presidential candidate John F. Kennedy addressed students at the University of Michigan in a 2 a.m. impromptu speech challenging them to give two years of their lives to help people in countries of the developing world. On March 1, 1961, President Kennedy issued an executive order creating Peace Corps. On September 22, 1961, Congress approved legislation formally authorizing the Peace Corps, giving it the mandate to "promote world peace and friendship" with the following objectives:

1. to help the people of interested countries and areas in meeting their needs for trained manpower
2. to help promote a better understanding of Americans on the part of the people's served
3. to promote a better understanding of other peoples on the part of Americans.

President Kennedy's innovative Peace Corps program reinforced a new American reform emphasis in Iran. The first 43 American Peace Corps volunteers arrived in Iran in September of 1962. These and nearly 2,000 others that followed them moved into the Iranian countryside, where they lived and worked alongside the Iranian people, much like the Missionaries that preceded them.

Another Conflict

For years the United States Department of Defense had pressured the Iranian government to grant exemption to Americans serving in military advisory positions in Iran from Iranian law. Considering such a concept as an assault on Iranian national sovereignty, and recognizing that such a policy would result in widespread and strong condemnation by the people, the Iranian officials resisted the idea. Under tremendous and continued pressure from the United States, however, on October 13, 1964, a reluctant Iranian parliament approved the long sought law. The final vote was 70-62, with a large number of the deputies intentionally absconding themselves from the session. Based on this law, American military officials could no longer be held accountable in Iranian courts for any crimes that they may have committed. This came to be known in the United States as the Status of Forces Agreement (SFA). In Iran it was known as the Capitulation Agreement.

Iranians were especially sensitive regarding the issue of immunity for foreigners as they remembered with horror stories of the British and Russian officials taking advantage of their immunity from 1828 to 1928. The explosive anti-American sentiment that rose in reaction to the passage of this law was clearly expressed by T. Cuyler Young of Princeton University in his statement:

> The news was met by a bitter and vehement public reaction, which was reflected in the press; this must have been condoned by the government, such is the close and continuous surveillance accorded the press. The depth and breadth of the bitter resentment among the people was highly deserving to one visiting the country a few weeks after the event.[38]

This thorny issue remained as a deep source of resentment among Iranians. American involvement in the United States continued undaunted.

In May 1970, a group of 35 American investors and heads of huge corporations were invited to attend a six-day conference in Iran. They were warmly welcomed by the Iranian political and economic elite. At the meeting with these investors, the Shah told them that they were most welcome but they would have to make their money as minority shareholders. On January 10, 1972, the Iranian Minister of Economy, Hooshang Ansary, and Vice President, Spiro Agnew delivered addresses at the Second Iranian-American Investment Conference that was convened in New York City. On November 2, 1973, Iran and the United States agreed to establish a joint economic commission to accelerate further commercial relations of all kinds between the two countries. Between January of 1973 and September of 1974, United States companies signed a number of contracts and joint ventures with Iran that totaled 11.9 billion dollars.

In March of 1975, another economic accord was signed between Iran and the United States for 15 billion dollars. This agreement included the construction of eight large nuclear power plants, which were to provide Iran with some 8,000 mega watts of electricity. The Iranian-American commercial and military agreement reached its peak when an accord was signed in August of 1976 for a hefty 50 billion dollar trade program.

The economic growth and material advances that had started in 1973 led to an increase in per capita income - in 1977 it had increased 1,100% since 1963 - and enabled many Iranians to travel abroad, especially to the United States. In 1977, the number of Iranian students in America reached 60,000. At the same time, the number of Americans living in Iran reached 50,000.

The End of Relations

February of 1979, a revolutionary regime replaced the Shah's government. On November 4, 1979, the United States Embassy in Tehran was invaded by extremist students. On April 7, 1980, United States severed diplomatic relations with the Islamic Republic of Iran.

A mass exodus ensued whereby hundreds of thousands of intellectuals and highly-educated Iranians took refuge all over the world from Japan and Australia to Canada and the United States. The process was termed The Brain-drain, and the biggest beneficiary was the United States, which became the host for over one million professors, scientists, physicians, professionals, and artists who unlike many other immigrants, came solely in pursuit of liberty and brought along their intellectual and monetary wealth.

ENDNOTES

1. See Fredreick J. Heuser, Jr., A Guide To Foreign Missionary Manuscripts in the Presbyterian Historical Society (New York, 1988), p. 71. Also see William E. Strong, The Story of American Board: An Account of the First Hindered Years of the American Board of Commissioners for Foreign Missions (Boston: Pilgrim Press,1910).

2. Grant, Asahel, M.D., Account of the Nestorian Christians Settled in Oroomieh, 1840.

3. Perkins, Justin, D.D., *A Residence of Eight Years in Persia* (Andover, N.J.: Allen, Merrill and Wardwell, 1843).

4. Perkins, Rev. Henry Martin, Life of Justin Perkins, D.D., Pioneer Missionary to Persia, Chicago, 1887.

5. The original text of Farman (decree) is on file in the records of the Central Board of the Presbyterian Mission, and a certified copy was available in the office of the local mission.

6. See Fredreick J. Heuser, Jr., A Guide To Foreign Missionary Manuscripts in the Presbyterian Historical Society (New York, 1988).

7. For a history of the school see "Mission to Persia" by Rev. John Elder, Church council of Iran, Tehran. pp. 28-31.

8. For Farrokh Khan's diplomatic mission see Sarabi's *Makhzan-ol-Vaghaye*, Tehran University Press, 1955.

9. R.R. Dawes, A History of the Establishment of Diplomatic Relations with Persia (Marietta, Ohio, Aldeeman and Sons, Printers, 1887).

10. Benjamin, S.G.W., *Famous Nations, the Stories of People Which have Attained Prominence in History*. Vol. II, Part II, the Story of Persia. New York and London, 1892.

11. Benjamin, *The Nations of the World, Persia*. 1889. Preface, pp. IV & V.

12. Foreign Office Bulletin dated 1956, pp.28-45; the First Diplomatic Relationship between Iran and America, by Abbas Eghbal, Yadegar Magazine, dated 1944.

13. For the Saga of his arduous task, see *"The Strangling of Persia"* by W. Morgan Shuster, Mage Publishers, Washington D.C. , 1987.

14. Ibid., p. 298.

15. Browne, Edward Granville.-*"The Prose and Poetry of Modern Persia"*, Cambridge, 1914.pp.250-252.

16. See his book entitled *"The American Task in Persia"*, London and New York, The Century Company , 1925.

17. bid., pp. 187-188.

18. "Memorandum by John D. Jernegan of the Division of Near Eastern Affairs: American Policy in Iran," Washington, D.C., Jan. 23, 1943, as printed in Yonah, Alexander and Allan Names, eds., *The United States and Iran.* (Frederick, MD.: Aletheia Books, 1980), P.95

19. Ibid., p.104.

20. Arthur C. Millspaugh, *Americans in Persia*, (Washington, D.C.: Brookings Institution, 1946), pp.49-50.

21. George Kirk, *The Middle East in the War*, Survey of International Affairs, 1939-1946 series, ed. Arnold Toynbee (London: Oxford University Press, 1952), pp.150-51.

22. OSS 61429, Feb. 15, 1944, as quoted in James A. Bill, "The Eagle and the Lion - The Tragedy of American Iranian Relations", New Haven and London: Yale University Crest, 1988), p.23.

23. Hossain Kay-Ostovan, *Seyasat-e Movazeneh-e Manfi dar Majless-e Chahrdahom (the policy of negative equilibrium in the fourteenth Majless)*, Vol. 1 (Tehran, 1949), p.123.

24. Mark H. Lyte, The Origins of the Iranian-American Alliance, 1941-1953 (New York Holmes and Meier, 1987), pp.103-4.

25. Saleh in *U.N. Security Council Official Record*, 6th Year, 563d Meeting, 15(S/PV 563, 1951), as quoted in Jerrold L. Walden, "The International Petroleum Cartel in Iran: Private Power and Public Interest," *Journal of Public Law* 11(Spring 1962), p.70.

26. David S. McLellan, Dean Acheson: *The State Department Years* (New York: Doddd, Mead, 1976), p.387.

27. Dean Acheson, *Present at the Creation* (New York: W.W. Norton,

1969), p.506.

28. Eden, Anthony, *Full Circle* (Boston: Houghton Mifflin, 1960), pp. 214-15.

29. Krock, Arthur, Memoirs (New York: Funk and Wagnalls, 1968), p. 262.

30. Bill, The Eagle and the Lion, p.83.

31. A very comprehensive account of this event is given by Mark J. Gasiorowski in Aug. 1987, Vol. 19, #3 of International Journal of Middle East Studies entitled *The 1953 Coup d'etat in Iran.*

32. Warne, William E., Mission For Peace. Point 4 in Iran (Indianapolis/New York: The Bobbs-Merrill, 1956), pp.277-78.

33. "Joint Chief of Staff Joint Intelligence Committee Memorandum for the Joint Strategic Plans Committee and the Joint Logistic Plans Committee [enclosure draft]," Apr. 13, 1955, Alexander and Nanes, *United States and Iran*, p.273.

34. Ibid., p.306.

35. Ibid., p.307.

36. Armin Meyer as quoted in Abbas Amirie and Hamilton A. Twitchell, eds., *Iran in the 1980s* (Tehran: Institute for International Political and Economic Studies, 1978), p.382.

37. Alexander and Nanes, *United States and Iran*, pp.345-48

38. T. Cuyler Young, "U.S. Policy in Iran since World War II," paper presented at seminar, Problems of Contemporary Iran, Harvard University, Cambridge, Mass., Apr. 17, 1965, pp. 22-23

APPENDIX

THE ORIGINS OF U.S. SUPPORT FOR AN AUTOCRATIC IRAN

At a time when the history of relations between the United States and the former Iranian regime (as well as other autocratic states) is being reconsidered, it is important to recognize that U.S. support for one-man rule in Iran did not commence in 1953 subsequent to the fall of the government of Dr. Mossadegh. A study of the diplomatic records of the U.S. State Department and the British Foreign Office indicates an earlier beginning.

The above records reveal three important facts about the subject of our study: (1) as soon as the 21 year-old Crown Prince Mohammad Reza Pahlavi replaced his father on the throne in September 1941 as a result of the invasion of Iran by the Anglo-Soviet forces-with the proviso that henceforth, in accordance with Iran's constitution, he must reign rather than rule-the young shah launched a gradual but persistent campaign to regain the absolute powers of Reza Shah and to reverse the movement toward a constitutional monarchy;[1] (2) within five years after the reestablishment of constitutional government, Great Britain and the United States decided to assist the shah to become "the strong man" of Iran because they concluded that through a single "strong" individual-rather than through a parliamentary democracy-they could better protect and promote their geopolitical as well as commercial interests; (3) the State Department and the Foreign Office were surprisingly well aware of the consequences and the risks inherent in their decision to assist the shah to gain absolute power.[2]

Much has been said (mostly off the record) about the inappropriateness and the prematurity of constitutional government for Iran[3]-for that matter for most "developing" countries.[4] Incompatibility with third-world history, tradition, character, and culture are often cited. It is true that Iran's experience with a working constitutional government has been brief and inconclusive-probably no more than a total of twenty years since the constitutional revolution of 1906. What is important to remember, however, is that on the two occasions when Iran endeavored to learn to live under the rule of law (1906-25 and 1941-53) the experience was aborted as a foreign power intervened on the side of Iranian opponents of constitutional government.

From 1941 to 1946 Iran was probably closer to being a functional constitutional monarchy than at any other time before or after. During these years executive powers lay with the prime minister and the cabinet and not with the person of the shah. The Majless (parliament), particularly the XIVth. session (1944-46), asserted its constitutional prerogatives, demanding and achieving some accountability by the executive branch. It is true that men of wealth and power, representing a very small minority of the population, continued to control the majority of the seats in the Majless (mainly those of the provinces). Still, there were important departures from the previous autocratic rule of Reza Shah (1925-41). The Majless majority, not having been hand-picked by the monarch, no longer followed his will; rather it considered the interests of its own constituency. One would expect that such a Majless would have totally disregarded public opinion-as had its predecessors. But this was not the case. The limited freedom provided by the return of constitutional monarchy was sufficient for the people of Tehran and a few other major cities to send their own representatives to the Majless. Because some of these deputies enjoyed wide public support, they were able, in spite of their small number, to transform the Majless into an open forum for the expression of views of the middle and lower-middle class Iranians.

Bills presented by the government were vigorously debated in and out of the Majless and then truly voted upon. The Majless also became a sanctuary and a court of appeals for individuals and groups to present their grievances against the excesses of the executive branch and the military. A free press, though on occasion acting irresponsibly, provided another means of exposing governmental abuses, informing the public about important issues before the Majless, and even occasionally forcing the Majless majority to vote with the minority. Perhaps as a result of this experience, the shah in later years rejected the advice of some advisors to allow a token number of freely elected deputies to enter the Majless so as to give the appearance of a genuine legislature. In short, as an observer of Iranian history has stated, Iran's political system during this period became plural-istic although not democratic.[5]

Iran's post-war constitutional government, however, received a major setback in October 1946 when Great Britain, once again, and the United States for the first time, played a critical role in ousting a legally elected prime minister. This was done by urging the shah to threaten Prime Minister Qavam with arrest if he did not offer the resignation of his cabinet. With this move, the two Western powers pointed Iran, once again, toward absolute monarchy.

It had been obvious for some time that the shah was discontent with the secondary and inactive role assigned to him by Iran's constitution. In this connection a review of the relevant articles of the constitution of 1906 may be of interest.

According to Article 44 of the Fundamental Laws: "The person of the shah is exempted from responsibility. The ministers of state are responsi-ble to the Majless in all affairs." Article 66 made the relationship of the monarch and cabinet ministers even more explicit. It stated: "The minis-ters cannot use verbal or written orders of the shah to divest themselves of responsibility."

As far back as December 1942, slightly over a year after taking the throne, the shah-then only 23 years old-had urged Prime Minister Qavam to resign and place the government under the military-over which the monarch already had some influence. Qavam, however, supported by the British Minister Sir Reader Bullard,[7] had repelled the shah's first attempt "to dominate the government through his own trusted supporters (acting) as ministers."[8]

The monarch was not about to abandon his dream of continuing in his father's footsteps. In July 1943, the Office of Strategic Services (O.S.S.) told Washington that the shah had been energetically, though cautiously, strengthening ties with the officers of the army.[9] In August, the same source reported that the shah had succeeded in taking control of the army. Although a high level commission had concluded that under Iran's con-stitution, the General Staff was subordinate to the minister of war (and thus under the control of the prime minister), the shah had refused to sign regulations implementing this decision. Instead the shah had ordered the minister of war to tell the press and the Majless that he (the minister of war) was fully responsible for the army and the General Staff.[10]

By September 1943, the monarch was issuing orders directly to the General Staff, thus undermining the constitutional authority of the min-ister of war.[11] He justified this seizure of executive powers by contending that constitutional government was premature for Iran. In December 1944, the shah had said to the visiting Averell Harriman: "The country could not be truly democratic, which he desired, until the people had acquired sufficient education to understand the principles of democratic government and be able to form intelligent individual opinion."[12]

It is not recorded that dignitaries such as Averell Harriman ever asked the youthful shah how many decades were to pass for the Iranian people to understand the principles of democratic government, when only 3-6 percent of the national budget was being allocated to education-while 30 to 40 percent was devoted to the army and police. This rationalization (unpreparedness of the people) in support of one-man rule was repeated frequently by the shah and echoed by his foreign and domestic supporters for the next thirty-five years. For example, only two weeks after the shah's meeting with Harriman a report by the O.S.S. officer in Tehran stated: "Iran, like a small child, needs a strong governing hand until education has done its work, political consciousness has developed, and a group of properly trained public officials been established."[13]

Possibly the shah, in some moods, initially did wish to see Iran become a democracy, and so assumed autocratic powers with mixed feelings. Abbas Eskandari, a veteran politician who knew both the shah and his father well, said in 1948 of the young shah: "He is one-half the son of Reza Shah and one-half a sincere democrat." Because of bad advisors, however, "the son of Reza Shah is in the ascendancy ... and the democratic, social justice-minded young king less and less evident."[14]

Still, in 1941 after sixteen years of absolute rule by Reza Shah, a large number of middle- and working-class Iranians were unwilling to easily surrender their newly found political freedoms. Workers in most factories and civil servants in the central government, for instance, had formed their own trade unions. Wages had been increased as a result of unionization. Workers discharged without cause could appeal their case through their union, the press, and even the Grievance Committee of the Majlis.[15] Consequently, the shah may not have succeeded in seizing greater power without the support of the two Western powers who (with the departure of Soviet troops) were able to wield considerable influence in Iranian affairs by the summer of 1946.

The attention of the United States had been attracted to Iran as soon as American troops arrived in late 1941 to expedite war shipments to the Soviet Union. Even in September 1942, the means of gaining influence over the Iranian government was being considered by the American Legation in Tehran. One U.S. memorandum discussed: "The urgent advisability of placing Americans in strategic positions in the Iranian Government, and, in particular the necessity of sending a military mission to observe and, if possible, check any internal plots in the Iranian Army."[16]

During the war years, the aim of these arrangements may have been to prevent pro-German sabotage within the Iranian government. Later, however, the aim became the furtherance of post-war U.S. policy as it evolved. Subsequently, American missions took their places at the ministries of finance, interior, and war. According to an agreement signed with the United States in November 1943, the chief of American military advisors, who remained under the command of the United States War Department, was granted access to "any and all records, correspondence and plans relating to the administration of the Army needed by him." He was also given the power to investigate, summon, and question "any member of the Army" in "matters which in his opinion will assist him" in his duties; and the option to recommend appointment, transfer, or dismissal of Iranian officers to the shah.[17]

Appointment of foreign nationals to governmental posts invariably led to conflicts of interest. As an example, a January 1945 dispatch from Colonel Norman H. Schwartzkopf to the American ambassador in Tehran is noteworthy. Schwartzkopf, an American in command of the Iranian gendarmerie, was organizationally subordinate to the Minister of Interior. Still, in the concluding paragraph of the above letter, reporting an incident involving industrial workers at the Shahi factory in Mazandaran and a group of Russian soldiers, Schwartzkopf wrote: "It is my definite and expressed intention to conform with American policy, and information is respectfully requested as to what action on my part American policy dictates in this situation."[18]

As the war neared its conclusion, both military and civilian planners considered more seriously Iran's post-war strategic importance to the West-especially in the light of Britain's decline as a world power. In 1945, a United States military planner stated:

Unfortunately, Iran's position geographically, bordering Russia on the north, with British oil interests in the south, and its important strategic location in any war, will continue to make this country an object of basic interest to the major powers. It must be borne in mind that in any future war control of any part of Iran will allow the bombing either of the Russian oil fields in the north or of the British oil fields in the south. In the post-war period Iran's location is of importance in connection with transit-landing facilities for the various world airway projects. It is these inescapable factors that give Iran an international importance and one beyond what its size and population would otherwise warrant.

It is, therefore, not for any sentimental reasons nor even for any idealistic democratic principles, worthy as these may be, that the United States is forced to take a continuing interest in Iran.[19]

United States interest in Iran had been whetted by the Tehran Conference of December 1943, attended by President Roosevelt. In a memorandum to the State Department after the conference, the president stated: "I was rather thrilled with the idea of using Iran as an example of what we could do by unselfish American policy."[20] Dean Acheson's argument, in 1944, for American involvement in Iran was more pragmatic:

The military, political and commercial security of the United States requires stability and order in the vast belt of territory, from Casablanca to India and beyond, which constitutes the Mohammadan and Hindu world. Certainly we favor the evolution of self-government for the diverse peoples of that area, as we favor the restoration of their liberties to the democratic peoples of France and Spain. But we have a stake of our own in their political development.[21]

As the United States' major objective in Iran narrowed to "stability and order," American diplomats cast about for the means of achieving that goal. According to State Department records, at an early stage the shah became a key factor in this strategy. Reporting on his first audience with the monarch, Ambassador Leland Morris stated on September 15, 1944:

On the whole I received a good impression of the shah and it might be possible that the strengthening of his hand would be one of the roads out of the internal political dilemma in which this country finds itself. One thing is certain, that the weakness at the top which is apparent here must be eliminated either through the hands of the shah or by the rise of a strong individual.[22]

While the new U.S. ambassador was advocating "the rise of a strong individual," he was at the same time demonstrating impatience with Iran's infant constitutional government. In discussing the future of the Majless, the cornerstone of government of law, the ambassador reported that Iran's legislature by its past actions had not shown itself to be "an intelligent, patriotic, and sincere body."[23] As was often the case, the diagnosis was partially accurate but the prescription totally misguided.

If the Majless was not paying sufficient heed to the interests of the entire Iranian population, it was because the majority of its members represented a small fraction of the electorate; in particular, the court, the landlords, the merchants, and other members of the privileged classes. The XIIIth. session of the Majless, whose members had been "elected" during the authoritarian rule of Reza Shah, was the first to complete its term of two years after the abdication of the former monarch. The XIVth. session, in which for the first time in twenty years a handful of popularly elected deputies were seated, had been in session for less than a year when the ambassador was condemning the constitutional system rather than its implementation. If a legislature of a state in his own country was seen as "unpatriotic," the automatic remedy would have been to call for reform of the electoral process so as to make that body more representative of the electorate.

Instead of proposing in the host country the remedy that would have been prescribed in his home country, Ambassador Morris advocated "the rise of a strong individual."[24] Consequently, while warning Iranians of the evils of totalitarianism and working toward the defeat of the local communists, the representatives of the world's foremost democracies supported the reestablishment of a system of government in Iran that embodied many features of the political system they so fiercely opposed.

In the spring of 1946, George V. Allen replaced Morris as ambassador. During Allen's tenure, the United States became more deeply involved in Iran's domestic politics. Some researchers have suggested that the Iranians in these years were engaged in manipulating the United States government as actively and perhaps more successfully than the Americans were manipulating the Iranian government. One writer has contended that the U.S., after World War II, was "sucked" into involvement in Iran and that far from imposing itself on a reluctant Tehran government for its own purposes, the Iranian government was working hard to increase American involvement in Iranian affairs as a counterweight to Great Britain and the Soviet Union.[25] In June 1946, Ambassador Allen expressed a similar view contending that he was being besieged by "Iranians" urging a more active role by the United States in the internal affairs of their country.[26]

The "Iranians" referred to above were, in the main, Iran's men of wealth and power who opposed the implementation of the constitution which would lead to greater participation of the public in political affairs. As the Soviets endeavored to present themselves as the ally of the underprivileged, Iran's privileged desperately sought a new partner to replace the declining power of Great Britain. Thus in their frequent contacts with embassy officials, they urged greater U.S. involvement in Iranian affairs as the only means of preserving Iran's "independence." While the opinion of these men was duly recorded and reported by the embassy to Washington, little notice was taken of a much larger group of middle and lower-middle class Iranians who believed that national independence and political freedom were interdependent and that Iran's only salvation lay in a government of law and in the absence of foreign influence rather than its balance.

According to the U.S. military attaché in Tehran, a major advocate of United States involvement in Iranian affairs was the shah, whom he described as "extremely pro-American, even to the extent of urging...the United States to accept a valuable oil concession." [27] In return the shah wished to be fully supported by the United States in his quest for absolute power. Reportedly the monarch had told Allen: "The Iranian people had not reached the stage where the king could only be a symbol. If he continued to exercise no substantive authority in Iranian affairs, the people would become unaware, after a time, of the value of a monarchy and unappreciative of the needs thereafter." [28]

Ambassador Allen initially turned down the shah's proposal to strengthen the court by reducing the constitutional powers of the prime minister. In the words of Allen: "I was not confident the shah was strong enough to succeed, did not think a king should be meddling in politics anyway, and was not certain where he would stop if he did succeed in whatever actions he might attempt." [29]

In May 1946, Allen considered Prime Minister Qavam better equipped to achieve the main objective of the United States in Iran, which was "to prevent one more country from falling completely into the Moscow orbit." [30] In the American ambassador's view, Qavam was "the most energetic and forceful man on the scene in Iran at the present time. If anyone can steer this ship of state through the dangerous waters it is now traversing, Qavam is the most likely instrument for the purpose." [31]

Qavam, a true aristocrat, was about 70 years old in 1946. He had first served in government in 1909 as undersecretary of the Ministry of Interior. In 1921 he became prime minister, with Dr. Mossadegh as his minister of finance and Reza Khan as his minister of war. In 1923, Qavam was arrested for an alleged plot against the then Prime Minister Reza Khan, and his estates were confiscated. After his release, he retired from public life until August 1942 when he formed his first post-Reza Shah cabinet.

In January 1946, he was elected prime minister during the final days of the XIVth. Majless to deal with a number of acute political problems: to respond to Soviet demands for an oil concession in the north, to get Soviet troops out of Iran, to resolve the dispute with the province of Azarbaijan over the question of local autonomy, and to contain the growing influence of the Tudeh party. [32]

Qavam demonstrated his mastery of the political process by dealing effectively with each of the above. He signed an agreement with the Soviets giving them an oil concession. The Russians, in turn, agreed to remove their troops from Iran and to wait for the ratification of the agreement by the still-to-be-elected XVth. Majless. Qavam then opened negotiations with Pishevari's Democrats in Azarbaijan, thereby reducing tensions. He then formed his own political party, the Iranian Democrats, as a rival to the Tudeh. In August 1946, he formed a coalition cabinet including three Tudeh leaders. Without going into the details of this decision, the following passage from Ambassador Allen's dispatch makes Qavam's motives clear. It also discounts claims made only two months later that Qavam was a "helpless" tool of the Tudeh and the Soviet Union: "I feel confident changes of ministers resulted from Qavam's belief [that] he can handle [the] Tudeh better inside government than out and from his effort to absorb [the] Tudeh organization into his political party." [33]

Confirming Allen's prediction, no sooner had the Tudeh joined Qavam's cabinet than the provincial officials in Khoozestan, Esfahan, and other localities began to smash Tudeh organizations. The British ambassador confirmed the erosion of Tudeh power subsequent to their inclusion in the cabinet. He reported on October 8th that although during the first six months of 1946 the strength of the Tudeh party had developed rapidly, "during the last three months it has encountered set-backs in spite of the inclusion of three Tudeh leaders in the cabinet at the beginning of August." [34]

Ironically, as Qavam proceeded systematically to weaken the Tudeh party and to strengthen his own Democrat party, George Allen decided that it was time to join forces with the court and oust the prime minister. The background to this important event was the following: In early October 1946 Qavam had ended the tribal uprising in the south by forming an alliance with the Qashqais who promised to help him fight the Tudeh by supporting the Iran Democrat Party. This alliance had greatly displeased the monarch, who had wished to eliminate not only the Tudeh, but in the process also remove all obstacles to his one-man rule-even if they were anti-Communists. According to Ambassador Allen, in the above instance the shah: "had wanted to wipe out the Qashqais, and the agreement left them with their arms and also meant a major political victory for Qavam. But the shah could not do anything about it, and at any rate the Tudeh advance into south Persia was halted."[35] It was thus not surprising that a few days after the conclusion of the Qavam-Qashqai agreement a court emissary called on Allen asking him to confer his blessings on what the visitor described as a coup d'etat against Qavam.[36]

Consequently (as Allen reported it later to the State Department), on October 14, 1946, Ambassador Allen told the shah that he had "finally reached the conclusion that he [the shah] should force Qavam out and should make him leave the country or put him in jail if he caused trouble."[37] In explaining this totally new attitude, George Allen gave Washington several reasons-some of which were not totally consistent with the record, including that of the British Embassy quoted above. The major justification provided by Allen and the one cited most by other researchers of the period was the following:

Things had been going from bad to worse for several weeks, with the Tudeh members of the cabinet tearing the government to pieces, installing Tudeh party members in all the ministries they could control, and Qavam seemed helpless before their organized attack, engineered by the Soviet Embassy here.[38]

Another, and a more plausible, reason why Allen decided (apparently without prior State Department authorization) to throw his weight behind the shah was to prevent the conclusion of an air agreement with the Soviet Union:

The Soviets had some time previously suggested the foundation of a joint aviation company to have a monopoly of all air traffic in northern Iran. The Soviets were to furnish all planes, equipment, personnel, weather stations, etc., etc., with the Iranians furnishing merely the air through which the planes would fly. Profits were to be shared 50-50. !t was a wonderful proposition, generous to a fault! On October 11,...manager of Iranian Airways, told Randy Williams [an Embassy secretary] that he had learned that at a cabinet meeting ten days previously, General Firuz, Minister of Roads and Communications, had presented the Soviet proposal urgently to the cabinet and strongly supported its adoption. The only member of the cabinet to oppose it actively had been Hajir, Minister of Finance. Iraj Iskandari, President of the Tudeh Party and Minister of Commerce, had spoken in favor but had pointed out that since he had been told that the Soviet proposal might be contrary to the Chicago Aviation Convention, it might be better for Iran first to announce its signature to the Chicago Convention and then agree to the Soviet proposal.

Within 12 hours Muzzafar Firuz had told all the details of the meeting to the Soviet Embassy and the Soviet First Secretary had called on Iraj Iskandari, raising hell about Iraj's disloyalty to USSR by his suggestion for delay. Iraj protested his deepest friendship for the USSR.[39] As soon as the Secretary left, he went to Qavam complaining bitterly about 'the traitor in the cabinet who is telling the Soviet Ambassador that I am opposing the USSR.'

As soon as Randy Williams passed the story on to me I seized on it as just what I'd been looking for. As you will recall, I'd been trying to find means for driving the Soviet airplanes out of cabotage business in Iran and I was delighted with a chance to hit a blow on this subject and against the Soviet stooges in the cabinet at the same time. I did not realize what a gold mine [sic] we'd struck, as it turned out.

I asked for an appointment with Qavam immediately. I told him he had a traitor in his cabinet who was running to the Soviet Embassy with the most secret discussions in his official family,[40] thereby enabling the Soviets to hold a pistol at the head of any Minister who might be brave enough to express a patriotic sentiment in cabinet meetings.[41] I said he would have to do something about the situation promptly, since I desired to recommend to my Government whether to continue to consider his Government as independent and worthy of continued treatment as such.

I waited three days and nothing happened. It became clear to me that Firuz (and perhaps the Tudeh crowd) had too strong a hold over Qavam to permit him to break loose from them. His own party was not yet strong enough to challenge the Tudeh,[42] but perhaps more important, Qavam knew that if he lost the Tudeh and the Soviet support, the shah would be able to push him around. On October 14, 1946, I had the conversation with the shah which disturbed Dean Acheson and others in the Department considerably, and which the Shah now refers to as 'our famous talk of last summer.[43]

Thus, the American ambassador in pursuit of his own country's interests and perhaps in his perception of what was best for Iran, delivered a devastating blow to Iran's infant constitutional government-a blow from which Iran has not yet recovered.

Qavam himself unwittingly helped bring about his own doom. Having decided to delay elections for the XVth. Majless, Iran was without a parliament after March 1946. Consequently, Qavam was unable to enlist the support of the legislature, and through it the public, to prevent the shah's take-over of the executive branch. Under threat of arrest, Qavam succumbed to the shah and replaced six members of his cabinet with men more acceptable to the shah.[44]

Qavam's purge of his cabinet, which took place on October l6th, was correctly described by Ambassador Allen as "the turning point in Iranian history." This event alone, obviously, did not put an end to constitutional monarchy. Iran's return to autocracy was accomplished in stages. Within a period of two and one-half years-beginning with October 16, 1946-three different Western ambassadors gleefully referred to three specific instances of usurpation of power by the shah as "historical."

The second "historical" advance toward one-man rule occurred in December 1947. By that time Russian troops had been pressured out of Iran by the United States and the United Nations, the province of Azarbaijan had been brought back under central government authority (as a result of the joint effort of the shah and Qavam), the Tudeh party was put in disarray, the XVth. Majless (with a few exceptions) was packed with members of the so-called thousand families, and the Soviet oil concession had been rejected by the Majless.[45]

It was at this juncture that the two Western ambassadors finally agreed with the shah's long-standing desire to discharge Prime Minister Qavam, who now seemed expendable.[46] Using as a pretext an allegedly veiled criticism of himself by Qavam, the shah let it be known that continuation of Qavam's cabinet was intolerable. As a result, on December 4, 1947, all members of the cabinet (except two who were absent from Tehran) resigned, leaving Qavam totally isolated.

Following the resignation of the cabinet, the XVth. Majless, dominated by the supporters of status quo, gave the prime minister a vote of no confidence.[47] He was not only relieved of his duties, but was also refused the diplomatic passport normally granted to former officials. Instead, Qavam, the most powerful man in Iran only a year and a-half earlier was allowed to leave the country on an ordinary passport.[48] This was the first demonstration of the shah's ability to out-maneuver and defeat his potential rivals, even Qavam, the highly experienced Iranian politician under whom the shah's own father had once served.

This was not an ordinary change of cabinet. Clearly, the shah had acted after securing the blessings of the British as well as the American ambassador. British dispatches mention that their ambassador, John Le Rougetel, had discussed the removal of Qavam with the shah on November 12, 1947.[49] The tone of the following passage from the American ambassador's report indicates that he too was sympathetic with the move:

> The shah kept Qavam in power to make him assume responsibility for refusing the Soviet oil concession, since the shah did not want Qavam ever to be able to return to power with Soviet support. Finally, when Qavam had served his usefulness, the shah gave the nod and the Majless kicked him out.[50]

Thus December 1947 marked the second "historical" event that propelled Iran toward autocracy. In the words of the British ambassador:

> The fall of Qavam seems likely to mark the end of a phase in the development of Persian politics. Earlier in the year there had already been signs of increased political activity by the court. The shah had felt, since December 1946 (when the central government took control of Azarbaijan), that too much credit had been given Qavam and insufficient to himself.[51]

A most surprising aspect of the diplomatic records consulted was that neither the State Department nor the Foreign Office was under any illusions as to the consequences of reestablishing one-man rule in Iran.[52] Ambassador Le Rougetel correctly predicted in December 1947 that henceforth the shah would exert a direct and increasing influence, backed by the military authorities, in the government of the country.[53]

In the United States, the decision to support an autocratic monarchy was preceded by a vigorous debate within the State Department. Some officials argued that an increase of power by the shah "might not be a bad thing since strong governments in countries bordering the Soviet Union have generally been better able to resist Soviet domination."[54]

John D. Jernegan, acting chief of the Division of Greek-Turkish-Iranian affairs, made a spirited reply. Although subscribing to the principle of containing Soviet power by strong, bordering governments, he doubted the applicability of this principle to Iran and the person of the shah. The shah had deplored the lack of progress in Iran and attributed it to his personal lack of constitutional power, Jernegan said. But where he did have control, as over the army, his record had been less than inspiring.[55]

Oddly enough, George Allen, who had played a key role in the shah's rise to power, agreed with Jernegan's analysis:

One is tempted by the thought that, although a dictatorship of the Reza Shah variety should be undesirable, perhaps a middle ground of a somewhat stronger government would be preferable to the chaotic and corrupt conditions we now have. However, I have steadfastly resisted the temptation, and my policy continues to be based firmly on support of democratic principles no matter how badly they may be carried out in practice. The shah sometimes uses cogent arguments with one on the subject, but I continue to argue for the ways of democracy.

The best way for Iran to become a decent democracy, it seems to me, is to work at it, through trial and error. I am not convinced by the genuinely held view of many people that democracy should be handed down gradually from above.[56]

Unfortunately, neither Allen nor his successors followed this advice. Time and again when the shah took a critical step toward autocratic rule, they either applauded and justified his action or maintained an approving silence, explaining their behavior as "non-interference."

The position of the Foreign Office was similar. On November 1, 1947, the shah had solicited the British ambassador's advice regarding changes in the constitution.[57] After much discussion with the Foreign Office, Ambassador Le Rougetel concurred that the composition of the XVth. Majless made it virtually impossible for the shah's government to reform the administration or to enact a constructive economic policy.[58] No reference was made, however, to the fact that only a few weeks earlier the same Majless had demonstrated its willingness to collaborate with the shah by deposing Prime Minister Qavam who was the founder and leader of the political party through which most of the deputies had entered the Majless.

The third step toward the reestablishment of autocracy was taken in April 1949, when a constitutional assembly was hastily and undemocratically convened and the constitution amended to grant greater power to the shah. The assembly was precipitated, in part, by an assassination attempt on the shah two months earlier.[59]

Referring to the increased domination of the shah over the executive branch as a "turning point in the current history of Iran," the new American ambassador, John C. Wiley, stated:

Iran is now in a new orientation. It must be watched with greatest care. The shah must be prevented from leaping on his horse and charging simultaneously in all directions. There is so much good he wants to do and so much harm he might do-if he does not proceed wisely. It is important that we and the British leave nothing undone to follow closely the immediate course of events.[60]

Confirming the forecast of Ambassador Wiley that henceforth "the shah will rule and not merely reign,"[61] the monarch reduced the powers of the prime minister further by personally presiding over cabinet meetings. Wiley, reporting on his conversation with a former Iranian prime minister, stated that the shah was

Dedicating himself to the minutiae of administration. On even the smallest detail he was communicating directives, even to section heads. He was wasting his energy and time and undermining governmental coordination. The worst phase of the situation, according to [former Prime Minister] Ali Mansur, was the fact that the shah was so badly entoure. He was surrounded by sycophantic advisors who were constantly urging [upon] him the necessity of increasing his royal prerogatives, exercising authority and ruling in the pattern of his late father. He had been given the concept of regal strength on a basis of weakness of the government; namely, that the shah would be strong in the measure in which the government would be weak.[62]

Having revised the constitution in his favor and taken direct command of the executive branch, the shah focused his attention on the legislative branch with the intent of making it completely dependent upon himself. In September 1949, the U.S. ambassador reported that the shah had cast aside his plans for free elections for the XVlth. Majless because he believed that:

corrupt and venal political influences were effectively working to take improper advantage of free elections. The shah was now convinced that with the great illiteracy among and backwardness of the great mass of Iranian people any application of electoral principles of Western democracies would be premature and bad. His Imperial Majesty[63] was determined to have a Majless with which he could work in harmony. He intended moreover to make considerable reforms of governmental structure but he wanted me to be completely assured that he had no idea whatsoever of setting up a dictatorship.[64]

Despite his assurances to Ambassador Wiley, the shah was indeed bent on setting up a dictatorship. Gradually he removed all semblance of independence from the Majless, the judiciary, the press, political parties, trade unions, universities, professional associations, and even the chambers of commerce. Thus no institution or public figure remained who could question his decisions and actions.

One would have thought Great Britain and the United States, being themselves democracies, would have expressed sympathy for constitutional government in Iran. But they decided that a "stable autocratic monarchy" better protected their interests in Iran than an "unstable constitutional monarchy."

The West's perception of political realities in Iran was not totally inaccurate. The initial stage of political development in Iran was inherently uncertain. The communists could take advantage of the dissatisfaction of the masses and perhaps gain control of the government. The West's response to the situation, however, was shortsighted and eventually self defeating. Instead of using its considerable influence to promote the development of democratic institutions and thus assist the people (or at least the educated middle class) in gaining a stake in their country's political system, it shattered the fragile institutions that were just beginning to form. Whereas this course of action may have been the safer of the two, and certainly the more profitable in the short run, it was also an indication that Great Britain and the United States held little faith in the applicability of their own democratic system of government to third-world countries. In the long run, this attitude would mean the surrender of a great advantage to their communist adversary who in contrast truly believed that its political system was applicable to the entire world.

ENDNOTES

1. This revelation adds a new dimension to the impression held by critics of the former monarch who viewed him in the 1940s as weak, ineffective, and pleasure-seeking.

2. John C. Wiley, May 12, and June 23, 1949. Records of the Foreign Service Posts of the Department of State, Tehran Embassy, Record Group 84 (hereafter indicated as RG-84), Box 2259, Washington National Records Center (hereafter indicated as WNRC), Suitland, Maryland.

3. For an unpublished statement of this view refer to United States Office of Strategic Services, December 15, 1944, Modern Military Records Division, Record Group 226 (hereafter indicated as RG-226), ID 50737, National Archives Building (hereafter, records in the National Archives Building are indicated as NA), Washington, D.C. For a public, but indirect, statement of this position (support for authoritarian leader rather than opposition to constitutional government) see George Lenczowski, Iron Under the Pahlavis (Stanford: Hoover Institution Press, 1978).

4. Jeane Kirkpatrick, Commentary, 68, 5 (November 1979), pp. 34-45.

5. Ervand Abrahamian, "Social Bases of Iranian Politics: The Tudeh Party, 1941-53," Ph.D. dissertation, Columbia University, 1968, p. 4.

6. See George V. Allen, May 21, 1946, Diplomatic Branch, Civil Archives Division, Record Group 59 (hereafter indicated as RG-59), Numerical File 891.00/5-2146, NA; and George V. Allen, June 6, 1946, RG-84, Box 2255, WNRC.

7. Louis G. Dreyfus, Jr. to the Secretary of State, December 9, 1942, RG-59, Numerical File 891.00/ 1962, NA.

8. United States Office of Strategic Services, June 30, 1943, RG-226, ID 83820, NA.

9. United States Office of Strategic Services. July 5, 1943, RG-226, ID 30178, NA.

10. Louis G. Dreyfus, Jr. to the Secretary of State, July 23, 1943, RG-59,

Numerical File 891.00/2032, NA.

11. United States Tehran Military Attaché, August 28, 1943, RG-226, ID 43824, NA.

12. Leland Morris to the Secretary of State, December 6, 1944, RG-59, Numerical File 891.00/ 12644, NA.

13. United States Office of Strategic Services, December I5, 1944.

14. James Somerville to the Secretary of State, December 21, 1948, RG-84, Box 2257, WNRC.

15. See Habib Ladjevardi, "Politics and Labor in Iran: 1941-1949," D.Phil., University of Oxford, 1981.

16. Paul H. Alling, September 4, 1942, RG-59, Numerical File 891.00/ 1914, NA.

17. Keivan Tabari, "Iran's Policies Toward the United States During the Anglo-Russian Occupation, 1941-1946," Ph.D. dissertation, Columbia University, 1967, p. 66. For a discussion of the military mission see Thomas M. Ricks, "U.S. Military Mission to Iran," Iranian Studies, 3-4 (Summer/Autumn 1979), pp. 163-193.

18. Colonel H. Norman Schwartzkopf to the United States Ambassador in Tehran, January I, 1945, RG-84, Box 2243, file 710, WNRC.

19. Colonel Harold B. Haskins, February t9, 1945, RG-84, Box 2244, WNRC.

20. F. D. Roosevelt, January 12, 1944, RG-59, Numerical File 891.00/3037, NA.

21. Dcan Acheson, January 28, 1944, RG-59, Numerical File 891.00/2844, NA.

22. Leland Morris, September 15, 1944, RG-84, WNRC.

23. Leland Morris, September 25, 1944, RG-84, WNRC.

24. Thus, there was just as much reluctance thirty-seven years ago as there is today in 1982 to recognize that the "strong individual" does not limit the use of his unchecked authority for "economic and social reform." The strong individual, after the initial period of consensus, removes the checks end balances required under constitutional government and suppresses all forma and channels of

debate and criticism. Having removed the legal and institutional brakes on arbitrary rule, the strong individual then proceeds with "economic development" projects that mainly benefit and appeal to a small segment of the urban population that is necessary to run his machine. In implementing projects, his administrators invariably indulge in favoritism, mismanagement, end corruption without fear of exposure, punishment, or even criticism.

25. Stephen McFarland, "A Peripheral View of the Origins of the Cold War: The Crisis in Iran, 1941-47," Diplomatic History (Fall 1980), p. 333.

26. George V. Allen, June 6, 1946, RG-84, Box 2255, WNRC. For an example of such invitations of intervention see George V. Allen, October 14, 1946, RG-59, Numerical File 891.00/ 10-1446, NA.

27. United States Tehran Military Attaché. May I. 1947, Modern Military Records Division. Record Group 319, ID 37085, NA.

28. George V. Allen, May 21. 1946.

29. George V. Allen to John D. Jernegan, January 21, 1948, RG-84, Box 2257, File 800, WNRC. This letter was written near the end of Allen's tenure in Iran, summarizing and reflecting upon the major events of the previous two years.

30. George V. Allen, June 6, 1946, RG-84, Box 2255, WNRC.

31. Ibid.

32. L. P. Elwell-Sutton, Persian Oil: A Study in Power Politics (London: Lawrence and Wishart. 1955). PP. 113-II8.

33. George V. Allen, August 6, 1946, RG-84, Box 2255, WNRC.

34. John Le Rougetel, October 8, 1946, F.O. 371, Registry Number G-575/54/46, Public Record Office, London. (Hereafter, records in the Public Record Office, London are indicated as PRO.)

35. George V. Allen to John D. Jernegan, January 21, 1948.

36. George V. Allen, October 14, 1946.

37. George V. Allen to John D. Jernegan, January 21, 1948.

38. Ibid.

39. Compare Ambassador Allen's private version of events with that published by the then chief of the Political Section of the United States Embassy in Tehran, Robert Rossow, Jr., "The Battle of Azerbaijan, 1946," The Middle East Journal, 10 (Winter 1956), pp. 27-28 in which he states: "At a meeting of Qavam's cabinet at which the issue was discussed in supposed secrecy, four of the non-Tudeh members forcefully opposed the granting of concession [Allen mentions only Hajir]. Less than two hours after the conclusion of the meeting, strong men of the Soviet Embassy [The First Secretary of the Soviet embassy] appeared at their residences [only Iraj Iskandari, the leader of the Tudeh party was allegedly visited], berating them and threatening physical violence to their persons and families [Allen reports no such violence] if they continued their opposition."

40. Allen said nothing about his own source of information about cabinet discussions.

41. Allen was referring to Iskandari, one of the ministers he hoped to remove.

42. On the contrary, Qavam and his party were strong enough to challenge the Tudeh. By mid September they had removed nearly all Tudeh leaders from the important industrial centers of Khoozestan and Isfahan. In Isfahan, the Tudeh leaders were arrested by the personal orders of Mozzafar Firouz. See Lajevardi, "Politics and Labour in Iran," pp. 355 and 415.

43. George V. Allen to John D. Jernegan. January 21, 1948.

44. Ibid. Mozzafar Firouz denied and ridiculed the allegation that he leaked cabinet discussions to the Soviets. While unaware of the role played by George Allen in the fall of the coalition cabinet, Firouz knew that he was intensely disliked by the American ambassador. After giving Firouz the unexpected news that he had resigned, Qavam "like a child put his hand in his pocket and said 'but 1 have got another order to form a new cabinet.'" In discussing a post outside the country for Firouz, Qavam asked: "What have you done to these Americans?" Firouz was just as puzzled. He said that he had only implemented the government's policies: "It is not only in our national interest but it is to the interest of the Americans to have Azarbaijan freed, to have the Russians no longer in the country."

Yet he refused to follow Qavam's suggestion that he should discuss his differences with Allen over a private dinner. See Mozzafar Firouz, in an interview recorded by Habib Ladjevardi. December 6, 1981, Paris, Iranian Oral History Project, Center For Middle Eastern Studies, Harvard University.

45. The Majless on October 23, 1947 voted to consider the Qavam-Sadchivkov agreement of April 1946 regarding the oil concession as null and void.

46. John Le Rougetel, December 8, 1947, F.O. 371, E-1200/40/34, PRO.

47. Princess Ashraf played a critical role in organizing the anti-Qavam vote in the Majless. See Ashraf Pahlavi. Faces in a Mirror (Englewood. NJ: Prentice-Hall, 1980), p. 90. Also on the same subject. but from the point of view of a Majless deputy, see Mohammad Ebrahim Amineymour (Kalali), in an interview recorded by Habib Ladjevardi, January 25. 1982, Tape II, La Jolla, California. Iranian Oral History Project.

48. United Kingdom, Tehran Embassy, Report for the Quarter Ended 31 December, 1947, F.O. 371, E-293/25/34, PRO.

49. United Kingdom, Political Situation in Iran, November 13, 1947, F.O. 371, E-1069/40/34, PRO.

50. George V. Allen to John D. Jernegan, January 21, 1948.

51. United Kingdom, Tehran Embassy, Report for the Quarter Ended 31 December 1947.

52. It is therefore somewhat incredulous to be told thirty years later-after the fall of the monarchy in 1979-that the Western diplomats were unaware of the consequences of the shah's mode of governance.

53. United Kingdom, Tehran Embassy, Report for the Quarter Ended 31 December 1947.

54. John D. Jernegan, December 4, 1947, RG-59, Numerical File 891.00/12-447, NA.

55. Ibid.

56. George V. Allen, December 26, 1947, RG-59, Numerical File 891.00/12-2647, NA.

57. United Kingdom, Political Situation in Iran, November 13, 1947.

58. John Le Rougetel, January 6, 1948, F.O. 371, PRO.

59. Although the would-be assassin, Nasser Fakhr-Arai, had closer ties with an Islamic religious group than with the Tudeh party, General Razmara and others decided to place the total blame for the assassination attempt on the Tudeh in order to deal a final blow to it. This tactical move was strongly supported by the U.S. Embassy. For more details see Ladjevardi, "Politics and Labour in Iran," pp. 223-22S.

60. John C. Wiley. May 12, 1949. Wiley succeeded Allen as ambassador in the winter of 1948.

61. Ibid.

62. John C. Wiley, June 23, 1949.

63. Subsequent to the increase in the power of the shah, he was thereafter referred to as "His Imperial Majesty" in the embassy dispatches rather than the "shah."

64. John C. Wiley, September 17, 1949, RG-84, Box 2259, WNRC. Illiteracy of the masses was a convenient excuse for many of the repressive measures adopted by the government. The shah also cited illiteracy when preventing the formation of political parties.

PART II

CHAPTER TWO

ANCIENT IRAN

For many centuries the words Iran and Persia have been used interchangeably to identify the same country. The peoples of the land have always called it Iran, while Westerners, influenced by the Greeks, have referred to it as Persia. In 1935 Reza Shah Pahlavi, believing that the name Persia denoted a backward country to the peoples of the west, ordered that henceforth it should be called Iran, a new name to the westerner, to demonstrate the modernity of the country under his rule. Ever since the Second World War both terms have come back into vogue.

Persians have a long history and they are very conscious of it. Stone scrappers/axes found in 1973 in Zagross Mountains near Kermanshah proved humans inhabited Iran as far back as 100,000 years ago. Tests of flints and similar material found in a cave in Gonbad-e-Ghaboos (Gunbad-Qabus) near the Caspian Sea in early 1960s by Dr. McBurney from Cambridge University, showed that they originated at least 40,000 B.C. and possibly as far back as 65,000 B.C., being used by hunters of rhinoceros, wild horses and bears.[1] Cave paintings west of Khorramabad date from 40,000 B.C. They are believed to be the only known examples between the Mediterranean and the Indian peninsula. Tests of findings in yet another cave near Kermanshah prove them to be 35,000 years old.

The residents of Iran belong to the people called Aryans. Aryan is a term primarily used to denote a family of languages and secondarily refers to the people who speak those languages. In other words it is not meant to denote a race.

Much has been written on the original homeland of the Aryans. The region north of the Black Sea, Eurasia, the Oxus region, and the plateau of Iran have been mentioned. It was first believed that the Aryans came to Iran about the first millennium B.C., but thanks to recent archeological discoveries in Sialk in central Iran, Hasanlu in Azarbaijan and other places, it is presumed that the Aryans were in the region long before then. This would seem to support some Persian scholars who believe that Aryans originated in the Iranian plateau and from there migrated eastward to India and westward to Europe. The excavator of the Sialk [2], however, believes that there were different invasions of Iran by the Aryans. The Persian and some other tribes were relative newcomers, invading the country through the Caucasus and from Transoxiana, thus from both sides of the Caspian Sea. While the previous Aryan invaders, such the Hurrians, the Mitanni, and the Kasites had been absorbed by the " natives," the new Aryan tribes, the Persians and the Medes, who settled in the Zagross Valley, were not absorbed but became one of the three principal rivals for the supremacy of the region. These three rivals were Assyria, the dominant power at the time; the kingdom of Urartu, which later became Armenia; and the Iranians, who comprised two groups known as Medes and Persians.

For several thousand years Persians have had the sense of Iran and Iranians as particular and special; they have regarded their place on earth as part of the continuing renewal of the whole creation. For over a thousand years Persians in many walks of life have chanted their history in the matchless poetry of Ferdosi, very much as the Greeks used to recite the exquisite poems of Homer. It was after the Eslamic conquest of Iran that Abolghasem Ferdosi of Toos spent 30 years in research and writing to create sixty thousand couplets depicting the history of Iran from mythological times to the coming of Eslam. The book is called Shahnameh, Book of Kings. It is a great literary masterpiece which has been an inspiration to generations of Persians.

Four dynasties in the pre-Eslamic Iran have been discussed in Shahnameh: the Pishdadians, the Kiyanians, the Ashkanians, and the Sasanians. The first two are semi-mythological, ending with the fall of the Achaemenian Empire. The third is the Persian name for the Parthian dynasty, and the fourth is the Sassanids, whose dynasty was in power for four centuries immediately before the advent of Eslam.

The first king of the Pishdadi dynasty, named Kayumars, is the same as the first man in the Avesta (the Zoroastrian Holy Book), Gayomareta. He subjugated the beasts of the field and the demons, who eventually killed his son Siyamak. The next king was Hooshang, who separated iron from the rock and accidentally discovered fire. To celebrate the discovery, he established the festival of Sadeh, still celebrated in some parts of Iran. His son Tahmoores domesticated animals and taught people the carding and spinning of wool. He conquered the demons but spared their lives, and in return they taught him the art of writing.

The most famous king in this dynasty was Jamsheed. He had a cup in which he could see the entire world. He ruled seven hundred years over men and beast and divided society into four: clergy, military, farmer, and artisan. He also inaugurated the festival of Norooz (also Now-Ruz), or New Year, at the vernal equinox (the first day of spring). This has always remained as the national festival of the Persians.

Jamsheed's kingdom was usurped by Zahhak who had two snakes growing out of his shoulders which had to be fed fresh human brain. After a thousand years of tyranny, a blacksmith called Kaveh, raised his apron as a banner of revolt and brought Fereydoun, a scion of the dynasty of Kiyan, out of hiding and proclaimed him king. The young shah imprisoned Zahhak on the summit of Damavand volcano, about 60 miles north east of Tehran. After that, he divided his kingdom among his three sons. Saam, the eldest, inherited "Rome" and the West, Tour received Touran (Central Asia) and China, and Iraj, the youngest, gained Iran. The older brothers were jealous of Iraj, and a good portion of Shahnameh is taken up with the rivalry and exploits of their descendants.

The first recorded reference to Persians (Parsua) and the Medes (Madai) is found in the records of Shalmaneser III - king of Assyria - in 844 and 836 B.C. respectively. These two were by no means the only Aryan tribes. The Zikirtu were scattered in Azarbaijan (northwest), the Parthava (Parthians) in the Caspian region, and the Haraivais in Khorasan (northeast). Perhaps during the eighth century B.C., when the power of Assyria declined, the Persians broke out of the Zagross Valley and went eastward to the mountainous region north of the Persian Gulf. There they settled and gave their name Parsa (modern Fars) to the region, which eventually became Persia. The Medes, however seem to have stayed in western Iran in the region of Ecbatana (from the old Persian Hagmatana, place of meeting, modern Hamadan) and continued the struggle against Assyria. Cayaxares, the king of the Medes, in alliance with Nabopolassar put an end to the Assyrian empire in 612 B.C. by capturing Ninevah. Western Asia, thus divided between the Babylonians and the Medes, did not remain tranquil for long. Soon these two powers began to fight each other for supremacy.

The Achaemenid Empire 550-330 B.C.

Throughput the time that these two adversaries were busy fighting each other, the Persians took advantage of the confusion and strengthened themselves without hindrance. The founder of the ruling house of the Persians was Hakhamanesh, whom the Greeks called Achaemenes. He established the dynasty called the Achaemenid. The earliest text in existence is a gold tablet written in old Persian by Aryaramnes a grandson of Hakhamanesh, and son of Chishpish (Teispes to the Greeks). He refers to his father as the "Great King, King of Anshan,) and to his brother Kourosh (Cyrus I) as "King of Anshan,) and to himself as "King of Kings, King of Parsa." He lived about 640-590 B.C. and wrote, " This land of the Persians which I possess, provided with fine horses and good men, it is the great God Ahura Mazda who has given it to me. I am the King of this land." This rare document found in Hamadan is important in two aspects: first, it is written in a very advanced alphabet, and second, it contains this reference to Ahura Mazda as the supreme giver of power.

Aryaramnes' brother's grandson, Kourosh II, known to the Persians as Kourosh (or Cyrus) the Great, was the first to make the name of Hakhamanesh world famous. Cyrus, whose mother was a Median princess called Mandana, "wooed as much as conquered the Medes under his principles of conquest. First, persuasion and accommodation would take precedence over brute force. And second, the vanquished would never be humiliated. With a deft political touch, Cyrus granted the captured king Astyages all reverence due his position and preserved intact Media's existing military and administrative organizations along with the people who managed them. Avoiding needless reprisals against the subjugated, Cyrus created partners rather than adversaries in the expanding Persian Empire."[3]

He chose Ecbatana to be the administrative center of his forthcoming empire. From there he marched with his superbly disciplined army against Lydia in Asia Minor and after capturing Sardis, the capital, in 547 B.C., went against the Greek cities. After securing Asia Minor, Cyrus went eastward and established his suzerainty over the Aryan tribes and built fortifications beyond the Amu Darya (Oxus) river.

In 540 B.C., Cyrus once more took up wars of defense and conquest conducted according to the Zoroastrian mandate of justice. The Achaemenian king began his assault on Babylon, which was the last formidable threat to Persia, to the west.

"Deploying part of his army as decoy, Cyrus drew the corrupt king Nabonidus and his army from the city. Then he and the remainder of his forces stood before the walls of Babylon. Once inside, the king of Persia walked down a carpet of fragrant leaves strewn on the great processional mall of once mighty Babylon liberated from the unjust rule of Nabonidus. Rejecting the image of conqueror, Cyrus assumed the traditional titles of Babylonian kingship and reached out to embrace the Babylonian Gods."[4]

Babylon's report of surrender written on a cylinder states: " All the inhabitants bowed to him. Happily they greeted him as a master through whose help they had come again to life from death and had been spared damage and disaster and they worshiped his very name."[5] This acknowledgement of Cyrus as a liberator was also confirmed by non-Persians:

"That said of Cyrus: He is my shepherd, and shall perform all my pleasure."— Isaiah, XLIV-28

"Thus said the Lord to his anointed, to Cyrus, whose right hand I have holden, to subdue nations before him — Isaiah, XLV-1-3

"All ye, assemble yourselves and hear; which among them hath declared these things? The Lord hath loved him: he will do His pleasure on Babylon, and his arm shall be on the Chaldeans." — Isaiah, XLVIII-14

Herodotus, the Greek historian, writes:

"Cyrus was a king of strong character, simple, and brave. He treated his subjects with great benevolence and in a parental spirit. He aspired always for the well-being and happiness of his subjects, so much that they were accustomed to referring to him as "Father'."

Plato spoke of him in these terms:

"Cyrus was a great leader and a great friend of his people...He gave to all of them the rights of free men. And by that he won their hearts...If among his subjects there was found someone who could offer just and reasonable advice he was not angry; rather he gave the subject complete freedom of speech...."

It was Cyrus, the liberator, who freed the Jews from their Babylonian captivity, restored to them remainder of their gold and silver confiscated by Nebuchadnezzar, and sent them home to rebuild their temple in JeruSelim."[6] In 1879 a clay cylinder with full text in Babylonian cuneiform characters was discovered in Babylon. The cylinder which is being kept in the British Museum, is the first declaration of human rights. This is the decree of Cyrus the Great granting national and religious freedom to the peoples of Babylon. Cyrus says:

"When I entered Babylon...I did not allow anyone to terrorize the land of Sumer and Akkad. I kept in view the needs of Babylon and all its sanctuaries to promote their well-being. The citizens of Babylon...I lifted their unbecoming yoke. Their dilapidated dwellings I restored. I put an end to their misfortunes

He not only liberated the Jews, but also freed other groups that had been taken captive.

Cyrus tolerated, understood and appreciated other cultures. This tolerance stemmed from Persian's Zoroastrian ideological orientation that God had entrusted Persian kings — the just rulers- with the task of uniting the people of this world in one kingdom of justice and peace. Iranians would give their support and allegiance only to the good ruler who maintained the Farr (sign of divine favor) and destroyed the evil and presided over a just society. This tolerance is clearly documented in the Encyclopedia of Religion and Ethics:

"...the Persians realized what had never occurred to Assyrians and the other imperialist powers of that age: that national interest does not have to express itself solely in vindictiveness, that it is not necessarily impaired by respect for lesser national interests, and that tolerance paid off." [7]

Iranians to this date have maintained the hope that someday myth and history would somehow converge to create happiness for all mankind.

During Cyrus' era the Persian Empire covered the largest lands from Africa to China, and from Aegean and Mediterranean Sea to the Indus River. Its size exceeded those of the Egyptians, Assyrians, and the Babylonians. This efficiently administered Persian Empire generally lived in peace. Cyrus's last battle happened in the Northeast at age 70 against the restless nomads. He was killed in battle, and his body was brought back to Pasargade and placed in a tomb that stands to this day.

Appraisal of this noble human being and the builder of the first documented empire is best illustrated by Professor Ghirshman, who speaks of him thus:

"A great captain and leader of men, he was favored by the fate that befell him. Generous, benevolent, he had no thought of forcing conquered countries into a single mould, but had the wisdom to leave unchanged the institutions of each kingdom he attached to his crown. We never see Cyrus, like the Romans, ally himself with a rival people, treat it as an equal, and then, turning upon it in a moment of weakness, subject and suppress it. The Persians called him father, the Hellenese whom he conquered regarded him as master and lawgiver, and the Jews as the anointed of the Lord."[8]

Cyrus's son, Kamboojieh (Cambyses) (530-522 B.C), continued the program of his father and added Egypt to the empire. It seems that he followed the conciliating policy of Cyrus, but scandalous events together with his probably impulsive nature have not left him with a good name. He is accused of the mysterious death of his brother Bardiya (called Smerdis by Herodotus). When Cambyses was in Egypt he heard that a man had ascended the throne of Iran who claimed to be the slain Bardiya. Cambyses rushed for Iran but died on the way. Whether he died in an epileptic fit or committed suicide is not known. Meanwhile, the false Bardiya, whose real name was Gaumatu the Magian, was accepted as the new ruler. Dariush (Darius), son of Hystaspes the Achaemenian, however, with the help of the army that had remained loyal to the real throne, overthrew the pretender and proclaimed himself king. The whole affair took only a few months in the year 522 B.C. On a highway near a rocky bluff overlooking the road between Kermanshah and Hamadan known as Beestoon, one can still see Darius under the protection of the winged Ahura Mazda, stepping on the body of the pretender. The inscription relates the story of the revolt and the restoring the throne of Hakhamanesh very much as described above.

After quelling the rebellion that had sprouted in many parts of the country, Darius continued the expansion of the empire. He led his army eastward into the present-day India. Later, having perfected the chariot, he went as far as Libya in North Africa. He then became deeply involved with the Greeks of Europe. The difficulty was that the European Greeks were enticing the Greeks of Asia Minor, who were under the Persian rule, to revolt. In 512 Darius crossed the Bosporus and advanced through Thrace and beyond the Danube. In the end, however, Darius felt obliged to squash the rebellion at the source. The campaigns of Darius against Greece ended in the famous Battle of Marathon (490 B.C.) in which the Persians were defeated. However, in the withdrawal back to Persia, Darius won more than forced the submission to Persian rule by both the Greeks of Thrace on the Aegean coast and the king of Macedonia. Dariush respected and defended the standards of just rule established by Cyrus the Great. A carved tablet at his tomb at Naghsh-e-Rostam reads:

"Saith Darius the king: by the favor of Ahura Mazda I am of such a sort that I am a friend to right, I am not a friend to wrong. It is not my desire that the weak man should have wrong done to him by the mighty; nor it is my desire that the mighty man should have wrong done to him by the weak. What is right, that is my desire."

At the death of Darius in 486 B.C., his son Khashayar (Xerxes I), the last of the great Achaemenian kings, continued the campaign and succeeded in taking Athens in 480 B.C. The victory, however, was short-lived due to the defeat of the Persian fleet at the Battle of Salamis. Once again the Persians had to withdraw to Asia Minor. Although the Greeks were justly proud of their victories, they did not destroy the Persians. At the most, Persians had to give up their ambitions in Europe. In Asia Minor, the Persians were successful in stopping Greek interference. The Persians were able to create friendly relations with the Ionians and continued unhampered until the rise of Alexander in 330 B.C.

133 years after the death of Xerxes, Alexander the Greek crossed the eastern side of the Hellespont and defeated Darius III. With more than twenty five thousand horses, mules and camels, he emptied the riches of the country. Then, Alexander, the student of Aristotle, the avowed servant of truth and beauty, ordered Persepolis- the 181,500 square yard ceremonial palace of gold-plated doors, jewel-embedded walls, gold lace curtains and rich tapestries which had taken 200 years to build, burned. "Committing one of the most senseless acts of destruction in human history, Alexander intended to take from the Persians their sense of self. He was only the first in a long line of conquerors who would consume the Persians' territory but not their identity."[9]

Administration and Economy

The Achaemenid dynasty, which lasted some 230 years, created not only the first great empire of recorded history but the first world civilization. It was not one culture imposed on others but a bringing together of diverse nations under one canopy. It was the first commonwealth of nations in which the king was the symbol of unity as well as the center of power. The Achaemenians were tolerant, conciliatory, and appreciative of the contributions and the talents of other cultures. In contrast to the rigidity of empires before and after, they were flexible and changed with the requirements of the times and the needs of each nationality. Each group had the freedom of its own culture and language. The Persians did not impose either their religion or customs upon the conquered people. Perhaps the only exception was the celebration of Norooz (New Year) when representatives of all the nationalities of the empire were required to present themselves before the king. The magnificent relief on walls of the grand stairway of Persepolis depicts these representatives, each in his national costume bringing his gifts.

Persians' tolerance and flexibility was implemented through a superb system of administration. Herodotus, the Greek historian, relates that the empire was divided into 20 provinces. Each was headed by a satrap, who was usually a person appointed by the king. In addition to the satrap each province had the military commander and a tax collector. Periodically a special inspector, called the "eyes and ears of the king," would visit the provinces unannounced to examine the conduct of affairs. All the provinces were connected with each other and with the center by a system of roads that can be traced even to this day. To facilitate communications within the empire, post stations were built along all routes to provide rest stations for the caravans and fresh horses for couriers on government business. Post stations were precisely spaced at intervals equaling one day's ride connecting the royal road stretching 2000 miles. Strong, skilled men riding fast, muscular horses carried royal messages as far as 1600 miles in one week. Herodotus marveled, "Nothing mortal travels so fast as these messengers. They will not be hindered from accomplishing at their best speed the distance which they have to go, either by snow, or rain, or heat, or by the darkness of night" This system of communications was unmatched in speed until the telegraph doomed the horse to obsolescence. In addition to this network of roads built for communication and commerce, Dariush also ordered the construction of the canal connecting the Red Sea with the Mediterranean, which is called the Suez Canal in modern times. He ordered four stone tablets erected along the waterway. In one of the tablets presently kept in the Cairo Museum, Darius says: "Ahuramazda is great, who created the sky, the earth, the humans, happiness for them, appointed Darius the king...I ordered this canal to be dug from the Nile to the sea coming from Persia...." The canal, ordered filled by the order of a Roman emperor, was subsequently dredged by Ferdinand De-lesseps, a French engineer in 1869.

The unity and stability of the empire encouraged the flow of commerce, and merchants were able to travel all over the empire. There is evidence that Kharazmians from eastern Iran were plying their goods in upper Egypt.[10]

To help the flow of commerce the empire adopted uniform weights, measures, and coinage. The Persians established private banks and businessmen were able to make loans, deposits, invest in land and other ventures, and transact their business by writing checks. Banking houses such as the House of Murashu and Egibi not only carried out the normal activities of banking but were tax collectors as well.

Even though there was industry to take care of the basic needs of the empire such as clothing, shoes, furniture, and the like, the main source of wealth in the empire was agricultural and pastoral. In an arid country like Iran, water was (and is) a precious commodity. The government built underground canals (Ghanats or Qanats), a method still used in Iran, and regulated the use of water. The government also transplanted fruit trees, carried out a program of forestation for economic purposes, and established mines, quarries, and fisheries.[11]

One of the most interesting discoveries of ancient Iran is the system of wages established for laborers throughout the empire. The numerous tablets found in the treasury at Persepolis, and translated by Professor George G. Cameron,[12] reveal an amazing array of regulations concerning wages, work, modes of payment, labor exchange, and the like. In these treasury tablets, which are really pay sheets for the building of Persepolis, it is quite evident that payment for different classes of workers such as skilled and unskilled laborers, women and children, were strictly regulated. Based on these documents, one can safely say that the Persian economy ran opposite of the Roman Empire and the Athenian society, where democracy was limited to the free citizens and excluded the slaves. The slaves of the Achaemenid Empire were "juridical persons" and were sometimes better paid than free men.[13]

Foreign Policy

Professor H.F. Farmayan states that ancient Iranians believed that their prosperity and security of their empire depended on adherence to four principles:

First, the boundaries of the empire must for the greatest security expand where possible to natural frontiers. This meant the Caucasus in the north, the Persian Gulf and Indian Ocean in the south, and Transoxianixa in the east. History has repeatedly demonstrated that from the sixth century B.C. to the present time whenever these frontiers could not be protected Iran was in danger.

Second, the creation or support of a series of buffer states along the frontiers which as vassals to Iran acted as exterior defense lines of the empire.

The third principle looked to the empire's economic welfare. Its gigantic landmass was crisscrossed by the greatest commercial routes of the age. Protection of their terminals was of vital importance. In ancient times, the most significant of these were the Greek port cities on the Mediterranean coast of Asia Minor, which connected Asia with Europe.

The fourth principle involved cultural considerations. The Persian Empire embraced all or portions of five of the ancient great civilizations: the Indian, Mesopotamian, Syrian, Egyptian, and the Greek. The Persian ruling class wisely placed these rich and varied cultures under their protection rather than forcing them to conform to Iranian ways. Throughout history it has been proven that when a ruler deviated far or long from this basic policy, disaster followed.

Art and Architecture

The same tolerance and flexibility which characterized the Achaemenid Empire, administration, and commerce permeated its art, architecture, and religion. It was not a question of the conqueror's religion, art, and culture imposing themselves on all others, but a blending of the civilizations of the ancient world-Mesopotamia, Egypt, Syria, Asia Minor, the Greek cities, and even India-into one distinctive and original whole. The inscription by Dariush describing the building of the palace in Shoosh (Susa) depicts the cosmopolitan and cooperative nature of the empire. Skilled workers were brought from Sind, Egypt, Bactria, Greek cities of Asia Minor and other localities.

Generally, the style of art and architecture of the Persians differs from other Middle Eastern peoples. There is a greater plasticity and roundness of figures, and there is a more realistic relationship of clothing to the contours of the body. On the whole, Persians rarely used large canvases. It must be noted that in Persian art and sculpting, in stark contrast to those of Assyria and Babylonia, there is no depictions of savagery or war. All in all, a person strolling through the ruins of ancient Achaemenid palaces, be it Susa, Pasargad, or Persepolis, finds the art and architecture more contemplative and the conflicts more spiritual, such as struggle between good and evil, rather than crude.[14]

The flexibility of the empire was further evidenced by the fact that the court was not fixed in one place. Cyrus used Ecbatana (Hamadan), which was the ancient capital of the Medes. Dariush used Babylon for a while, but later he built Susa as the winter capital and the administrative center of the empire. He built a strong citadel separated by a wide avenue from the houses and villas reserved for officials and merchants. It was indeed the capital of the world to which kings, ambassadors, artists, and scientists came.

The palaces that best represented the inner spirit of Persians, rather than the necessary outer trappings of the empire, were located deep inside Parsa, the native homeland of Hakhamanesh. One of these was Pasargadai (Pasargad) and the other, Persepolis. Pasargad was something of a national shrine. The name, which is the Greek form of the original word, is almost certainly misspelled. It probably should have been Parsa rather than Pasar, and perhaps the original name was Parsagerd, 'fortress of Persia' or Parsagadae, 'throne of Persia' or Parsakadeh, 'house of Persia'.[15] It was located on the plain of Morghab between the Morghab and Polvar rivers on the Shiraz-to-Esfahan road. This location was the ancient capital of the Achaemenid princes and the home of their temple. This was also the area where Cyrus the Great built his palace. All erected in original Persian art and architecture.

The Achaemenid kings were crowned in Pasargadai, where they would don the robe of Cyrus and eat a peasant's meal as part of the ceremony. About the only buildings which are relatively intact are the Ka'beh-e- Zardosht (Ka'aba of Zoroaster), a temple in the proximity of the royal tombs in Naghsh-e-Rostam, and the tomb of Cyrus the Great, which dominates what used to be the royal gardens. Since the time of the Eslamic conquest, the tomb of Cyrus has been called the "Tomb of mother of Solomon," Pasargad the "Martyrdom of the Mother of Solomon," and one of the palaces as the "Throne of Solomon." It is quite likely that the Persians invented these names to prevent desecration of the tomb and other buildings by the intolerant Moslems- the latter being convinced of the holiness of Solomon and in awe of his expolits.[16]

If Pasargad was the spiritual shrine of the ancient Persians, Takht-e-Jamsheed (Persepolis) was the Portal of all Nations, symbolizing the internationalism of its builders. Its construction started with Dariush and was almost completed by Khashayar Shah (Xerxes). Its style is generally that of Pasargad but more developed and suited for its cosmopolitan use. It was built on a raised platform overlooking the plain of Marv (Marvdasht) and consisted of living quarters, a treasury, and an audience hall (Apadana) of a hundred columns, a large enough hall to hold ten thousand people. All of this was built on a terrace 52 feet above the surrounding plain which was approached by a double flight of stairs leading to the "Portal of all Lands" and then to the audience hall. Its most important ceremonial use was at Norooz (New Year) when the representatives of the commonwealths within the empire would present themselves before the King of Kings with gifts. In the midst of cosmopolitanism and the diversity of cultures, the Norooz ceremony was the symbol of the unity of the empire created in which all peoples participated.

"Norooz, perhaps more than any other event in Achaemenian Persia, demonstrated the growing body of customs and traditions which stamped Persian culture as unique. For at Persepolis on Norooz, the Persians knew who and what they were- a special people sitting at the center of the universe."[17]

Some of the better preserved monuments of ancient Egypt, Greece and Rome are perhaps more famous, but none are as moving, or as vital to Western history and culture, as Persepolis. One of the reasons cited by historians for the importance of Persepolis to Western civilization was its possession of a comprehensive library, which Alexander had translated into Greek before destroying it. Thus Persepolis, by way of Greece, exerted a profound influence on all human culture.

Alphabet and Writing

The Gold tablet of Aryaramnes, great grandfather of Darius, was important on two points. The first, that it is written in a very advanced alphabet, and the second, that it contains a reference to Ahura Mazda. The discovery of this tablet has allowed professor Ghirshman to conclude that the "invention of the cuneiform writing to express old Persian probably goes back to Teispes (700 B.C.). "[18] Inasmuch that this tablet is written in a "very advanced" alphabet, it indicates that the alphabet was known to the Persians long enough for them to experiment with it. Indeed the most recent discovery (1970) at Tappeh Yahya of a similar alphabet written around 3500 B.C. reveals that the alphabet was prevalent in Iran and India before Assyrian or Babylonian times. Notwithstanding this fact, European scholars believe that the Achaemenids wrote their decrees and kept their books and archives in an alphabet which is commonly called Aramaic.19 Presumably, because this form of alphabet was better known than the Persian, the Aramaic alphabet was used for writing Persian. The word Aramaic, however, is a late nineteenth-century discovery or invention. Aramaic was formerly known as Syriac, and no grammar has yet been deciphered for Aramaic because there are not enough samples for the purpose. It is of interest to note that European scholars, in tracing the origin of alphabet and especially of writing in ancient Iran, have not used the Pahlavi or the Arabic and Persian sources written in early Eslamic times about pre-Eslamic Iran. These writers are Mas'udi, Ebn-e-Moghaffa', Hamzeh Esfahani, Ebn-e-Nadim, Abu Reyhan Biruni, Mohammad Kharazmi and others who have written extensively on this subject. Even Avicenna, the great Persian physician, mathematician and scholar, has an important monograph on the alphabet and writing.

According to these Persian and Arab sources, the pre-Eslamic Persians had seven different sets of the alphabet soup and each was used for a special purpose. These were:

1. Am Dabireh. The common alphabet, which has 28 characters but only seven are recorded. These deal with legal papers, city, Treasury, national accounting, and so on.
2. Gashteh Dabireh. This alphabet had 28 letters and was used for treaties and royal decrees.
3. Nim-Gashteh Dabireh. This also had 28 letters and was used in medicine and philosophy.
4. Farvardeh Dabireh. This had 33 letters and was used in keeping royal records.
5. Raz Dabireh. This had 40 letters and was used for codes and classified documents.
6. Din Dabireh. This unique alphabet had 60 letters and was used for writing religious hymns and prayers to be chanted in worship. With this alphabet all the peculiarities such as intonation and length of vowels of a word could be designated so that the reader would not mispronounce the holy word.
7. Visp Dabireh. This was an international alphabet by which all languages and all sounds, even the "sound of falling water" could be written. This alphabet had 160 letters for all languages 205 letters for all sounds.[20]

Religion

As stated earlier, one important point in the inscription of Aryaramnes (640-590 B.C.) is that he was proclaimed to be king by the grace of Ahura Mazda. This provides the opportunity to discuss the religion of ancient Iran, founded by Zoroaster (Greek form of the Persian Zaratushtra, modern Zartosht or Zardosht), which without doubt is the most significant contribution of the Persians to the world. Indeed, the tolerance, flexibility, devotion to truth, and all other progressive attributes heaped upon the ancient Persians by friend and foe, are all rooted in Zoroastrianism.

Where Zoroaster was born, whether in the northeastern or northwestern Iran, is insignificant to the heated controversy of when he was born. European scholars used to claim that he was born in the middle of the sixth century B.C. In direct contrast is the claim of Zabih Behruz,[21] who believes that Zoroaster was born on the 21st of March 1767 B.C. Recent non-Persian research suggests that the Persian Prophet "lived somewhere between 1400 and 1200 B.C. This is important because it makes him the first of the prophets of the world's major religions, older than Moses, Buddha, or Confucius."[22] This claim is further confirmed by Jacques Duchense-Guillemin who states: "Zoroaster is, in fact, in the full sense of the word, the first theologian."[23]

Zoroaster was a prophet who claimed to have a special revelation from Ahura Mazda. He preached the coming of a new kingdom and, like many prophets, he was ignored and sometimes ridiculed. After many years of struggle and disappointment, he at last won over Prince Vistaspa who ruled in a principality in eastern Iran. Until the end of his life he preached the Kingdom of Goodness, Life, and Light. The way of Zoroaster revolutionized the old religious practices of the Aryans who accepted him.

If it were not for Zoroaster, perhaps the religion of the Iranians would have developed along a line similar to those followed by the religion of their kinsmen, the Aryans of India. The revolution of Zoroaster reversed the process so that the Gods (daiva) whom they shared with the Hindus became devils (deev) to the Iranians. Professor Frye is correct when he says that the old Aryan religions were "rite-centered " while the reforms of Zoroaster were "belief-centered." The belief proclaimed by Zoroaster was trust in the goodness and justice of Ahura Mazda and having faith that in the end, it is only He who would be victorious. Zoroastrianism is based on what later became known as Dualism. In the Gathas, Zoroaster proclaimed:

"I will speak of the two spirits
Of whom the holier said unto the destroyer at the beginning of exis-
tence: Neither our thoughts nor our doctrines nor our minds' forces,
Neither our choices nor our words nor our deeds,
Neither our consciences nor our souls agree."

The "holier" person in the hymn is Ahura Mazda and the "destroyer"
is Ahriman. Ahura Mazda is the creator of life, light, and goodness while
Ahriman is the lord of death, darkness, and evil. The greatest difficulty
in all theistic religions has been to explain how an all-powerful and all-
loving God can conceive of evil, let alone allow it. Either He is all-powerful and not all-good or He is all-good and not all-powerful. In Zoroastrianism Power is sacrificed in favor of love and goodness. Ahura Mazda
and Ahriman are always at war with each other for supremacy in the world
at large, in every community, and in the heart of each person. Each wages
war with the aid of his "hosts," which are called Angels and demons, but
the most important soldier in each army is man. Inasmuch as man joins
the hosts of Ahriman, then death, darkness, and evil will dominate the
world, society, and a person's life. And to the degree that man joins Ahura
Mazda, the forces of life, light, and goodness will conquer in the world,
the community, and in the individual. Man, therefore, stands between the
primordial goodness and evil and by his choice can help in the expira-
tion of falsehood and death, and aide in the establishment of truth and
life. The essence of the revelation of Zoroaster is to encourage man to choose
Ahura Mazda. It is a secret revealed only to Zoroaster and may be
accepted by all who believe. The revelation in this is that all are between
Ahura Mazda and Ahriman and will be won by the former. Ahriman may
win some battles, but in the end, goodness shall defeat evil, light shall
vanquish darkness, and life shall overcome death.[24]

Both Ahura Mazda and Ahriman help and guide men who volunteer
in their service with their "spirit"- Ahura Mazda with the "Holy Spirit,"
Sepanta Mainyu (modern Persian Minoo), and Ahriman with the "Evil
Spirit," (Angra Mainyu).[25] Those who give their allegiance to Ahura Mazda
are enjoined to battle with foes using weapons of good or pure thought,
pure speech, and pure deed.[26] There is a well-developed system of rewards
and punishments as well as eschatology and apocalypse in Zoroatrianism.
Every person's thoughts, words, and deeds are recorded. On the Day of
Judgment, if evil outweighs good, then the person is destined to go to hell,
but if the good outweighs the evil, he is destined to go to paradise (original Persian Paradis, modern Pardis or Ferdows). There is no forgiveness

in Zoroastrianism, and each person is rewarded and punished in an intermediary state called hamestagan, a prototype of Roman Catholic purgatory. Unlike purgatory, however, hamestagan is not controlled from the earth. The Last Judgment will take place at the Chinvat Bridge, where the victorious Ahura Mazda himself will separate the good from the bad and the soul, urvan (modern Persian ravan) of the good will live in the abode of light.

The number of Zoroastrians today is not great, but the fact that after over 1,300 years of subjugation and persecution, there are still some people who have kept the "Good religion" alive is quite remarkable. Upon the conquest of Eslam, a number of devout Zoroastrians left their homeland to settle on the west coast of India to freely practice their faith. As the British developed the island city of Bombay in the seventeenth century, the Persians, or the Parsis (people of Pars) migrated to India's commercial capital. There they began to acquire positions of real importance, dominating much of Bombay's trade, commerce, industry, education and politics. During the period of British rule in India, only three Indians were ever elected to the English parliament. All three were Parsis. Parsis were also very active in the establishment of the Indian National Congress.

Parsis migrated throughout the British Empire such as East Africa, Hong Kong, Singapore, Australia, and Britain. After political changes in East Africa, Pakistan and Iran, a good number of Zoroastrians have settled in the North American continent. It is interesting to note that although the number of Zoroastrians has shrunk, the "Good Religion" is now more widely spread around the world than it has ever been.

ENDNOTES

1. Sylvia A. Matheson, Persia: An Archeological Guide (London: Faber & Faber Ltd., 1976), p.26.
2. R. Ghirshman, Iran (Baltimore, MD.: Penguin Books, 1965), p.73ff.
3. S. Mackey, The Iranians: Persia, Eslam and the Soul of a Nation (New York: The Penguin Group, 1996), p.18.
4. Ibid., p.22.
5. Clive Irving, Crossroads of Civilization: 3,000 years of Persian History (New York: Barnes and Noble Books, 1979), p.19.

6. The Iranians, p.22.

7. Encyclopedia of Religion and Ethics, quoted in Adda B. Bozeman, Politics and Culture in International History (Princeton, N.J.: Princeton university Press, 1960), p.46.

8. Ghirshman, Iran, p. 133.

9. Mackey, The Iranians, p. 31.

10. Richard N. Frye, The Heritage of Persia (New York: World Publishing Company, 1963), p.120.

11. Ghirshman, Iran, p.182.

12. George G. Cameron, ed., Persepolis Treasury Tablets (Chicago: University of Chicago Press, 1948).

13. Frye, Heritage of Persia, p. 109.

14. William Cullican, The Medes and the Persians (New York: Praeger, 1965), p.104ff.

15. For this and a detailed description of Pasargadai, see Ali Sami, Pasargasdai, trans. R.N. Sharp)Shiraz: Mousavi Press, 1956).

16. Ibid., p.22ff.

17. Mackey, The Iranians, p.27.

18. Ghirshman, Iran, p.163.

19. Ibid., p.163ff; and Frye, Heritage of Persia, pp.127ff. and173ff.

20. Zabih Behruz, Khat va Farhang (Alphabet and Culture), Iran-Kudeh no.8 ed. Mohammad Moghadam (Tehran, 1950).

21. Zabih Behruz, Taghveem va Tareekh dar Iran (Calendar and History in Iran), Iran-Kudeh no.15 (Tehran, 1952).

22. John R. Hinnells, Persian Mythology (New York, Peter Bedrick Books, 1973), p.9.

23. The Hymns of Zarathustra (Boston, Beacon Press, 1952), p.2.

24. Job, which is very likely a Judaized Zoroastrian story, illustrates this truth in that Job with un-replenished power of God overcame the replenished power of Satan.

25. This concept borrowed by the Hebrews and Arabs is expressed in both languages by the word wind ('ruwah,' 'ruh') but does not approach the fullness of the meaning of Mainyu.

26. Fire as light and also as the best purifier has been the symbol of Ahura Mazda. Even to this day on the last Wednesday eve of the year Persians in general and Zoroastrians in particular, make bonfires and jump over them purifying themselves for the new year. Water, which is the second purifier, also has a place in Zoroastrian symbolism. John the Baptist baptized with water and promised the coming of a greater One who would baptize with fire.

CHAPTER THREE

THE INVASION & DEFEAT OF THE WEST

Noble and world encompassing as the ideas of Alexander may have been-ideas such as the fusion of races and civilizations under one authority, the founding of intercultural colonies, freeing the world from economic divisions, and establishing a peace which was both Eastern and Western-all came to naught with his premature death in 323 B.C. This was a mere seven years after his conquest of Persia. His death relegated all those ideas to their realm of the "might have been." What really did occur is so vastly different from what might have occurred if he had not died that all the luster of "Hellenism" and its "contributions" fades as the subject is studied more carefully.

Hellenism

Professor Frye expresses the opinion which other western authorities have expressed in diverse forms, namely, that "the conquest of the Achaemenid empire by Alexander marks the end of that ancient history and the beginning of a new era, an era of ecumenical (universal) culture generally called Hellenism."[1] In the light of the fact that all these authors, without exception, have devoted a greater portion of their books praising the ecumenicity, open-mindedness, tolerance, and internationalism of the Persians and how under the Achaemenids all nationalities were allowed to develop their talents freely, one is amazed to read that Hellenism *started* an ecumenical culture rather than, at least continued the tradition already started by the House of Hakhamanesh.

In any case the heirs of Alexander did not continue such a spirit. It is commonly accepted by all historians that, following the death of Alexander, his fledgling empire was plunged into a bloody struggle between his generals. The bloodshed and destruction continued for forty years until, at long last, the situation was stabilized by the formation of three kingdoms: European Greece under a Macedonian monarchy, Egypt under Ptolemy, and western Iran under Seleucus. The Seleucid kingdom, which controlled the western part of the Achaemenian empire, was highly centralized and autocratic. It had to be because it was not a national dynasty and could not trust the Iranian majority. The Seleucids did not " continue the policy of the fusion of races."[2] They established Greek centers in different cities in the empire, and the most they could do was to preserve Greek supremacy for a while. The fact that some Greek inscriptions have been found in these centers is not an indication of a new wave of Greek influence. After all, part of the Golden Age was at a time when, thanks to the open door policy of the Achaemenids, there was a great deal of interchange between the two peoples. It was not as though the Persians had built a dam waiting to be destroyed by Alexander in order to let the waters of Greek culture overrun the land of Iran. Scholars, from Theodor Noldeke until the present, have agreed that "Hellenism never touched nearer than the surface of Persian life."[3] It seems that inasmuch as it did, if one has to judge the Seleucids as the chief missionaries of Hellenism, it destroyed the spirit of tolerance, good will, and dialogue that the Achaemenids had started. Never again do we see in that part of the world, or anywhere else for that matter, another empire based on tolerance as was that of the Achaemenids. At the time of the Achaemenids the boundary of political struggle between the rulers of the major portions of Europe and Persia was the Straits of Bosporus and Dardanelles. Alexander pushed this boundary eastward to include Asia Minor within the western orbit. The Parthians and the Sassanids fought against the Romans and the Byzantines respectively. To show that it was not really the West against the East as Professor Ghirshman would have us believe when he talks about "the *conscience Europeenne* of the 4th century B.C. that led to the campaign of Alexander,"[4] the Ottoman Turks who occupied the same territory as the Byzantines before them and who most certainly were not led by *"conscience Europeenne,"* fought the Safavids, the Afshars, and the Ghajars(Qajars) who occupied the same territory as the Sassanids and Parthians before them, along the same borders, and heaven knows for what reasons.

To be sure, the Seleucids, who ruled Iran proper for about a century, were not without influence in art and architecture as well as in commerce and social life. This is especially so because the Persians have been able to adapt themselves to new situations and to adopt new ways. This is true now as it was in the days of Herodotus who wrote: "There is no nation which so readily adopts foreign customs as the Persians. As soon as they hear of any luxury they instantly make it their own. " But whether the normal influences of an occupying power, which admittedly was itself influenced by the occupied people, should be magnified to such exaggerated proportions as Hellenism has been in the history of Iran and the Middle East is a question that should be scrutinized. Further in this regard, Professor Mackey remarks in *The Iranians*:

> In the Seleucid territories of Syria and Asia Minor, Hellenism flowered and bore the fruit of new cultural patterns. But in Iran, it remained only an influence.... Consequently, one generation after another of Persians sustained their basic identity and sense of belonging to the Iranian plateau. That the Persians... should have remained indifferent to Greek culture, one of the most potent in history, is extraordinary. Thus in 160 years of Seleucid rule, the Greeks succeeded only in laying a veneer over the Persian body. They never seduced the Persian heart that dwelled in the blackened ruins of Persepolis.[5]

The Parthians

By the time the grandson of Seleucus II (261-246 B.C.) succeeded to the throne, the Parthians had become a serious menace in Eastern Iran. It is believed that Parthians were originally from an Aryan tribe who came down from the east side of the Caspian Sea around the time Alexander died. They gradually began to absorb the Persian culture. In 246 B.C. Arsaces I, known to the Persians as Ashk I, established a kingdom. The Seleucids were caught between the growing power of Rome on the west and the Parthians on the east. The Roman encroachments, at the expense of the Seleucids, enabled Merhdad I (Mithridates I 171-138 B.C.) to extend his power over Bactria, Parsa, Susa, Media, and Babylonia by severing the main artery connecting Persia from the rest of the Seleucid empire. Persia was reborn. The destruction of the Greek Empire was assured. The star of the Parthian fortune was on the rise and the successors of Mithridates strengthened their hold on their gains and expanded the empire. By the time of Mehrdad II (Mithridates II 127-87 B.C.) the Parthians had a bona fide empire extending from India to Armenia, and the ruler took upon himself the title of "King of Kings."

The Romans, in the meantime, were gradually advancing eastward. The inevitable conflict between the two advancing empires, who did not know very much about each other, began under the reign of the Phraates III (69-57 B.C.). For about 300 years Parthians having perfected a new breed of larger horses with much stamina which were outfitted with armor and mounted by powerful archers, fought against the Romans, ensuring that Persia would not become a satellite of the West. In one battle, the Parthian army killed twenty thousand Romans. In 36 B.C., in the northwestern part of modern Iran, the Persian mounted bowmen defeated the famous Roman general Mark Anthony in a confrontation, forcing him to flee to the arms of Cleopatra. During this war, the Roman forces lost about 35,000 soldiers. Rome retreated to the west of the Tigris river, and the world of west Asia and Europe was virtually divided between the Romans and the Parthians. These wars were not just for the advancement of prestige and power. Iran was astride the trade routes between East and West. The Romans wanted the silk, spices, ivory, perfume, and precious stones of India and China, while the manufactured goods of Rome such as bronze, glassware, wines, oils, and gold especially had customers in the East. Iran, in the main, was the entrepreneur and a specialist in transportation, both on land and water.[6]

In the beginning, the Parthians tried to steer a middle course between the Greeks and the Persians. While they considered themselves restorers of the Achaemenid Empire, they introduced themselves on their coins as philhellene to the Greeks. Their records were kept in Greek and their diplomatic language, during the early years, was Greek. As time passed, however, they forsook the Greek and became the Iranians that they were, adopting consciously many things from the old Persian Empire. They spoke Middle Persian, wrote in Pahlavi script, and their bards sang about the heroes, *pahlavans*. Some parts of the songs later became the source of the epic of *Shahnameh*.[7]

Foreign Policy

During the long Parthian period the dynamic leadership of one great king after another caused foreign policy to occupy much of the time of the entire ruling class as well as the military. Some of the international problems which have plagued us for centuries have their origins in those distant times. A classic example is Armenia, a geopolitical security blanket for possession of which Rome and Iran quarreled over for several hundred years. In the end, it was skillful diplomacy backed by military strength which achieved peace in Armenia for a notable period. The remarkable entente which was established between Iran and Rome during the reigns of Augustus and Nero was an extraordinary victory in diplomacy for Iran. It was agreed that Armenia be ruled by a Persian prince who would be crowned by the hand of the Roman emperor. Thus occurred one of the most bizarre events in ancient history when Tirdad (Tiridates), accompanied by his family and three thousand cavalry, arrived in Rome and amid magnificent festivities was crowned King of Armenia by Emperor Nero. Ill-concealed behind the pomp and lordly bestowal was the fact that mighty Rome had been forced to renounce its claim upon this crucial state. Iran had achieved a major goal, security in the Caucasus, as one of her princes assumed rule of Armenia.[8]

Even though the Parthian kings were mostly involved in the affairs of Mesopotamia and their struggle with Rome, they did not neglect their contacts with the East. As early as 115 B.C. an embassy from China visited Iran and concluded a treaty with Mehrdad (Mithridates) on the movement of caravans through Iran. These contacts are recorded in the Chinese sources as well. Furthermore, Parthian coins found on the Volga attest to the relationship.

Great Changes

Practically all scholars believe that during the Parthian period great changes occurred in Iran in religion, art, and literature. Usually Western scholars consider Hellenism to be the source of these great changes which occurred during the second century B.C. and on into the middle of the Parthian period. This may well be, but it is useful to consider a theory advanced by Iranian scholars, professors Zabih Behruz [9] and Mohammad Moghadam [10]. The great event, according to these scholars, was the birth of Mehr (Mithra) or the Christ, on Saturday night, December 25, 272 B.C. He died at the age of 64 by natural causes, but his message was accepted by many, and the missionaries of the faith took the message to all parts of the world from China to Ireland. The Parthians adopted Mithraism as their official religion; and up to the fourth century A.D., not only was it prevalent in Rome, but it was the official religion of the Roman Empire. "It is one of the great ironies of history that Romans worshiped the God of their chief political enemy, Persia.... It has been said that Mithraism was so strong that if the Roman Empire, and after it the Western world, had not become Christian it would have become Mithraic."[11]

In as much as this person, Mehr (Mithra), was born of a virgin named Nahid Anahita ("immaculate"), and in as much as the worship of Mithra, and Anahita, the virgin mother of Mithra, was well-known in the Achaemenian period, it is as yet not clear whether the religion adopted by the Parthians and accepted in many parts of the world was a revival of the old Mithra worship (about 4,000 years ago), or was caused by a religious leader named Mithra.

Not much is known about the life and works of Mithra, but what little information is available is strangely similar to the life and works of Jesus of Nazareth; about the only differences are the location of birth and the fact that Mithra of Iran died a natural death while Jesus was crucified. Another striking similarity is the most famous relief relating to the Mithraic ritual meal. This relief, which is kept at Zemaljski Muzej in Sarajevo, depicts Mithra at a dinner table, denoted by grapes, wine and bread. This is amazingly similar to Jesus' Last Supper. While Christianity was based on prophetic Judaism, Mithraism was based on Zoroastrianism, which would probably account for the idea that "The Parthians in a sense rescued the Zoroastrian religion, giving it the basis of a canon which was passed to the Sassanians and down to the present day. " [12]

It must be noted that there is a great mass of archeological and linguistic evidence that shows the tremendous influence of Mithraism in Europe, Iran, and as far east as China and Japan. Later, it became the rival of orthodox Zoroastrianism in the Sassanian Empire and of Christianity in Europe. In Christian church history it is known as one of the "mystery religions." In the gradual disappearance of Mithraism its temples were destroyed and churches, fire temples, and even mosques were built over them. The Churches of St. Prisca and St. Clemente in Rome are good examples of this fact. Temples of Mithraism have also been found in London, Austria, Hungary, Ireland, and other locations in Europe. The ideas and rituals of Mithraism, however, are so mixed with the ideas and rituals of the religions which supplanted it that "even though on the surface they destroyed the religion of Mithra, in reality the religion of the person whom Iranians called 'Victorious' and the Romans named the 'Undefeatable Lord' is alive within our religions and actually has remained undefeatable." [13]

In Mithraism, the bull, Persian *gav* or *gow*, was the symbol of the passion of man, which is also alluded to in Persian Sufi poetry. Since Mithra killed the bull in a cave, Mithraic temples were usually built in caves, examples of which are to be found in the mountains of the Italian Alps and the Balkans. In localities where there are no mountains, the "holy of holies" of the Mithraic temples was given a cave-like appearance by building special domes over it. The Persian word for dome is *Aveh* (English abbey). *Mehrabeh* (Mehr+ aveh or abeh) found its way into Arabic as *Mehrab*, which is the holiest place in the mosque. Since the shedding of the bull's blood was for the remission of sins, this act was ritualized in Mithraic worship. A holy table (Persian *meez*, Latin *mass*, Spanish *mesa*) was set on which wine and bread and sometimes meat were placed symbolizing blood and the body of the bull. This was called the *hu khoresht*, good food (Greek *eucharist*) which was partaken of by the worshippers. Reliefs of drawings of this and other Mithraic rituals are found wherever Mithraic temples have been found. In Iran evidences of Mithra worship may be seen in Saveh, Tagh-e-Bostan, Shoosh (Susa), Bishapour, Sistan, and other places.

It has been recorded that the cult of Anahita was very popular in the Parthian period, and it was exported beyond the western frontiers of Iran. Anahita, exalted as the "Mother of the Lord," probably gave rise to the exaltation of Mary as "the Mother of God" and the naming of many churches after her. Putting together all the evidence and certain archeological sites and recent studies of archeology in Mithraism, it appears that Mithraists believed the human soul descended into the world at birth. The goal of the religious quest was to achieve the ascent out of the world again, involving its passage through seven heavenly gates corresponding to the initiate's ascent through the grades of initiation. On the side benches of a temple near Naples are a sequence of paintings of Mithraic initiation. The epithets applied to the higher grades in inscriptions imply that the path through the grades, and so for the soul through the heavens, was life-long, arduous and ascetic. For the ascent of the soul the initiate needed a map of the heavens, directions along the path for which he might hope for the aid of other forces. The main relief provided just such a map.[14]

In about 464 years, some 35 kings ascended the Parthian throne. They tried to restore the ancient Achaemenian culture and added significantly to it. They also tried to create a united states, as the Achaemenians had done, and had the custom of choosing their kings.

The Sassanians A.D. 224-642

Per Foerdosi's Shahnameh, Sassan was a shepherd whom Papak (or Baback), the king of Estakhr (between Persepolis and Pasargad), liked very much and gave his daughter Dinak to him in marriage. They had a son named Ardeshir who founded the Sassanid dynasty. The inscription of Shapour I, found on the Ka'beh of Zoroaster in the outskirts of Pasargad, leads historians to believe that Ardeshir Babakan, was the son of Babak and a grandson of Sassan. Sassan and Babak were probably priests in the temple of Anahita in Estakhr. In about A.D. 208, Babak's son, Ardeshir became the king of Fars province and by adding force to Cyrus the Great's policy of conciliation, began to put together the Persian state. About A.D. 224, when Parthian king Ardavan, accused Ardeshir of usurping his power, Ardeshir's response echoed the Achaemenian tone when he said: "This throne and this crown were given me by God". [15]

It is interesting to note that the two kings, rather than starting a war between their armies, decided to engage in a hand-to-hand combat. Ardeshir won. From then on he claimed the title of "King of Kings."

The Sassanians claimed to be the descendants of the Achaemenians whose name carried a great deal of weight among the Iranians. The Parthians, who were also Iranians, never gained the prestigious position of the Achaemenians. In time Zoroastrianism was adopted as the state religion, and it was interpreted to voice and approve the policies of the state. Between the fall of the Achaemenians and the rise of the Sassanians, the Moobads (priests) of Persia had preserved the "Good Religion". Ardeshir realized that in order to maintain his kingship, he needed to acquire the aura of divinity prescribed by Zoroastrianism. He also recognized that religious conformity served his need to centralize authority within his kingdom. It was at this juncture that politics met religion. The priests granted legitimacy to the king, and the king ensured the survival of the priests.

In over four centuries of rule, the Sassanians extended the frontiers of their empire and built a civilization which was basically Persian and which rivaled that of Rome. Professor McKay writes in *The Iranians:*

> The Sassanian epoch constitutes one of the notable ages of Iranian history. It took form in a Renaissance of Persian culture, the charisma of kingship, and the religion of Zoroastrianism. Even today the artistic footprints of the Sassanians track Eslamic Iran. The dome and the vault so identified with Iranian Eslamic architecture are, in fact, Sassanian. The first known Persian carpet, "Spring of Khosro," came out of a Sassanian royal palace. The technique of miniature painting developed by the Parthians reached a new plateau during the Sassanian era.

One of the great kings of the early Sassanian period was Shapour I (A.D.2 40-272). In the Sassainan period, Iran, was menaced from two sides, on the west by the Romans and on the east by the Kushans, who dwelt around Peshawar in modern Pakistan. Shapour I went against the Kushans first, and after dealing them a severe blow he captured Bactria. He then crossed Amu Darya, (Oxus) and returned via Tashkand (Tashkent) and Samarghand (Samarkand). Now it was the time to deal with Rome. In a series of wars that lasted over fifteen years, he defeated the Roman army in two successive campaigns. In the third he crushed it, capturing the emperor Valerian in the process (A.D. 260) along with some 70,000 Roman troops. Shapour I immortalized his victory on rock reliefs at Bishapour and Naghsh-e- Rostam, below the tomb of Dariush, depicting the Roman emperor cowering before the mighty Sassanian king, the King of Kings of resurrected Persia. The Roman soldiers were settled in communities in different parts of Iran.

Shapour had great interest in peace as well as war. He completed the reorganization of the empire that had been started by his father. He also ordered the translation of scientific and philosophical works into Persian. He was tolerant enough to extend his protection to Mani, a religious visionary and the founder of Manichaeism. Mani was the promoter of one of the long line of syncretistic religions which found fertile ground in Iran, the most recent of which is Bahaism founded in1844. Manichaeism, a blending of Zoroastrianism, Buddhism, and Christianity into a universal religion, found many adherents in Iran and in the west. But the Zoroastrian Moobads (priests), who had become powerful as an arm of the state, could not allow such a heresy any more than could the Christian priests whose religion would soon become the official religion of Rome. Soon after the death of Shapour, his son Bahram I, goaded by the Mazdian priests, killed Mani in 272. This did not end Manichaeism, but Mani's followers were persecuted as heretics by the Zoroastrians and Christians alike. It is interesting to note that a famous Manichaeian who later converted into Christianity was St. Augustine.

During the thirty-seven years between the death of Shapour I in 272 and the accession of Shapour II in 309, no less than six kings ascended the Sassanian throne. During this period of confusion, Iran was not strong enough to curb the pressure of Rome or resist the raids of Kushans. It seems that Shapour II (309-379) had to do the work of his namesake all over again. He subdued the Kushans, annexing their territory, and expanded the boundaries of his empire to the borders of Chinese Turkestan. Then he faced Rome and recovered the territories they had overrun.

In the protracted wars between Iran and Rome, Armenia was caught in the middle and suffered the most, now being annexed by one or occupied by the other. During the Parthian period, one of the Arsacid (Parthian) princes had been appointed king of Armenia and the region enjoyed semi-independent and sometimes independent existence. During the Sassanian times, however, and the wars with Rome, Armenia became the buffer state. Quite naturally two parties developed in the area, one inclined toward Iran and the other toward Rome. When Christianity became the official religion of Rome after the conversion of Constantine, and later when the Armenians became Christians, their situation altered. Christianity, which had been tolerated during the Parthian and early Sassanian period and was allowed to spread in the empire and build churches and establish bishoprics, became suspect as the official religion of the of arch enemy, Rome.

As stated before, the Sassanians set about to establish a strong central empire in which unity was achieved through conformity. In such a society each segment that enjoys a certain amount of power and has developed a vested interest, is in turn centralized and becomes very jealous of its power and privileges. Often these different segments cooperated with each other in the face of a common enemy to keep their power, and sometimes they vied with each other to gain more power at each other's expense. In the early Sassanian period, toward the top of the pyramid of power there were the king and his worriers, the priests, and the nobility. Later on the scribes, who served the ever increasing activities of the central government, and the lesser nobility (*dehghans*) joined in the power struggle. In the struggle for power between the king and the large landowning nobility, the priests were in the middle sometimes helping the king against the nobility and sometimes joining the nobility in opposing the king in favor of another member of the royal family. Apparently the tradition of legitimacy in the royal line was quite strong. Only once did a strong member of the nobility and a popular general, Bahram Choobin, lead a coup d'etat in about A.D. 590 and tried to be king. But he failed, mostly because he was not a member of the Sassanian family.

The established Zoroastrian church, under the Sassanians, developed a hierarchy as well as an orthodox theology. The Avesta — the Zoroastrian Holy Book - was put into writing, and Zoroastrianism developed a rigid theology which matched the rigidity of the state it served. In this hierarchy the office of *hirbad* was in charge of the fire temples. Above this was the *moobads*, the priests who were headed by the *moobadan moobad*, the chief religious leader of the realm. There is also mention of the "*moobad of Ahura Mazda*," which must have been an honorary title bestowed upon an individual by the king. As a centralized organization, the church could not tolerate innovation. The killing of Mani and prosecuting his followers is a good example. The Zoroastrian priesthood was also very jealous of the spread of Christianity and encouraged the persecution of that group as well. They relegated the worship of Anahita and Mithra to the background and gradually destroyed it. The persecution of the Christians came to an end, so far as the government was concerned, when during the reign of Bahram V (421-439) the new Catholics summoned a synod which made the Christian Church of Iran independent of that of Byzantium. Since that time, the Persian Church has been usually called "Nestorian."

The Communism of Mazdak

There were over 30 Kings in the Sassanian dynasty, and some of them did not accomplish much. Since the Byzantine Empire was going through similar vicissitudes, it could not take advantage of the Sassanian weakness. In the East however, a new group from Central Asia had succeeded the Kushans. They were called Ephthalites who were probably members of an Iranian tribe or one greatly influenced by them. In the second half of the 5th century they defeated the Sassanians. For intermittent decades until about 531, they had the upper hand and the situation in Iran was confused. There were pretenders to the throne and rivalries among the nobility and the army generals for power. The greatest sufferers were the peasant masses, who had to provide soldiers for the civil and national wars and paid taxes to carry on the struggle for power among the nobles. Persia was ravaged by famine, drought, and military defeat, all signs that the king no longer possessed *Farr*, the divine aura. Some of the vassal estates revolted, and there were fresh raids from the Ephthalites, who demanded and received tribute. Aggression and famine encouraged the masses to join the revolt of Mazdak.

The revolt of Mazdak was the socio-religious movement, partly based on neutralizing, abstinence, and the avoidance of hatred (taught by Mani), discord , and war, and partly based on the equal distribution or sharing of goods, wealth and women. It was a kind of a "Communist movement" which demanded dispossessing of the rich in favor of the poor. King Ghobad I (Qobad 488-531), who was himself pressed by many problems, championed the cause of Mazdak, perhaps to free himself from the clutches of the nobility, and introduced new laws favoring the program of Mazdak. But the nobility and the Zoroastrian and the Christian clergy were against the Mazdaki movement and the king. He was deposed, but after two years he was reinstated to the throne with some help from the Ephthalites. In the meantime, the Mazdaki movement had become a full-fledged social revolution. Ghobad, who had very likely compromised his support of the Mazdaki movement as a price for the crown, was cool toward the revolutionaries. In 524, he allowed the Mazdaki centers to be destroyed, Mazdak assassinated, and his followers massacred.

But neither Mazdakism nor Manichaeism totally died in Iran. Their influence survived in part because it touched the deep concerns of the Persian culture with the aim and purpose of life. In its most basic terms Manichaeism retained the Zoroastrianism principle of opposing forces of good and evil, of light and dark, by teaching that man must redeem his soul by the rigorous denial of fleshly appetites; and Mazdakism summoned each individual within society to fight for truth against darkness and lies. Both sought to level the class hierarchy in order to establish a just society.[16]

Sassanid Achievement and Decline

The most popular of the Sassanian kings in the folklore of Iran is Khosro I (531-579), whose very name became synonymous with "king," and whose title, *Anooshiravan* "the immortal soul," shows the legend which has been built around him. Although he was called " The Just," he was an absolute monarch who had instigated the massacre of Mazdak and his followers. He was a strong king, worthy of comparison with Shapour. Like many of his predecessors, he built his charisma on heroic legend and fed the mystique of the throne by embellishing his court. Khosro exercised justice both as philosophy and political pragmatism. He restored the land taken from the landed by gentry by the followers of Mazdak. He repaired roads, bridges, and canals which were destroyed in the civil strife and inaugurated extensive legislation in fiscal matters. He ordered the survey of the land and a census of population as well as livestock, date palms, and olive trees. He helped the peasants by changing the tax system from a fixed amount to one proportionate to the yield. Even though he returned the property of the nobility, he did not allow them to regain their lost power. Instead, he created a new class of landed nobility called *dehghan* (dehqan), who became the backbone of the local administration in Iran for centuries. He strengthened the bureaucracy so that the office of *Dabiran Dabir* (Chief of Administration) became very important in the empire. He also reformed the army by introducing compulsory military service and creating " peasant-soldiers." For the defense of the empire, he settled tribes at the frontiers and gave them the responsibility of securing the frontiers against foreign enemies. These *Marzbans*, " watchers of the border, " also called

Marzdars, " keepers of the border " became a permanent institution in Iran until the 20th century. Khosro did not forget the traditional enemies of the Sassanians. Successful in re-establishing Persia as a military power, he crushed the power of the Ephthalites and dealt a severe blow at the Byzantines.

The Sassanians as heirs of the Achaemenids, built a national empire. They indeed nurtured the "conscience Iranienne, " which they had inherited, by contributions of their own, and this consciousness has appeared and re-appeared in Iran in times of stress as well as of glory. Sassanian art, according to the experts in the field, was "the culmination of a millennium of development."[17] Typical of all periods of Persian art, " it was receptive to foreign influences, but it adapted them to the traditions of its native land, and as the art of the world empire it spread into far distant countries."[18] Strangely enough they did not rebuild the Achaemenian cities of Pasargad and Persepolis, but built cities of their own. Chief among them were Bishapour in Fars, Gondishapour in Khoozestan, and Teesphoon (Ctesiphon) which the Parthians had built on Dajleh (Tigris) river. Works from Byzantine as well as India on literature, philosophy, and medicine were translated. Gondishapour became "the greatest intellectual center of the time," and boasted a prominent medical college which lasted well into the Eslamic times. Borzuyeh, the famous minister and physician of Khosro, is reputed to have translated many books on medicine from India. His famous translation however, is the fables of Bidpaai. He is also credited with bringing the game of chess from India and creating the game of backgammon (*Nard in* Persian) to match it.

Since Iran and Byzantium were the two most civilized empires of West Asia and Europe, one should expect great interchange between them. There was trade in spices, precious stones, and silk. The most important commodity was silk, in which Iran had a monopoly. Although Iran and Byzantium had contiguous boundaries for over three hundred years, there was little cultural exchange. Constant wars and insecure peace no doubt attributed to this paucity. War had become a habit, most of it as senseless as it had been between the Romans and the Parthians before and was to be between the Ottomans and Safavids centuries after them.

The twin empires produced two more giants to continue the useless war: Khosro Parviz (591-628) in Iran and Heraclius (610-641) in Byzantinum. For 19 years Persians under Khosro Parviz swept everything before them, took Damascus, Allepo, and Antioch. In 614 the Persians took Jerusalem and carried away the "True Cross" of Jesus, the most cherished Christian possession. By 617, the Persian army was poised across the

Bosporus from Constantinople. The inevitable counter attack was started by Heraclius in 622 and six years later it was the Byzantine army that stood at the gates of Ctesiphon, the Persian capital. The victories of both Parviz and Heraclius were empty. Even though Khosro Parviz was killed by his own sons and the country once more plunged into chaos, Heraclius was too exhausted himself to pursue his victory. He satisfied himself with retrieving the "True Cross." The two empires had bled each other to death and the end for both came from unexpected source- the desert of Arabia.

The Sassanian dynasty fell, yet the Persian culture that came to life under the Achaemenians survived. The themes of ethics and behavior bred by religion, kingship and justice, art and customs, tolerance for diversity and an eagerness for assimilation lived on as they had lived on after the Achaemenians. The Sassanians must be credited for taking the traditions they inherited and casting them into a distinct kind of identity. However, in the end, it was the Iranians themselves who defended a unique form of nationalism which came from an emotional commitment to culture. When Iran fell to the Arabs in the 7th century, Persian culture stayed intact to fertilize Eslam and define it for Iran.[19]

ENDNOTES

1. Frye, Heritage of Persia, p.124

2. Ghirshman, Iran, p. 225.

3. Theodor Noldeke, Aufsatze zur Persischen Geschichte (Leipzig, 1884), p.134.

4. Ghirshman, Iran,p.352.

5. The Iranians, pp.31-32

6. The fact that empires in Iran did not build strong navies has led scholars to the mistaken conclusion that Iranians were not seafarers. Linguistic evidence alone refutes this because words such as anchor, helm, barge, captain, lateen, and others prevalent in Arabic (and some in English) are derived from Persian. Furthermore, place names on the shores of the Indian Ocean from Zanzibar to Malabar

are Persian. See George F. Hourani, Arab Seafaring in the Indian Ocean, trans. Into Persian by M. Moghadam (Tehran: Franklin Publications, 1959),pp.173ff., Under "Comments by the translator."

7. Frye, Heritage of Persia, p. 170.

8. H.F. Farmayan, The Foreign Policy of Iran, A History Analysis 559 B.C.-A.D.1971(Salt Lake City, University of Utah Press 1971), pp.7-8.

9. See his Taghveem va Tarikh dar Iran (Iran-Kudeh no.15).

10. See his Mehrabeh ya Parasteshgah-e Deen-e Mehr (Mithraism or the Temple of the Religion of Mithra) (Tehran: Iran-e Bastan, 1965).

11. John R. Hinnells, Persian Mythology, pp.76-78

12. Frye, heritage of Persia, p.170.

13. Moghadam, Mehrabeh, p. 48.

14. Hinnells, Persian Mythology, p86.

15. Irving, Crossroads of Civilization, p. 76.

16. Mackey, The Iranians, p.36.

17. Frye, Heritage of Persia, p. 222.

18. Ghirshman, Iran, p.318.

19. Mackey, The Iranians, p.39.

CHAPTER FOUR

THE ARAB INVASION OF IRAN
AND ITS AFTERMATH

The harsh climate and inhospitable desert of the Arabian peninsula were not at all enticing for the Persian or Byzantine empires to conquer that land. Moreover, trade with the nomadic Bedouins was not so great to induce the empires to fight over it. Roaming desert people would periodically raid the boundaries of the two empires. In order to protect themselves from such raids, the two empires had agreed to give autonomy to two strong tribes and had given them the responsibility for keeping the raiders in check.

It is generally presumed that many waves of raiders have emerged from the Arabian peninsula and have settled in the Fertile Crescent- a territory that covers modern Iraq, Syria, Lebanon, Jordan, and Israel. Assyrians, Babylonians, Chaldeans, and Hebrews are supposed to have come from the desert. The last large raid in known history occurred about the middle of the seventh century A.D. and created an empire and established a religion. The people who emerged from the desert are known as Arabs and the religion they preached is called Eslam (Islam).

Eslam is the religion of submission to the will of Allah, a deity who was vaguely familiar to the pre-Eslamic Arabs and the same as *El-loh* or *Elohism*, the deity described in the Old Testament. Mohammad is said to have received his revelation from Allah in A.D.610 at age forty, when he was a prominent member of the Ghoraysh (Qoraysh) tribe in Makkeh (Mecca). Mohammad, and other important members of the tribe did not only have the business monopoly in the city of Mecca but were also the custodians of the holiest shrine in Arabia, the Ka'beh (Ka'ba), which was located in the city and attracted thousands of Bedouins every year, who came for pilgrimage as well as trading.

The message of Mohammad was monotheistic and against the pantheon of Gods and Goddesses which surrounded the Ka'ba. Since Mohammad identified Allah with the God of Jews and Christians, he considered his message to be in line with the Judeo-Christian tradition. Other religions, such as Zoroastrianism, Buddhism, and so on, were outside the tradition and, therefore, were not acceptable as authentic.

Mohammad clashed with other fellow businessmen of the tribe, who saw in his message the destruction of Ka'ba and, with it, the business opportunities the pilgrims brought every year. For twelve years he campaigned without much success. In 622, Mohammad along with a number of his followers escaped to Madineh (Medina), two hundred miles north of Mecca. This migration or *Hejrat (Hejra)* marks the beginning of the year one of the Moslem lunar calendar. This move transformed Mohammad from a private person preaching a new faith to a leader wielding political and military authority.

In Madineh, Mohammad was both the new head of the state and at the same time the prophet of Allah. As head of the state he was the judge, legislator, organizer, and the person responsible for the welfare of the community. As a prophet he had to see that the will of Allah was proclaimed. In his mind and in the opinion of his followers the two were combined. As prophet he revealed the will of Allah, and as head of the state he enforced it. He subdued Mecca and ordered the destruction of the idols; but preserved Ka'ba, which embodied the holy black stone (a meteorite), and continued it as a shrine for Moslem pilgrimage in exactly the same manner as it had been in pagan times. By his death in 632, he had unified Arabia under the banner of Eslam.

Mohammad's death created one of the most thorny problems to disturb the body of politic of Eslam throughout the centuries to this day. The problem was that of the succession to his political office. Even before the internment of his body, a bitter struggle arose over his succession. There were three different opinions. On the one side there were the legitimists, who were later called Shi'ieh (Shi'ites). They believed that succession belonged exclusively to the descendants of the prophet. Since Mohammad did not have a male issue, the prize, they believed should go to Ali, who was the first cousin, adopted son, son-in-law of the prophet, and one of the first to accept Eslam. He would be followed by his two sons and their descendants.

The next group, whose opinion on the caliphate was accepted by the Sunni sect of Eslam, believed that since the prophet himself was a member of the Ghoraysh tribe, that only a member of this tribe could succeed him. This group prevailed.

The third group, a minority, believed that the caliphate should not be limited to a family or tribe. They took Mohammad at his word that greatness was based on piety and not on blood. These claimed that even a slave could become a caliph.

When Abu Bakr was chosen the first caliph, he had to spend his whole term of office — less than three years- in subduing the rebellious tribes. These tribesmen's allegiance to Mohammad had been superficial and, with him gone, they severed their relations and reverted to their old ways. Some of them even claimed prophets of their own.

The Invasion of Eslam

After the death of Abu Bakr in 634, Omar was chosen caliph. It was under the inspired leadership of Omar that the Arabs of the desert erupted like a volcano and consumed everything before them. There has been much debate concerning the real cause of the collapse of the Persian Empire- undoubtedly one of the most important events in world history. One factor was the fact that the Byzantine and the Sassanian empires had bled each other to death. The heavy taxes to finance the war must have been unbearable to masses. Also, the Mazdaki revolt had not been able to break the stratification of society, which had closed the door of opportunity to others. Furthermore, religion in Iran had become an arm of the state and an oppressor of the people. Under these circumstances, it is not too surprising that the Arabs defeated the Persians. The Sassanians did not expect attacks from the bedraggled Bedouins any more than the Romans expected the Huns, or the Chinese the Mongols.

It cannot be determined whether Mohammad had visions of a world empire. It is known that Abu Bakr, who had his hands full with the rebellious tribes, was reluctant to order his brilliant general, Khaled ebn-Valid to go to Syria. Even Omar, who was certainly enthusiastic for conquest beyond the borders of Arabia, did not set out to conquer according to a studied plan. The whole thing started more like a raiding party, which Arabs were used to, than a full-fledged military campaign. Also it should be noted that it had become necessary for Omar to send the Bedouins out to war. The new religion, imposed on the Arabs by Mohammad and again by Abu Bakr, had disrupted their mode of life. Among other things, they were asked to pay taxes, which they had never done before. Furthermore, they were forbidden from raiding, which had been a habit of generations and could not be abandoned so easily. So Omar encouraged them to fight non-Moslems outside of Arabia, thereby ridding himself of Bedouin intransigence at home and affording the new government the prospects of victory abroad. The nomadic Bedouins, who had heard of the fabulous wealth of Iran and Byzantinum, were very eager to go, especially when they were exempt from paying taxes.

The adventure of raiding and prospects of rich economic reward were strengthened by a new faith that what they were doing was for the cause of Allah. What was heretofore a raid was elevated into *Jahad (Jihad)*, holy war, which, in case of death, would assure them entry into paradise. Without Eslam, the victories of the Arabs would not have been much more than raiding sorties, and without the military victories, Eslam would not have become much more than a tribal religion in Arabia.

From the start of the raids against Iran in 634 until the death of Yazdgerd III (632-651), the Arabs and the Persians were engaged in no less than thirty-three battles, the most important of which were the battles of Ghadessiyeh (Qadisia) in 637, Teesphoon(Ctesiphon) shortly afterward, and Nahavand in 642.

At Ghadessieh, a small town on the west side of Forat river (the Euphrates in modern Iraq), well-armed Iranians looked with contempt at about ten thousand Arabs- sun-scorched, dusty nomads in sandals and torn, dirty clothes, carrying swords sheathed in rags. Demoralized as a result of futile campaigns against Byzantium, the famous Persian cataphracts became clumps of fat, immobile men battling a swarm of wasps. In 638, the vaulted palace at Teesphoon (Ctesiphon) fell to the Arabs. Its fabulous prizes dazzled the poor, unlearned tribesmen of the Arabian Peninsula. A life-size silver camel and a golden horse with emerald teeth and a garland of rubies around its neck were among the thousands of objects looted by the Arabs. The legendary Spring of Khosro or Baharestan, a carpet ninety feet square, woven of silk and embellished with gold and silver threads representing the traditional Persian garden- where diamonds were used for water, emeralds for greenery, rubies and pearls for blossoms- was cut into pieces as booty and distributed among nomads. The destruction by ignorant Arabs went on. The massive libraries carefully collected by Persians were burned or destroyed based on the Arab edict that maintained:

If the books herein are in accord with Eslam,
Then we don't need them.

If the books herein are not in accord with Eslam,
Then they are kafer (of the infidel).[1]

In 642, the Arab victory in Nahavand opened the passes through the Zagross Mountains and into Fars province, where the Arab armies met Persian defenders refusing to surrender historic Persia to a foreign conqueror. These Persians proved to be the most difficult adversary in all of the Eslamic conquests. In the end, after slaughtering about forty thousand people, the Arabs rode toward Persepolis- the emotional center of Persian history and culture- broke the crowns and faces that had been so artfully carved in stone, and inscribed the story of their destruction next to the justice and tolerance stories of the Achaemenian kings.

Thus it was that in the course of a decade the Arabs of the desert had reduced the size of the Byzantine empire by half and had vanquished the Sassanians altogether. For an understanding of the history of Iran it is essential for the reader to realize that the defeat of Iran at the hands of the Arabs has always been considered by the Persians as a great calamity and has not been forgotten by them. Iran has been invaded by many nations in its long history, but the Persians have forgotten about practically all of them except the Arab conquerors.

After the first victories over the Byzantine and the Persian empires, it became evident to the Arabs that these colossi were not invincible. Omar and most of the Omayyeh (Omayyad) caliphs desired to create an empire ruled by the Arabs in which Eslam was the dominant religion and Arabic was the official language. Of course, the early Arab Moslems were not the first people in the history of the world nor the last to dream such a dream, but they succeeded more than most. What is of interest is to note that the Persians brought about the defeat of the Arab dream. It was the Persians who, after recovering from the shock of defeat, consciously tried to destroy the Arab hegemony and were successful in A.D.750. It was the Persians who, unlike the Egyptians, Syrians, Iraqis, and others who adopted Arabic as their mother tongue, refused to speak Arabic and, as soon as they could, stopped writing it. It was the Persians who changed Eslam before accepting it; and since 1500 they have belonged to a sect which sets them apart from the majority of the Arabs.

The peoples of the Fertile Crescent, Egypt, and North Africa were under a foreign power, Byzantium. In the victory of the Arabs, all that happened to them was a change of masters, and they had every reason to welcome such a change. A vast majority of them became Moslems, and they all adopted the Arabic language. If they remember the surrender of

Dameshgh (Damascus), Jerusalem, Alexandria, and other cities to the Arabs, they do so with pride for the victory of Eslam. This was never so with the Persians. The lament of the Persian poet, Khaghani Shirvani, (1106-1185) when he visited the ruins of the palace of Teesphoon (Ctestiphon), Tagh-e –Kasra, is known by every Persian, and the story of the battle of Ghadessiyeh in Ferdosi's Shahnameh, has been memorized by most of the schoolchildren in Iran. On the eve of the battle, Rostam Farrokhzad, the commanding general of the Persian forces, has a premonition of defeat and writes a moving letter to his brother in Teesphoon (Ctesiphon). Two lines are indicative of the feelings of the Persians:

From drinking camel's milk and feeding on lizards,
So have affairs of the Arabs prospered.
That they long for the crown of Kiyan,
Shame on thee, O circling Heaven, shame!

The Persians did not forget their defeat neither did they forgive Omar, who was the main cause of their defeat. Perhaps it was no accident that the second caliph of Eslam was assassinated by a Persian on November 23, 644.

Shi'ism

More than 95 percent of the people of Iran are Shi'is and Shi'ism is the official religion of Iran, therefore a description of Shi'ism origins and tenets is essential to the understanding of the Persian scene.

It may loosely be stated that the first four caliphs of Eslam were "elected" to the high office. Of these, the first three, Abu Bakr, Omar, and Osman (Othoman) were members of the Ghoraysh(Qoraysh) tribe but did not satisfy the requirements of the legitimists: they felt that Mohammad had actually left a will in which he had nominated Ali and that Abu Bakr and his friends had destroyed it. When Osman was assassinated in 656, Ali simply assumed the office, as the fourth caliph, to the satisfaction of all those who believed that he was the only legitimate successor.

As soon as Ali was proclaimed caliph, other claimants challenged his right. The most important of these was Mo'aviyeh, a relative of Osman, who was the governor of Sourieh (Syria) with headquarters in Dameshgh (Damascus). He accused Ali of the murder of Osman and refused to pay allegiance to him. The dispute culminated in a battle at Saffain, on the

Euphrates in July 657. In the heat of the battle, when the soldiers of Ali had the upper hand, Mo'aviyeh asked for a truce and arbitration. Ali accepted. Some of the soldiers who were disgusted by this decision, left the battleground crying: "There is no arbiter except Allah." These were named Khavarej (Kharejites), the abandons. Before any conclusive decision was issued by the arbitration board, one of the Khavarej assassinated Ali in January 661.

Hassan, the oldest son of Ali was proclaimed caliph, but Mo'aviyeh offered him protection and royal pension and asked him to withdraw. Hassan accepted, and Mo'aviyeh became the ruler of Eslam with Damascus as his capital. This, however, did not end the claim of the partisans of Ali that the caliphate should remain in the household of the Prophet. Now that Hassan had withdrawn, the only rallying point was Hossain, his younger brother who was willing to press his claim and lead a revolt against the Bani Omayyeh (Omayyads). In 680, when Yazid became caliph, Hossain did not acknowledge him and secretly left Madineh (Medina) to join his followers in Kufeh (Kufa) on the Persian Gulf. The plot was discovered by the agents of Yazid; and the small party of 72, including women and children, was ambushed at Karbala, south of Baghdad on the 10th of the Arabic month of Moharram. Hossain was beheaded and the women and children were taken captive.

Hossain was considered the "Lord of Martyrs" for the cause of Allah, and his death became the rallying occasion for the opponents of the caliphate. With a cause and Ali and Hossain as martyrs, the followers separated themselves from the main body of Eslam and found a religio-political community with a philosophy, theology, government, and ethics of their own.

Professor Arberry states in The Legacy of Persia: "From the earliest times there can have been scarcely a belief or a dream, a cult or a hope, that was not eventually either integrated into, or held in suspension in that potent elixir which is Persian culture." If there is any truth in the above statement, then Eslam went through this process and one of the results was Shi'ism and the other was Sufism. Albeit, both have their roots in Eslam and the Ghor'an (Qor'an), but there is no question that both show characteristics that are integral part of the Persian culture. It should also be noted that Hossain had married a daughter of Yazdgerd, the last Sassanian king; therefore it is believed by Persian Shi'is that Shi'i religious leaders are legitimate rulers as descendants of both the Prophet and the Sassanian kings.

As a religion, Shi'ism is speculative with Zoroastrian and Christian overtones, and incorporates within itself mysteries, saints, intercessor, belief in atonement, and the spirit of high cult, all of which are repugnant to the majority of the Sunnis. In Sunni Eslam, only the Ghora'n is infallible, while in Shi'ism infallibility has been extended to include Ali and his eleven descendants who are called Emam (Imam). The doctrine of the Emamate in Shi'ism believes that Mohammad and the twelve Emams are sinless.

In Sunni Eslam, Mohammad is the last of God's prophets. The Shi'is confess this also, but they seem to qualify it by stating that Ali, as the "rightful heir," has received the "light of prophecy" from Mohammad and has passed it to his descendants, the twelve Emams. This doctrine has two significant ramifications. The first is that while in Sunni Eslam, the Ghor'an and the Sonnat (Sunna)-the practices of Mohammad- form the sole bases of Eslamic law, the Shi'is believe in *ejtehad*. This means that the Emams, and in their absence, their spokesmen, have the right of interpretation. Second, is the political theory that evolves from this doctrine. Since the spiritual and temporal powers of Mohammad have been passed on to Ali and successively to the other Emams, the only legitimate government belongs to the Emam. Consequently, governments which are not under the Emam or his agents, among them all the Sunni caliphs including the first three, are "usurpers."

The Shi'is also have a doctrine of the *Return*. This is similar to the return of the deliverer in Zoroastrianism, the coming of the Messiah in Judaism, and the "second coming" of Jesus in Christianity. The majority of the Shi'is believe that there were twelve Emams and that the twelfth, the Mahdi, "Messiah," disappeared in 878 and shall return at the end of time when he will bring the whole world under the jurisdiction of Shi'i Eslam.

Iran and the Bani Omayyeh (Omayyads)

The Omayyads Continued the Eslamic conquest. In the West they conquered Spain and in the East they crossed the Amu Darya (Oxus) as the Sassanians had done. They also went south toward India and captured territory along the Sind river and the Punjab area.

Omayyads tried to establish an empire that was Arab first and Moslem second. There were others who thought that the prophet would have wanted an empire that was Moslem first and Arab second. Only a small minority believed that in Eslam there should not be a " second " place to be given to the Arabs or any other nationality. The Omayyads, however, preached the superiority of the Arabs, and in this they were following the policy set by Omar, who has sometimes been called the "second founder " of Eslam. Eslam believes in the brotherhood of all Moslems. Omar interpreted Eslam to be a brotherhood of Arabs who had become Moslems. The non-Arab converts could join in this community but would not be part of its inner governing circle, a privilege reserved only for the Arabs. To this end Omar banished all non-Moslems from Arabia in order to keep the home base purely Arab and Moslem. He forbade Arabs from obtaining land in conquered territories in the hope that without land of their own, " home " would always be Arabia. He discouraged intermarriage, even with converts, in order to keep the blood pure and the Arab military intact. In order to prevent the Arab warriors from mingling with the conquered peoples, he ordered the building of military cantonments where the conquerors and their families lived.

In keeping with the above principles, the original egalitarian message of Eslam had given way to the stratification of society into four groups, very much as the Sassanian society had been stratified. At the bottom were the slaves. These were white, black, and yellow and were captured from all parts where Arab arms had been victorious. Judging by the number of slaves in both the Omayyad and Abbasid societies, one may safely conclude that early Moslem society was based, to some degree, on a slave economy.

Above the slaves were the *Zemmi* (Arabic *dhimmi*), members of the tolerated religions, Judaism and Christianity, whom the Moslems called the " people of the book." Every zemmi had to pay a special head tax, called *jezyeh*, but he was free to practice his religion and was judged in his own religious courts. The Zoroastrians of Iran were not considered zemmi at first, but very early the Arabs realized that they could not kill all of those who did not belong to the "people of the book." Consequently they extended this status to the Zoroastrians also and taxed them accordingly. On the whole, the zemmi was a third-class citizen and was restricted in his dress, hairdo, manner of riding, holding of politic office, and so forth. In practice, however, many Jewish and Christian zemmis held important public offices, but such a privilege was denied a Zoroastrian.

Above the zemmis were the non-Arab Moslems, *mawali*, or clients. In theory, every non-Arab convert to Eslam had to have an Arab sponsor, whose client he became. This second-class status of the non-Arab Moslem became the bone of contention and the source of rebellion.

At the top of the pyramid was the Arab Moslem, who not only did not pay any taxes, but as a soldier, received an annual stipend from the public treasury.

The doctrine of Arab superiority was easier claimed than demonstrated. About the only thing that early Arabs, who emerged from the desert, could do well was to fight. They considered agriculture beneath their dignity and did not have the expertise and experience to administer the large empire they had acquired. They depended heavily on the Persians and the Greeks. They borrowed the satrap system from the Persians and adopted the tax laws of Khosro Anooshiravan.

Caliph Abdolmalek (685-705) started a program of Arabization. He ordered all government records that were kept either in Persian or Greek to be changed into Arabic. This caused bloodshed in Iran and was not fully implemented until 741. But once the Persians saw that it was inevitable, quite characteristically accepted it. Sibveyh, a Persian scholar, wrote the most authoritative grammar for the Arabic language which has been used by generations of Arabs.

When oppression and corruption spread, branches of the Ghoraysh tribe and the religious Moslems who thought the Omayyads too worldly rose against them. The Persians encouraged them all and offered them hospitable location in Khorasan (northeast of modern Iran) which was quite distant from the capital. The leader of this upraising was a young Persian known as Abu Moslem Khorasani, whose real name was Behzadan. Around 740, the descendants of al-Abbas, the Prophet's uncle, claimed their right to the caliphate and asked Abu Moslem, who was in Kufa at the time, to go to Khorasan and lead the movement. Pro-Abbasid forces that finally emerged, were commanded by Behzadan (Abu Moslem), who unfurled the Abbasid flag and marched against the Omayyad strongholds. After nearly two years of battle, the *Siah Jamegan* "Black Robes" of Abu Moslem defeated the main Omayyad forces in January of 750. In April of the same year Damascus was captured, and the unity of the Arab Empire was shattered, never to be revived again.

The Abbasids and Iran

The victory of the Abbasids was not simply a transfer of power from one Arab group to another. It rather ushered in a new era. With the victory of the Abbasids, the caliphate and the empire altered geographically and politically. The center of cultural emphasis shifted from Syria to Iran. As a result, the distance between Mecca and Eslam's capital lengthened again not only in miles but in culture as the new caliphate oriented itself more to Persia than to Arabia. The Arab aristocracy of Medina and Mecca that had exercised control over the empire since its first days gradually diminished. And Arabs as a separate identifiable group faded into the geography of the Eslamic Empire.

The Abbasid capital built at Baghdad carried the hallmark of the Persians more than that of the Arabs. The city's walls formed a circle just like the walls of the classics Sassanian city of Firoozabad. The caliph's palace incorporated the architectural style of the imperial Persia. Within the court itself, everything from the clothes the caliph wore to the servants' attire carried the stamp of Sassanian Persia. Persians occupied the chief positions in the new government, and the non-Arabs felt a sense of liberation. The doctrine of Arab supremacy was made obsolete, and a large number of Arabs themselves, who had emerged from the desert a short century before, receded to the desert not to be heard of again until the twentieth century. To be sure, the Abbasids were Arabs, but they ruled actually only until 842, and only nominally until 1258. Eslam remained, but its destiny was not in the hands of Arabs alone.

The Abbasids had come to power with the help of many groups, and each group saw in the Abbasids its own triumph. Especially, the first two caliphs found themselves embarrassingly dependent on Abu Moslem Khorasani and his many devoted followers to keep order in their new dominions. Noteworthy is the defeat of the Chinese in central Asia by Abu Moslem's lieutenant in July 751, after which Chinese influence in this area greatly decreased. The Abbasids, however, were not interested in any of these groups except as a means of gaining power. They began to rid themselves of those who had been their allies. It is said that Mansour, the second Abbasid caliph, had four obsessions: an exaggerated dislike for spending money; love for his son; hatred for the Shi'is; and hatred for Abu Moslem.

Mansour's hatred of Abu Moslem was reciprocated. It is said that Abu Moslem wanted to get rid of the Abbasids after using them to destroy the Omayyads. The Abbasids had already used Abu Moslem and did not need him anymore. Mansour tricked Abu Moslem into accepting his invitation to a feast in 754 and then put him to death. This treacherous deed caused such an uproar in Iran that took the Abbasids a century to suppress; in the process they weakened themselves to the point of extinction.

Soon after the Abbasids came to power they realized that it was not politically expedient to antagonize the majority Moslems in favor of the minority Shi'is and checked their own pro-Shi'i proclivities. This did not endear them in the eyes of the Shi'is, who thenceforth became the enemies of the caliphate.

When the Abbasids came to power, a large segment of the population of Iran, especially in the rural areas, was not Moslem. The Abbasids, however, who had discarded Arab supremacy, concentrated on religion and aroused the animosity of the masses. Unlike the Omayyads, they imposed Eslam and became dogmatic to the point of organizing the first inquisition in Eslam. The history of Iran during the first century of Abbasid rule is the story of religious uprisings all over the country. After the first century, the Abbasid caliphs were only figureheads and were used by leaders of principalities in Iran who had such an important part in the creation of the Parisian Renaissance.

Persian opposition to the Abbasids took three forms - religious, literary, and political. The most spectacular of the three was the religious uprising, mainly because it was the movement of the masses. These numerous uprisings had many common characteristics: they were anti-Arab and sometimes anti-Eslamic; they had speculative and bizarre beliefs and an exaggerated system of eschatology; they were communal and took care of the social and economic needs of the members; and practically all of them attached themselves to Abu Moslem Khorasani (Behzadan) by preaching the doctrine of transmigration of souls to show that the leader was the incarnation of the fallen hero. These uprisings began in 755, when Sandbad (Sinbad) the Magian, a good friend of Abu Moslem, set out to destroy the Ka'ba, and slackened with the execution of Babak in 839.

The most famous was the "Veiled Prophet of Khorasan," who rebelled in 766 and claimed that he was the reincarnation of Abu Moslem. His followers, who numbered in the thousands, wore a white uniform and were known as the "White Robes." They destroyed mosques and killed those who prayed or gave the call to prayer. Equally famous is the rebellion of Babak Khorramdin in Azarbaijan and Arran whose religion was a mixture of Zoroastrian and Mazdaki beliefs, called *Khorramdin*, or "Happy religion." His followers, who kept the forces of two caliphs occupied for over twenty years, were called the "Red Robes." Babak was defeated in 838 by Afshin, a Persian general in the service of the caliph, and was dismembered and killed in Baghdad.

The second form of Persian opposition to the Abbasids was literary. During the Omayyad period when the Byzantine and Persian secretaries and other officials could not tolerate the claims of Arab superiority any longer, they started to combat these claims by writing about the good points of their own nationality and the weaknesses of the Arabs. They were called the *Sho'ubieh*, or the nationalist writers. As the people of Syria became Arabized, the movement became more and more Persian and reached its peak during the Abbasid caliphate. Through original writing and translation of Pahlavi books, they tried to revive the Persian culture and re-establish the Persian tradition and social structure. They were avant-garde literary critics and dominated the Mo'tazelite movement, which was a nationalist movement that questioned, among other things, many Eslamic dogmas, especially the dogma of the infallibility of the Ghor'an (Koran). The caliph Mamoon came so much under their influence that he raised the green flag of the Shi'is and appointed the eighth Emam, Ali al-Reza, as his heir. The uproar created by this move forced Mamoon to leave Baghdad. After two years of struggle he recanted. He is accused of having ordered the poisoning of Emam Reza. He also removed his support for the liberty lovers, but the intellectual and religious controversy continued until after the middle of the tenth century. Two of the members of this group, literary genius ebn-Moghaffa and the blind poet Bashshar ebn-Bord, were executed for heresy by the caliphs Mansour and Mahdi, respectively. Ebn-Moghaffa, whose real name was Roozbeh Parsi, was a secretary in the court of the Omayyads and continued in the same position with the Abbasids. He translated *Khodaynameh* (Book of Lords) into Arabic and called it *Sayr al Molook al-Ajam (Attributes of the Kings of Iran)*, for the use of caliphs. His more popular translation was the ancient Sanskrit classic, *Panchatantra*, which had been rendered into Pahlavi by Borzoo under the name of "Fables of Bidpaai." Roozbeh translated it into Arabic as *Kalileh va Demneh*. In this delightful story animals take on the characteristics of humans and discuss all sorts of philosophical and moral subjects. Both of these translations set the norm for Arabic writing until recent times. It is said that Roozbeh Parsi claimed that his Arabic was much better than that of the Ghor'an. He was accused of being a *Zendigh*, a heretic, and was burnt to death.

The third form of Persian opposition was political. Afshin, the Persian general who captured Babak, was typical of this group. He was an aristocrat and an anti-Arab, but he did not care for the masses and felt that their uprisings confused the issue. The main issue was to control the government from the top. They indeed did penetrate the early Abbasid caliphate and were quite successful in "Persianizing" the administration. The aristocratic Persian family which exerted the most influence was named Barmak, whose distinguished members, Khaled, Yahya, Fazl and Ja'far, occupied ministerial posts for half a century. They had charge of civil and military affairs and appointed and deposed governors and generals at will. They organized the postal service, inherited from the Achaemenids and Sassanians, to serve the public. They built roads and caravansaries and made Baghdad the hub of commerce and industry. They also established a Bureau of translation in which manuscripts from many languages were translated into Arabic. Due to the fact that the Barmakis were Shi'is, coupled with a probable scandal that involved the sister of the caliph Harun-al-Rashid and Ja'far, the latter was executed while Yahya and Fazl died in prison.

On the whole, the early Abbasids kept the pretense of piety and dealt harshly with non-Moslems. Even the Zemmis could not build a house of worship, could not have homes taller than their Moslem neighbors, and their testimony against Moslems was not admitted in court. The Omayyad doctrine of Arab supremacy was resented by the Persian aristocrats, but the Abbasid religious zeal persecuted the rest of the population. Freedom came with the rise of independent principalities and the renaissance of Iran.

ENDNOTES

1. Frye, Heritage of Persia, p.214.

CHAPTER FIVE

THE PERSIAN RENAISSANCE

Before the universalization of Eslam and its culture was completed according to either the Persian or the Arab model, the Iranians revived their specifically Persian identity. The Persian renaissance, which began roughly about the end of the 9th century and reached its peak in the 12th, only to be arrested temporarily by the Mongol invasion, had basically two aspects. One was political and the other cultural, namely religious, intellectual, and literary. The origins of the renaissance are to be found in the almost constant struggle of the Persians to exert their national and cultural identity and in the ability of them either to dominate the culture of their conquerors or to "Persianize" it to suit their mood and needs.

During the 1st. century of their rule, the Abbasid dynasty had relatively strong and distinguished caliphs like Mansour, Haroon al-Rasheed, and Mamoon. Without them they probably would not have been able to establish themselves. The Omayyads had deliberately relied upon an Arab base. Their satraps and military commanders were always Arabs and could be dependent upon to enforce the use of the Arabic language and values. The Abbasids, on the other hand, had abandoned the Arab base. Moreover, they did not use their enormous wealth to weld the different elements and keep the empire intact. The Golden Age of Eslam did not begin until the 10th century when all the Abbasids could do was to keep themselves alive, and some of them did not succeed in even that. The period of borrowing, however, in which most of the available manuscripts of the non-Eslamic world were systematically collected and translated into Arabic, was begun during the early Abbasid period. Haroon al-Rasheed and especially Mamoon, who had come under the influence of the Mo'-tazelites, did support the intellectuals and strengthened the foundation which made the Golden Age possible.

After Mamoon, whose espousal of the Shi'is had alienated the Ortho-dox Arabs and whose later recantation had not left many friends for him among the Persians, the caliphs felt even more insecure. The last of their Khorasani bodyguards, who had been weakened because of the murder of Abu Moslem (Behzadan), had left in disgust. In the struggle between Mamoon and his older brother Amin for the caliphate, the Persians had sided with Mamoon and brought about the death of Amin. Fazl ebn-Sahl, a Shi'i convert from Zoroastrianism, became powerful in the court of Mamoon and further alienated the orthodox Arabs.[1] Mamoon's change of heart and his alleged order for the execution of Emam Reza, fanned the fires of revolt in Khorasan. The *coup de grace*, as it were, was delivered by Mamoon himself when he sent his trusted general, Taher, to quell the rebel-lion. Taher, who was from a Persian from Khorasan and also was close enough to the center of power in Baghdad to know its weaknesses, joined the rebellion as its leader. He founded the Taherid principality in 823.

Notwithstanding all the difficulties the Abbasids were having with the Persians, the Arabs did not come to their aid. They continued their own inter-tribal feud between the north and south and practically aban-doned the caliphs to their own devices. To protect himself and his house-hold, the caliph Mo'tasem (833-842) brought in the Turks to act as his bodyguards. These Turks, who were from the easternmost part of the empire, were devout Moslems and as brave and obedient as they were uncouth and unlettered. After several years, their debauchery and row-dyism caused so much uproar in Baghdad that the caliph was forced to move his capital to nearby Samereh (Samarra) and take his bodyguards with him. But the change of venue did not solve the problem. By 861 they had become strong enough to kill the caliph Motavakel and replace him with his son. Soon they became the virtual rulers of what was left of the empire. Under these circumstances, independent principalities mushroomed all over the empire.

Persian Principalities

The principalities in Iran from the middle of the ninth century to the coming of the Mongols in the second decade of the thirteenth century were numerous.

The first consciously Persian principality was the one established by Yaghoub (Ya'qub) ebn-Lays-e-Saffar in 867. In his youth he helped his father who was a coppersmith. Later, he joined a band of brigands and later entered the service of the local chieftain in Sistan province. Eventually he overthrew the chieftain and, with the help of his three brothers became the ruler of Sistan. From then on, it was a series of campaigns against the petty rulers of Sistan, Fars, and Khorasan, the Taherids, and also against the caliph in Baghdad. He seems to be the first to try to overthrow the caliph, and he almost succeeded. It is believed that one of the reasons for Yaghoub's lack of success was the fact that he fought on Easter Sunday, even though he knew that the group of Christians in his army would not take part. But he thought he could win without them. This is indicative at least of the religious distribution in eastern Iran. Yaghoub tried a second time but died in Gondishapour. His brother succeeded him, but the dynasty finally came to an end in 892.

Of undeniable importance is the Saffarid stimulus to the renaissance of new Persian literature and culture in the later part of the 9th century.

Another Persian principality which had a very important role to play in the Persian renaissance was the Samanid (874-999). They claimed descent from Saman, a Persian nobleman. The famous writer, *Abu Rayhan Birooni* , who wrote about A.D.1000, reports that the Samanids were descendants of Bahram Choobin , the Persian general who rebelled against the Sassanid king Khosro Parviz. Their area of dominance was Khorasan and Transoxiana, with Bokhara as their capital. The founder of the dynasty was Esma'il ebn-Ahmad (874-890) who defeated the Saffarids and other principalities to carve out his kingdom. The other well-known prince in this line is his son Nasr, who became Amir at the age of 8 and died at the age of 38. Nevertheless, thanks to able ministers, during his reign the Samanids conquered the most territory.

During the Samanid period, Persian literature came into its own. Samani rulers attracted such Persian scientists and poets as Razi, Avicenna, Roodaki, and others to their capital in Bokhara, contributing to the revival of the Persian language.

The third important Persian principality arose in Deylaman, the mountainous and wooded slopes north of the Alborz range overlooking the Caspian Sea. The Moslem soldiers were not able to cross the difficult Alborz Mountains to subdue the inhabitants. During the reign of caliphs Motavakel, Montaser and Mosta'in in the period of 847 to 867, the Shi'is were persecuted. A large number of them took refuge in the Alborz mountains and later found the *Alavi* (Shi'i) kingdom of Tabarestan (modern

Mazandaran). During their sojourn among the Deylamites, they converted a number of their leaders to Shi'i Eslam. Consequently the Deylamites, because of their strong Persian nationalism and Shi'i proclivities, were bitter enemies of the Abbasids.

The Deylamites are divided into two branches, Al-e Ziyar, known as Ziyarids and Al-e Buyeh, known as Buyids. They ruled contemporaneously, the Ziyarids from 911 to 1041, and the Buyids from 934 to 1055.

The Buyids crossed the Alborz and expanded their domain all the way south to the Persian Gulf and west beyond the Euphrates River. So far as is known, Buyeh was a fisherman, but he is claimed to have descended from Yazdgerd, the Sassanian king. He had three sons, Ali, Hassan, and Ahmad, who were at first in the service of the Ziyarid prince Mardavij and later crossed the Alborz range and started a kingdom for themselves. It was through the cooperation and ability of these brothers, especially Ali and Ahmad, that the Buiyds became masters of western Iran and most of Iraq.

The impotence of the caliph and the near anarchy in the court at Baghdad may be surmised in the fact that in the fourteen years between 931 and 945 the caliphate changed hands five times. It is said that the helpless caliph Mostakfi, in his desperate desire to be rid of his Turkish "protectors," asked a staunch Shi'i like Ali Buyeh to rush to his aid. Ali who was in Fars province at the time, asked his brother Ahmad, who had already captured Ahvaz on the Karoon River, to advance to Baghdad. Ahmad did not have much difficulty in defeating Tozan, the commander in chief of the Turkish guard, and entering Baghdad. The deliriously happy Mostakfi, forgetting the fact that Ahmad was a Shi'i, made him the new commander in chief, presented rich gifts to all the three Buyeh brothers, and bestowed upon each of them high-sounding titles.

Only a month after these events, Mostakfi was literally dragged to Ahmad's presence, blinded, and thrown into jail. His successor Moti' (946-974), whose name ironically enough means "obedient," obeyed every whim of Ahmad. He was not allowed to appoint his officials and was wholly dependent on Ahmad for his daily sustenance. It is said that Ahmad was seriously considering deposing the Abbasids altogether and appointing a member of the house of Ali as the new caliph. He was advised against the move, however, on the ground that as long as the Abbasids were caliphs, the Buyids could treat them in any way they pleased without arousing the criticism of their own Shi'i supporters. But if a scion of the house of Ali was made a caliph, then all the Shi'is would follow him as the only legitimate ruler and discard the Buiyds altogether.

The Buiyds during more than a century of their rule used Shiraz as their capital because there they had a better base of support and also because Baghdad had lost its luster. To emphasize their Persian origin, they were the first among the principalities to use the title of Shahanshah, "King of Kings,". In time they were divided into three groups with bases of operation in Fars, Khoozestan, Kerman, Hamadan and Esfahan. Gradually, the Buiyds lost their territory to the rising Turkish principalities.

Turks of the eastern shore of the Caspian Sea and central Asia had started coming west following formation of a Turkish guard by the Abbasid caliphs. At first, they had come in small groups, but their numbers increased as years passed. They came as soldiers, servants, and sometimes as slaves. As they saw the political confusion in Iran and they heard of the weaknesses of the caliphs, some of the adventurous among them joined the continuous battle among rival principalities and carved out kingdoms for themselves. It must be remembered that the Turks did not come as conquerors and it can not be said that they came with any great or established cultural background except their tribal mores and social values. The main motivation was love for adventure and personal ambition. Inasmuch as they were devout Sunnis, some of them, after they had been established, did feel the responsibility of propagating Eslam through conquest and did think it their duty to protect the Abbasid caliphs from their enemies. The collapse of Persian dynasties did not mean the end of the Persian renaissance. The Turks were swallowed up by the tremendous cultural activity of the Persians and became its enthusiastic patrons. Persian was the official language of their court and they conducted themselves in the manner of Sassanian kings.

The Ghaznavids

The founder of the Ghaznavid kingdom was a Turkish slave by the name of Saboktakin (Sebuk-tegin) who was bought in the Samanid slave market. Dealing in slave trade or charging transit taxes for slaves who were being taken to the western markets in Baghdad and Syria was a lucrative source of income for the Samanid rulers. Later, he was given to another slave named Alp-tegin who made himself very useful to the Samanid governor of Ghazneh, in modern Afghanistan. After the death of Samanid governor, Alp-tegin took over the governorship. At his death Sebuk-tegin, who is reputed to have been his son-in-law, announced himself independent of the Samanids.

The actual founder of the Ghaznavid dynasty and the one who gained real independence and made a name for himself was his son Mahmood (998-1030). During the thirty-two years of his reign, Mahmood carved out a large kingdom which included all the possessions of the Samanids, Saffarids, and a good portion of the Buiyd kingdom. In addition to this, he conquered western India and opened that subcontinent to the influence of Eslam.

Sultan Mahmood is well known in Persian history as the patron of men of science and letters. He was the contemporary of such luminaries as Avicenna, Birooni, Onsori, Farrokhi, and the most famous of them all, Ferdosi Toosi. Mahmood was unlettered and did not understand Persian well enough to appreciate its literature. Furthermore, as a devout orthodox Sunni, he was suspicious of philosophy and new learning. Nevertheless the love of learning and Persian was so prevalent in his day that the mark of distinction for any prince was to have a number of intellectuals around him. Mahmood carved this respectability even if he had to kidnap some of the men of letters, which he did. Ferdosi, who completed his famous *Shahnameh* in Mahmood's court, had a great deal of trouble with him and in the end had to escape to save his life. Five centuries later, the poet Jaami, assessing the life of Mahmood, wrote:

Gone is the greatness of Mahmood, departed his glory,
And shrunk to "he knew not the worth of Ferdosi," his story.[2]

The power of the Ghaznavids began to decline after the death of Mahmood. Even though the dynasty lasted in ever-shrinking territory until in 1186, they did not amount to much and had to make way for the larger Turkish dynasty of Saljoogh (Saljuq).

The Saljooghs

We read in the Cambridge History of Iran that when the Saljooghs first appeared in Transoxiana and Khorasan in the 11th century, they came as marauders and plunderers. They belonged to the Ghuzz Turkman tribes who converted to Eslam. One of them called Saljoogh, with the help of his three sons, Esra'il, Mika'il, and Musa Arsalan, founded a dynasty. Their zeal for Jahad (holy war) helped them to overrun so much of the Middle East. They carried on warfare against the Byzantines and the Christian kingdoms of Armenia and the Caucasus. The ease with which they took over Khorasan was to a considerable degree due to the misrule of the Ghaznavids. Sultan Mahmood, who was more interested in the plunder of the riches of India than on building a tranquil kingdom, did not find as rich a loot as he expected. The result was heavy taxation on the merchants, small shopkeepers, and peasants in order to make Mahmood's wars possible. During the reign of his son, Massoud, the situation became worse and the misuse intensified. When Toghrol, the grandson of Saljoogh, came into the Ghaznavid strongholds, he did not have much difficulty. In 1037 he was crowned king. Being a good Sunni, he developed a motivation for the Saljoogh empire. His purpose was to protect the caliphate from its Shi'ite enemies, the Buyids in the east and the Fatemids in Egypt; and to uphold Sunni orthodoxy against the encroachments of foreign and liberal ideas, be they twelver Shi'is, Esma'ilis, Mo'tazelis, or free thinkers of all description. What the Ghaznavids had started to do with zeal and fanaticism, the Saljooghs carried out through zeal and organized political and intellectual planning. The fact that the celebrated and able Persian vazir Nezam al-Molk, who undoubtedly had a great deal to do with the formation of the above policies, held the same office under two kings for thirty years, was responsible for the strengthening and success of that policy.

After the death of Toghrol in 1063, and during the reign of his nephew, Alp Arsalan, and the latter's son Malekshah (1073-1093), the rank and file of the Persians witnessed thirty years of comparative peace and prosperity while the intellectual advance, which had already started, kept pace with the prosperity. The intellectual ferment of the period is shown in the fact that Nasser Khosro, Mohammad Ghazaali, and Omar Khayyam flourished at this time. The first was an Esma'ili poet missionary, the second was the famous orthodox theologian opposed to the Esma'ilis, and Khayyam was a mathematician and poet of no particular religious view.

After the death of Malekshah, there was the usual struggle for succession. With the exception of the reign of Sanjar (1119-1157), when there was some stability, the Saljooghs could not rule the empire they had created. Eventually they were divided into three main groups. One was known as the Saljooghs of Iran (1037-1194), who after Sanjar were fragmented into smaller principalities. Another was known as the Saljooghs of Syria (or Shaam) who had their capital at Aleppo (1094-1117). The third was the Saljooghs of Asia Minor (Or Room) with their capital at Konya (1071-1299). During most of these years Crusaders were engaged in warfare against the Arabs, but the Saljooghs of Iran not only did not heed the plea for help from their fellow Moslems but did not go to the aid of the Saljooghs of Syria. Perhaps the most important effect of the Saljoogh rule in Iran was the saving of the Abbasid caliphate. They repulsed the Fatemids of Egypt and broke the Buyids' heavy hand on the caliphate. Even though the Esma'ili activity continued in Iran for a time, they strengthened the foundations of Sunni orthodoxy. The early Saljooghs did not deal much better with the caliphs than the Buyids but as the Saljooghs weakened, relatively capable caliphs, such as Nasser (1176-1222) exerted some power for a short time.[3]

Kharazmshahis

The region of Kharazam (Charasmia) is located in the lower region of Amu Darya as it flows into the southern coast of the Aral Sea. It was originally populated by Iranians, and the people spoke a dialect of Iranian related to Sogdian. The encroachment of the Turkish tribes from this steppe gradually diluted the Iranian nature of the culture, and by the time they established a dynasty they were Turks with perhaps some Persian proclivities. Anush-Tegin, the first of the Kharazm rulers, and his decedents, were hereditary governors appointed by the Saljoogh sultans. It was not until the last years of Sanjar that Atsez (1127-1143), the very able Kharazmi ruler, took advantage of Sanjar's defeat at the hand of the Ghara (Qara) Khatay, and took Khorasan. Later, as the Saljoogh's power waned, the Kharazmshahis increased their territory and power. Among the increasing number of petty principalities that arose after the fall of the Saljooghs, the Kharazmshahis have been chosen for consideration for two reasons. One is to show that despite the new lease on life that the Caliphs received from the Saljooghs, they were still in danger. The Kharazmshahis, though Turks, Shi'is or had strong Shi'i proclivities, had constituted a threat to the Caliphate. Indeed, Sultan Mohammad Kharazmshah (1217-1238) omitted the name of the Caliph Nasser from Friday prayers. The second reason is that Mohammad Shah might have been able to transfer the Caliphate from the Abbasids to the house of Ali had it not been for the attack of Chengiz Khan and his Mongol hordes which swept aside everything in their way, putting an end to the Kharazmshahis and eventually the Caliphate itself.

Social and Economic Conditions

A very resourceful author by the name of Abol Faraj Esfahani (897-967) wrote a book called *Ketab al-Aghani* (Book of Songs) in which he collected anecdotes, songs, poems, games, pastimes, and jokes about the Omayyad and Abbasid men and women of wealth and power. Judging by his observations, one can readily see that even proximity to the life and times of the Prophet did not prevent the city of Mecca and Medina under the early Omayyad period from becoming centers of leisure, pleasure, and vice. There were clubs and cabarets, house of ill repute and elegant salons, belly dancers, various musicians, and songsters from all parts of the empire. If such things did go on within a stones throw of the Ka'ba and the tomb of the prophet, then one can readily surmise that other cities throughout the period had such facilities for the enjoyment of those who could afford them.

Hunting and polo were the sports of kings and princes, and they shared chess with men of lesser ranks, while practically everyone played *nard* (backgammon) as they do today. The common people of Iran, as well as the nobility, enjoyed themselves at festive occasions, such as Norooz (New Year) and Sedeh (Autumn Equinox) except at times when such celebrations were forbidden by the Orthodox Saljoogh kings. Parents could buy their children toys of stuffed animals, wooden swords, and clay pipes.[4] The Buyids, who are Shi'is are reputed to have started passion plays, *Ta'ziyeh*, which depicted incidents in the life of the Emams, especially the martyrdom of Hossain. Traveling troupes of actors would go from town to town and put on performances for the edification and entertainment of the public. The common people had ample opportunity to use the bath houses in the cities, and even small towns and larger villages claimed such accommodations. Strangers were cared for in hostels, and if they were poor they could always sleep in the mosque.

Women were segregated, and their duty was in the home, except for slave girls, who would amuse the men by their song and dance. Polygamy was permitted to the extent of four legal wives. It being a slave society, one may assume that men of the upper classes availed themselves of the opportunities to have concubines. The upper classes sat on raised divans covered with mattresses and cushions, and the lower class used mats. The security and welfare of the people depended very largely on the nature and power of the Caliph, the prince, or the local governor. During the period of principalities, which lasted some three centuries, wars, pestilence, famine, invasions, banditry, and heavy taxation must have made the lot of the people hard to bear.

In spite of the disruptive effects of war and frequent changes in dynasties, commerce continued and merchants transported their wares to different parts of Iran as well as outside the country. The system of roads built in pre-Eslamic times, and improved upon during the early Abbasids, was still functioning. Insofar as Iran was concerned, Esfahan, seems to have been the hub to which roads converged from Tabriz, Zanjan and Ray; Baghdad, Kermanshah, and Hamadan; Ahvaz, and Shiraz; and extended northwest to Nishapur, Marv, and Sir Darya; and eastward to Kerman, Sistan and through the Ghur Desert to India. Travel was possible and caravans took to the road. In 1052, Nasser Khosro, the famous Esma'li missionary, visited Esfahan and reported that there were some 50 good caravansaries in the city as well as 200 brokers who handled the transaction of money for the merchants.5 Nearly two centuries later, even in a more troubled period, another famous Persian writer, Sa'adi, was able to travel to India, Kharazm, and west to Syria.

The old idea that all land belonged to the king continued into the Eslamic times with the difference that the Ommat, (*Umma , the Eslamic community)* replaced the King. The Caliph as the chief executive of the Ommat, administered the land. Later when different princes and sultans became powerful, they took the job over. Land grant, called Aghta (*Iqta*) were temporarily dependent upon the desire of the king. The grant did not include the land itself or the peasants who were working on the land; only the income from it. At first these land grants were given to military leaders in return for the support of the army; later they were also used to secure the support of bureaucracy. The expenses of the court came from revenues from the king's lands. For example, in the court of Malekshah, the expenses of his royal pantry came from the revenues of Kharazm and the man in charge there was responsible for collecting them. Inasmuch as Atsez, who was actually in charge, became an independent ruler, it is quite evident what could be accomplished with judicious land grants. The four chief bureaus of administration, namely secretariat, revenue, military records, and audit, each had an Aghta. There was always tension between the bureaucracy, *Divan*, headed by the chief minister, and the court, *Dargah*, headed by the king. Since the military was under the king, usually the Dargah was victorious.

Religion, Science and Literature

In this circumstance of general dynastic struggle and warfare interrupted by only short intervals of stability, Iran experienced one of the most brilliant eras of cultural renaissance in the history of any people. Inasmuch as most of the cultural activity during the early Abbasids was made up of the translation of available material from different parts of the known world, the period of creativity coincided with the turbulent period of principalities. During this time Persian theologians, scientists, philosophers, historians, and poets produced original works, and in the process revived the Persian language into a beautiful vehicle of expression. Two of the most important problems facing Eslam were the theological problems created by its contact with other religions and ideas and the problems connected with the caliphate. Questions such as free will and predestination, the attributes of God and his unity, the anthropomorphic connotations of the name of God in Eslam, and others were not purely theological questions. Perhaps because the *Shu'ubiyeh* were involved in the controversy, national rivalry got somehow mixed in it. According to the observation made by H.A.R. Gibb, the problem facing the Eslamic society was whether it should "become a re-embodiment of the old Perso-Aramaean culture into which the Arabic and Eslamic elements would be absorbed, or a culture in which the personal Iranian contributions would be subordinated to the Arab tradition and the Eslamic values". Professor Frye believed that, in the case of Persia, there was no question but that the former Perso-Aramaean view should prevail, while in the Arabic-speaking parts of the caliphate, it would seem the latter triumphed."6 It appears that the Persian's tradition won only after the Mongol Invasion when Iran became free from the inhibitions that the Arabic-Eslamic tradition had imposed. Although Shi'ism and Sufism have their routes in Eslam, and have branches among the Arabic speaking people, they became Persian vessels in which Arabic-Eslamic traditions and values were diluted.

It was not until the middle of the century that orthodoxy found a capable defender in the person of Abol-Hassan Ali al-Ash'ari. He declared the uncreated nature of the Ghor'an and the arbitrary nature of God by rejecting freewill. He said that man was responsible for his actions only because God willed it. He further stated that the meaning of the attributes of God are different from the meaning of the same attributes as applied to man, thus separating God and man altogether and removing God from the knowledge of man. The scholastic school somehow had to reconcile Eslam with the new learning. This task, ironically enough, was accomplished to the satisfaction of the orthodox by a Persian, Abu-Hamid Mohammad al-Ghazaali, and was politically enforced by another Persian, Nezam ol-Molk.

This dean of Moslem theologians, Ghazaali, was born in Khorasan in 1058, and after a tumultuous life died in his birthplace in AD 1111.

He studied every philosophy and religious thought and was converted to some in turn. He ended up in orthodoxy and taught at Nezamiyyeh College in Baghdad, founded by Nezam ol-Molk. In his book, *The Revival of the Sciences of Religion*, he had tried to reconcile Eslam, Greek rationalism and Persian mysticism into one harmonious whole. Thomas Aquinas, who had a similar task in the reconciling Christian revelation with Greek rationalism, read Gazaali's work, which had been translated into Latin and was influenced by it. Although Thomism was challenged by the Protestant Reformation and the philosophical systems which came after it, Moslem orthodoxy only began to be challenged in the 20th Century.

The other main problem facing Eslam involved the theory and the practice of the caliphate. Aside from the thorny question of succession, the main reason for the existence of the caliphate was to enforce the law of God as revealed in the Ghor'an and practiced in the daily life of Mohammad. This is known as the Shariat (*Shari'a*), which could not be enforced without a state, which in turn could not be held together without a caliph. With the gradual weakening of the caliphs and the rise of rival caliphates, the situation was quite confusing. The institution was forced to go through changes as suitable substitutes and justifications had to be found. Consequently, the Ghor'an and the Tradition did not remain the only sources of Eslamic political philosophy. At least two other sources were added during the period of Persian renaissance. One was the contribution of Moslem political philosophers; the other was the "practical percepts" written for the guidance of princes, which were taken from the Irano-Turkish tradition and mores.

All of the political philosophers were by no means Persians. Indeed, the foremost among them was Abu Nasr al-Farabi (870-950), the Turk from Transoxiana. To the Greek, law was the product of man's mind, while to the Moslem it was the will of God. Plato wanted a philosopher-king while Eslam already had a prophet-king. To resolve the dilemma, Farabi combined the two. He said that imagination was the function of prophecy and intellect the function of philosophy. By having a prophet-philosopher for a king, we have a person with intellect and imagination.

He was followed by one of the great geniuses of all times, Abu Ali Hossain ebn-Sina (980-1037), the Persian from Bokharka. He is known as Avicenna. A distinguished philosopher, as well as a prominent physician, he wrote learned essays on a half a dozen subjects. For a while, he was at the court of the last Samanid Prince in Bokharka, then in Kharazm and then from city to city until his death in Hamadan. Part of this time he was escaping the kidnappers of Sultan Mahmood Ghaznavi, who wanted him at his court. Nevertheless, he found time to write two works of encyclopedic proportions, one on philosophy called *Shafa*, and the other on medicine called *Ghanoon* or Qanun (The Canon). In political philosophy, he acknowledges his debt to Farabi, but goes a step further by declaring prophecy to be the result of the highest human intellect. In other words, the prophet was a philosopher with highest intellect. There is no dichotomy involved. One could conclude that since prophecy was the result of intellect, the revelation was not necessary. He agreed with Farabi that in the absence of a prophet, it was possible to have a good society. Furthermore, Avicenna integrated his political philosophy with the old Persian system of social classification and added a sociological dimension to the process of secularization. He divided society according to professions, such as rulers, administrators, artisans, and so forth, as against the division of society by lineage preferred by the Arabs. This gave an aura of legitimacy to powerful men who considered it their profession to rule even though they were not remotely related to the prophet.

More palatable to the tastes of the orthodox and more understandable to the rulers were the "Practical Precepts" or the "Mirrors to the Princes," which became popular during this period when so many strong men wanted to behave like the kings of old but did not have the proper education. Among these, one is *Ghaboosnameh* (Qabusnameh), written by Ghaboos (Qabus) Voshmgir of the Ziyarid principality and the other is the better known *Siyasatnameh* by Nezam ol-Molk, written for the edification of Saljoogh princes. They deal with every royal duty from playing chess to the administration of justice. The art of government is taught through anecdotes, maxims, and examples taken from Sassanid kings and other sources.

Even though the ideas of Farabi, Avicenna and others were considered heretical to the orthodox, the Shi'is, Esma'ilis, and free thinkers discussed them and were influenced by them. All along the caravan routes there was a string of large cities in which the merchants, artisans, and poets were affluent, cosmopolitan, and fascinated by new ideas. The Esma'ilis, with their network of missionaries, had a cell in every city. They not only fanned the grievances of the miserable masses against the caliphs and the Sunni rulers; they also organized discussion groups and encouraged the integration of Eslam with Persian culture. They formed semi secret fraternities called *Ekhvan ol Safa* "Brethren of Purity" and encouraged political activities against the government. It is important to note that philosophers like Farabi and Avicenna, scientists like Razi and Omar Khayyam, and men of letters like Ferdosi who were all accused of heresy were mostly either twelver Shi'is, Esma'ilis, or served under Shi'i rulers. It must also be noted that there was no talk of anti-Eslamism at this time. They were all Moslems and eager to propagate the faith, but they wanted a boarder Eslam than the one brought from the desert.

The orthodox, however, were not satisfied; sustained by the power of the Saljooghs, they tried to stamp out the heretical ideas. Nezam ol-Molk, the most effective champion of orthodox theologians, placed orthodox civil administrators in all departments of the government. He established colleges in different cities, the most important being the Nezamieh college in Baghdad, in which bureaucrats were trained to apply Moslem Shari'a to every aspect of government and society. He forbade the celebration of Persian festivals and took punitive measures against the twelver Shi'is and Esma'ilis. Indeed, some parts of Siasatnameh reads like witch hunting. He not only attacks the "heretics", but includes the members of the tolerated religions as well. He supports the statement that "It is better that enemies should not be in our midst." This led to an Esma'ili revolt under the leadership of Hassan Sabbah, who was the leader of the group in Deylaman from 1090 until his death in 1124. He fortified the fortress of Alamoot, in the Alborz Mountains, north of Ghazvin into an un-impregnable fortress. It remained their stronghold until 1257 when it was destroyed by the Mongols. Sabbah used terror and assassination as a political weapon. He organized the Esma'ili cells in the cities into armed bands. The devotees who were sent on missions of assassination were fearless, believing that their mission was holy and that if they were killed they would go to paradise as martyrs. One of their first victims was Nezam ol-Molk himself.

The Persian renaissance produced great physicians, mathematicians, astronomers, and historians as well. As stated before, GondiShapour was a medical center in Sassanian time and remained so in Eslamic times. Haroon ol-Rashid built a hospital in Baghdad after the Persian model and called it by its Persian name *Bimarestan*. The most original work in medicine was done by two Persians, Razi and Avicenna. Mohammad ebn-Zakariyya al-Razi (865-985) was born in Ray, south of modern Tehran, and lived most of his life under the Samanid patronage. For a time he was the chief physician in Baghdad. His book on medicine, *Al-Hawi*, is a comprehensive work in medicine in which he reports his medical studies on the kidney stone, smallpox, and measles, and describes his invention of seton (a method of suturing) in surgery. He is also credited to be the first person who made Alkahl (yellow) which today is called alcohol. Avicenna, who has been discussed as a philosopher, was a physician at the Samanid court at the age of 16. His encyclopedia of medicine, Ghanoon "Canon", was used in Europe well into the 17th Century.

In mathematics and astronomy, we must single out Mohammad-al Kharazmi, whose works introduced "Arabic" numerals, algorism, and algebra to the west; Abu Rayhan Birooni, who figured the latitude and longitude of many cities on the basis of the rotation of the earth on its axis; and Omar Khayyam, who in addition to his works on Euclid, produced a new solar calendar which has an error of only one day in 5,000 years and is still in use in Iran. Gregorian (Western) calendar leads to an error of one day in 3,330 years.

Of the contribution of these men, as well as scores of historians, geographers, and others to what is sometimes called "Eslamic civilization," suffice it to quote the late E.G. Browne: "Take from what is generally called Arabian Science — exegeses, tradition, theology, philosophy, medicine, lexicography, history, biography, even Arabic grammar - the work contributed by the Persians and the best part is gone."7 Very likely their work would not have been possible had it not been for the weakness of the caliphs and the freedom which this gave to the intellectuals to become creative. After the Saljooghs restored orthodoxy, scholarship and creativity began to languish in the world of Eslam wherever orthodoxy was in power.

During this period almost all intellectuals wrote their scientific and physiological treatises in Arabic, which was still the language of the learned. This is why many westerners today erroneously think of them as Arabs. Persian, however, was not forgotten, for this period saw also the renaissance of the Persian language, which eventually became the medium through which the meditations of the soul and thoughts of the intellect were expressed. "New Persian" as it is called, is new in that it has borrowed a large number of Arabic words, but it is old in that it is the same as Pahlavi (also called "Middle Persian") which was connected with "Old Persian" and so on to the original Aryan language. As Professor Frye writes in the preface of the Cambridge History of Iran, volume 4, "The Persian language was spread in the East, beyond the borders of the Sassanian Empire, by the conquering armies of Eslam, and Persian became the *Lingua Franca* of the eastern caliphate. The new Persian language written in the Arabic script, and with numerous Arabic words in it, became a marvelous instrument of poetry and literature, similar to the English language, which develops from a simple Anglo-Saxon tongue to one enriched by Latin and French usages after the Normal Conquest."

The language which is spoken in Iran, Afghanestan, Tajikestan, and the neighboring regions is one of the few languages of the world with an unbroken literary history going back to ancient times. It was kept alive by the masses with practically no literature during the two centuries of Arab rule; it was encouraged and made official by leaders of principalities, who had emerged from the masses and did not know Arabic; and it was formed by men of talent who enriched their spoken tongue by blending into it unencumbered grammar and syntax words from the Arabic vocabulary. *Shahnameh*, which is four times longer than Homer's Iliad, resurrected Iranian identity within the world of Eslam by celebrating the history and mythology of Persian Kingship. Writing a new Persian pruned of Arabic excesses, Ferdosi awakened the soul of the Iranians. The *Shahnameh* evokes a whole range of images - heroism, justice, national glory, and tragic defeat - that Iranians as a people hold essential to their culture and their identity. Ferdosi writes: "Let not this body live if there is no Iran." This is the essence of Ferdosi's composition, explaining why it has worked its extraordinary emotional power on the Iranian's for almost 1,000 years.

Another great Persian poet is Sa'adi of Shiraz, who in his writing uses Persian and Arabic at will. He is best known for his *Golestan* (Rose Garden). In short anecdotes, written in prose and poetry, Sa'di moralizes on all sorts of conditions and relations. His ethics is situational, sometimes cynical, and always existential.

The Mongol Invasion

The Mongol avalanche which started in 1219 in Sinkiang, had by 1224 destroyed a chain of cities on the Iranian plateau, such as Balkh, Bokhara, Samarghand, Marv, Harat, Nishabour, and Ray; it had killed men and women by the thousands; and it had left maimed the few who had escaped with their lives. Why the Mongols came so far from their base of operation in China is still vague. All that can be ascertained is that the governor of the border town of Utrar, under the principality of Kharazmshah, killed a number of Chinese merchants who were sent by Chengiz Khan and confiscated the rich merchandise. Chengiz Khan sent his envoys to the ruler of the dynasty, Mohammad, and would have been satisfied if the governor had been punished, but Mohammad was too proud to punish him and killed the envoys instead. This started the avalanche. On the other hand, Chengiz, who had become emperor of a settled and civilized Chinese empire, had difficulty controlling the restless Mongol tribesmen. The only alternative was to keep them fighting. In any case, in the words of a contemporary, "they came, they looted, they killed, they burned, and they left." Actually they did not leave. Many remained and were absorbed by the Persian people and culture. That the advance of the Persian renaissance was arrested there is no question, but it did not last long. Indeed, the speed with which the Persians were able to rise again is nothing short of a miracle.

After the death of Chengiz, his vast empire was divided into three parts. First was China proper, with Peking as capital; it's ruler had titular authority over the whole empire. The second, in Russia, was known as the "Golden Horde," with its capital at Saray. The third was in Iran, called the "Ilkhan," with its capital at Maragheh in Azerbaijan. Destructive as Chengiz had been in Iran, Holagu, the founder of the Illkhan dynasty, was a builder and a patron of art and sciences. Marco Polo, who traveled through Iran to Peking around 1271, described the thriving industries of the cities of Tabriz, Kashan, and Kerman. Holagu is also responsible for ending the Abbasid caliphate with the capture of Baghdad.

The Mongols, as pagans, were very tolerant of people of all religions. Some of the Ilkhan rulers were Christians and the Vazir of Argun in 1289 was a Jewish physician. But, in the end Eslam won, and Ghazan Khan (1295-1304) became a Moslem and with the zeal of a convert destroyed the "heathen" temples as well as the Christian and Jewish houses of worship.

The arrest of the Persian renaissance was short-lived. The Persians not only restored their own culture, but they also civilized the Mongols. Unlike the Arabs, the Mongols had not come with an ideology and therefore did not impose any restrictions on the Persian artists and scientists. The famous Persian miniature paintings showed the freedom under which the artists worked. The very power that was so destructive at first also freed the Persian culture from the limiting tendencies of Orthodox Eslam and brought Iran and Eslam into contact with the cultures of Asia.

By the time the Crusaders were driven away and the Mongols had been absorbed, the geo-political pattern of the Middle East reverted to what it was before Eslam. Iran was separated from its neighbors to the west, along the same line as the Sassanids had been separated from the Byzantines. Furthermore, Persian language replaced Arabic in practically everything except the recital of the Ghor'an and prayer. The Persians, however, have changed considerably since the Sassanian days. Their blood was mixed with Berbers, Arabs, Greeks, Turks, Mongols, Indians, and a few other nationalities. Their loyalty was not to a land, but to a language and culture. It was a form of "culturalism" or a cultural nationalism in which the Persians found their identity. Two centuries later, political unity followed in the establishment of the Safavid dynasty.

ENDNOTES

1. Abdol Hossain Zarrinkoub, Do Gharn Sokoot (Two Centuries of Silence) (Tehran:Amir Kabir, 1956), p.214

2. E.G. Browne, A Literary History of Persia, II (Cambridge: Cambridge University Press, 1964), p.95

3. C.E. Bosworth, "the Political and Dynastic History of the Iranian World," in the Saljoogh and Mongol Periods, p.201.

4. Ibid., p.278.

5. Ibid.

6. Frye, Persian Heritage, p.274.

7. Browne, Literary History, Vol.1, p.192.

CHAPTER SIX

CULTURAL RETROGRESSION

The Isolation of Iran

The experience of the Persians in absorbing the culture of all comers and blending it with theirs and producing something new was so enriching and rewarding that land and boundaries became insignificant. It did not make any difference whether this activity was carried out in Baghdad or Balkh. What was important was the culture, the outlook, and not land. What was considered essential was the language and the medium of the culture, and not race. Such a concept is more of a fulfillment of the tolerance and cosmopolitan ideas of the Achaemenids than the limited nationalism imported from 19th century Europe, which is based on a national state and race. This concept of cultural nationalism was strengthened during the Mongol period. As has been stated, the absence of a strong caliph to impose orthodoxy had provided the intellectuals and artisans in all fields the freedom to be creative and inaugurate the Persian renaissance. The Mongols, who did not have an ideology to impose, obliterated even the partial sanctions imposed by some of the Saljoogh rulers. The result was a period in which the Persian artists and writers were not bound by many restrictions imposed by the dogma of religion or government.

It is agreed by all historians of Iran that the four centuries from the founding of the Ilkhan dynasty in 1250 to 1650, or a century and a half after the founding of the Safavid dynasty, was one of the brightest periods of cultural advance in the long history of Iran. It is also agreed that from 1650 to the beginning of the 20th Century is a rapid period of cultural decline in Iran. Cultural activities slackened when the Safavids made

Shi'ism the state religion and carried out a period of forced conversion. By the time of Shah Abbas (1587-1629) the last bright light of the cultural advance was still in evidence. After that, when Shi'i heterodoxy became orthodoxy, state and religion became one, and the kings, with very few exceptions had to enforce the dogmas of the established religion, then the light of learning began to dim.

The purpose is not to minimize the destruction wrought by the Mongols; but it is important to note that it did not break the Persian spirit, nor did it destroy the Persian cultural advance except for the temporary arrest during the invasion and a few years after that. The Persians did manage to become advisors and ministers for the Mongols from Holagu on. They did survive the invasion through artistic creativity which reached its heights as evidenced by the magnificence of miniature paintings. Furthermore, they did withstand the onslaught through Sufism, which minimized the significance of the real world which had crumbled around them. Sufism was a reaction to the transitory nature of life - a phenomenon which was heightened by Mongol destruction - so that the mystic experience, which is the union of the self with God, became a means by which to free the soul.

Sufism

Sufism derives its name from the coarse woolen (suf) garment which the adherent wore. It has its roots in the Ghor'an, but it has picked up elements from older religious practices, as well. Sufism must not be confused with Shi'ism. It was thanks to the influence of Ghazaali that Sufism was given a niche in the orthodox temple and was tolerated by the Sunnis. Perhaps because it was tolerated by the Sunnis, the Shi'is did not have much use for it until after the Mongol invasion. There was not much love for the Sufis among the orthodox because Sufism was a reaction to the orthodox theology of the separation of God and man. According to Sufis, there are true similarities between the attributes of God and man, through which man can become "one" with God. The law of Eslam, *Shari'a*, according to the majority of the Sufis is like a "shell" which protects the kernel. Sufis do not all agree, however, on what to do with the shell once it is broken and the kernel is reached. Some believe that it is still useful as a protection; others think that it should be honored for having contained a kernel; and still others like the prince of old mystics, Jalal o-Din Roomi, believe that it is only good for animal fodder.

100,000-year-old scraper,
Kermanshah
(Photo by Ghazalle Badiaozamani)

Jurassic footprint in
Kerman

42,000-year-old rock painting,
Lorestan

(Photo by Ghazalle Badiozamani)

The first U.S.-Iran
Treaty of Friendship
(First Page)

(Photo by
Ghazalle Badiozamani)

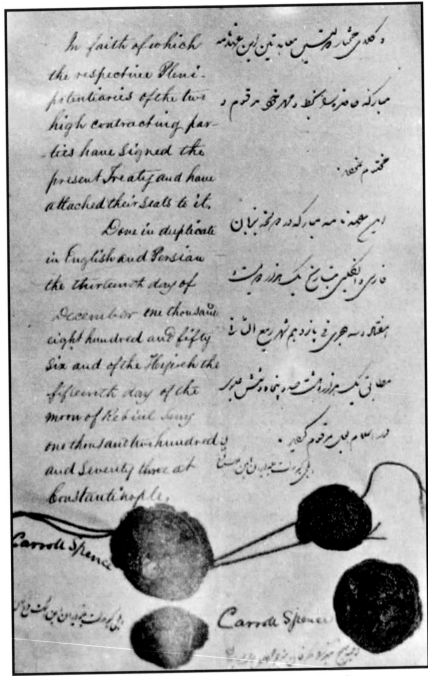

The first U.S.-Iran Treaty of Friendship (second page)

(Courtesy of the National Iranian Archives)

S.G.W. Benjamin,
America's first envoy to Iran

(Courtesty of the National Iranian Archives)

Haji Hossain Gholi Khan Mo'tamed-ol-
Vezareh, Iran's first envoy to the U.S.

(Courtesy of the National Iranian Archives)

Nasser-e-din Shah Ghajar

(Courtesy of the National Iranian Archives)

Howard C. Baskerville, an American who
gave his life for the freedom of Iran

(Courtesy of the National Iranian Archives)

Persian rug made in honor of Baskerville

(Courtesty of the National Iranian Archives)

Baskerville's tombstone in Tabriz

(Courtesty of the National Iranian Archives)

Morgan Schuster, the first American financial advisor
hired by the government of Iran

(Courtesty of the National Iranian Archives)

World leaders in the Tehran Conference: Churchill, Roosevelt and Stalin

(Courtesty of the National Iranian Archives)

Reza Shah

(Courtesty of the National Iranian Archives)

Dr. Arthur Millspaugh

(Courtesty of the National Iranian Archives)

Dr. Samuel Jordan

(Courtesty of the National Iranian
Archives)

Graduates of the American College of Tehran, 1917

(Courtesty of the National Iranian Archives)

Professor Arthur Upham Pope, the Great American Iranologist, in Tehran University

(Courtesty of the National Iranian Archives)

President Truman and Mohammad Reza Shah Pahlavi

(Courtesy of the National Iranian Archives)

President Eisenhower and the Shah

(Courtesty of the National Iranian Archives)

Mr. and Mrs.
Robert Dreyfus

(Courtesty of the
National Iranian Archives)

President Kennedy and the Shah

(Courtesty of the National Iranian Archives)

The World's first declaration of Human Rights (Cylinder of Cyrus the Great)
(Photo by Ghazalle Badiozamani)

Mausoleum of Dariush the Great where he has the following etched in stone: It is not my desire that the weak should have wrong done to him by the mighty; nor is it my desire that the mighty should have wrong done to him by the weak. What is right that is my desire.

(Photo by Ghazalle Badiozamani)

One of the three tablets found at the Suez Canal containing Dariush the Great's order for digging the canal about 2,500 years ago

(Courtesty of the National Iranian Archives)

Triumph of Shapour I over two Roman emperors eternalized in stone at Naghsh-e-Rostam (late 3rd century A.D.). Kneeling in front of his conqueror is Phillop the Arab. In his right hand, Shapour holds the uplifted arms of the Emperor Valerian; one of his hands is hidden in his sleeve as the sign of submission.

(Courtesty of the National Iranian Archives)

Mithra in Germany

(Courtesty of the National Museum of Iran)

Mithra in England

(Courtesty of the National Iranian Archives)

Mithra in Eastern Europe

(Photo by Ghazalle Badiozamani)

Sattar Khan

(Courtesty of the National Iranian Archives)

Reza Khan Sardar
Sepah

(Courtesty of the National
Iranian Archives)

Ahmad Ghavam

Dr. Hossain Ala

(Courtesty of the National Iranian Archives)

Dr. Mohammad Mossadegh

Persian Wheel

4,000-year-old tree in Iran

(Photo by Babak Borzooyeh)

Early Persians, guardians of the environment,
Persepolis, 500 B.C.

(Photo by Ghazalle Badiozamani)

Eternalized flowers and plants at Persepolis

(Photo by Ghazalle Badiozamani)

7,000-year-old Venus, Tappeh Sarab

(Courtesty of the National Museum of Iran)

7,000-year-old clay
container, Fars

(Courtesty of the National Museum of Iran)

6,000-year-old clay container, Shoush (Susa)

(Courtesty of the National Museum of Iran)

6,000-year-old clay container Shoush (Susa)

(Photo by Ghazalle Badiozamani)

6,000-year-old bowl, Shoush (Susa)

(Courtesty of the National Museum of Iran)

5,000-year-old clay figurine,
Shahdad, Kerman

(Courtesty of the National Museum of Iran)

3,000-year-old clay bull,
Marlik, Guilan

(Courtesty of the National Museum of Iran)

3,000-year-old
strainer, Sialk, Kashan

(Courtesty of the National
Museum of Iran)

A variety of pre-historic
pottery designs

7,000-year-old metal molding furnace, Natanz

(Courtesty of the
National Museum of Iran)

The trench where some of
the molding furnaces were
discovered

(Courtesty of the National Museum of Iran)

5,000-year-old silver beaker, Marvdasht, Fars

(Courtesty of the National Museum of Iran)

3,100-year-old cult ceremony depicted in a 3D artwork, Shoosh

(Courtesy of the National Museum of Iran)

3,000-year-old metal chair, Guilan

(Courtesy of the National Museum of Iran)

3,200-year-old bronze bell, Guilan

(Courtesty of the National Museum of Iran)

2,800-year-old man with a knife and
two dogs, Lorestan

(Courtesty of the National Museum of Iran)

3,200-year-old golden beaker, Marlik, Guilan

(Courtesty of the National Museum of Iran)

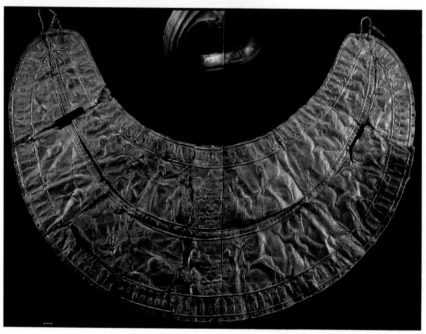

2,700-year-old Gold plaque, Kordestan

(Courtesty of the National Museum of Iran)

Goddess of plants
depicted in a
5,000-year-old seal,
Shahdad, Kerman

(Courtesty of the National
Museum of Iran)

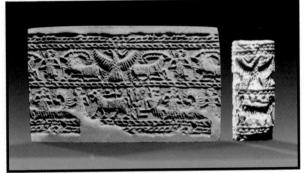

5,000-year-old cylinder seal, Sialk

(Courtesty of the National Museum of Iran)

2,500-year-old fabric, Pazyryk

(Courtesty of the National Museum of Iran)

World's oldest Persian rug, Pazyryk, 500 B.C.

(Courtesty of the National Museum of Iran)

World's first building model, Shahrood

(Courtesty of the Ghazalle Badiozamani)

World's widest brick vault, Teesphoon
(Courtesy of the National Museum of Iran)

Wheeled clay container, 1200 B.C., Marlik, Guilan
(Courtesy of the National Museum of Iran)

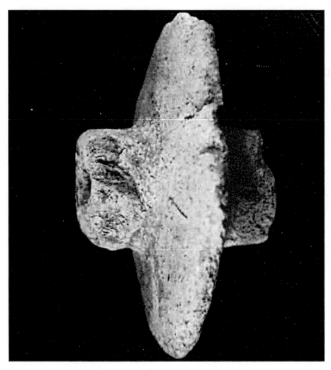

4,000-year-old clay wheel, Khoozestan

(Courtesty of the National Museum of Iran)

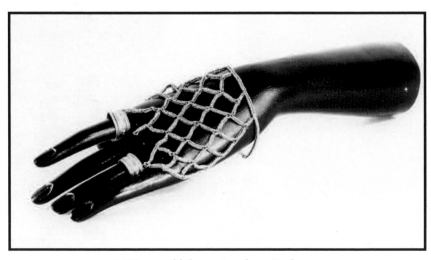

3,000-year-old decorative glove, Kordestan

(Courtesty of the National Museum of Iran)

Polo (Chowgan), the ancient Persian sport

(Courtesty of the National Museum of Iran)

2,500-year-old spread-winged eagle

(Courtesty of the National Museum of Iran)

2,500-year-old silver spoon

(Courtesty of the National Museum of Iran)

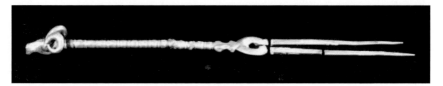

1,700-year-old silver fork

(Courtesty of the National Museum of Iran)

2,500-year-old Achamenian gold chariot

(Photo by Ghazalle Badiozamani)

2,300-year-old winged horse

(Courtesty of the National Museum of Iran)

World's first orchestra, 3,400 B.C., Choghamish, Khoozestan

(Courtesty of the National Museum of Iran)

4,000-year-old musician, Khoozestan

(Courtesty of the National Museum of Iran)

Clay figurine of a musician lady, 1250 B.C., Choghazanbil, Khoozestan

(Courtesty of the National Museum of Iran)

1,700-year-old perfume burner

(Courtesty of the National Museum of Iran)

World's first animation

5,000 year old
game boards

2,500-year-old Persian dog, Persepolis

(Courtesty of the National Museum of Iran)

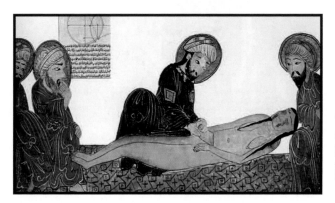

World's first
cesarean section
(Rostamzad)

(Courtesty of the National
Museum of Iran)

The Sufis, like the early Christians, called themselves "people of the way," *ahl-e tarighat*. The idea is that the soul of man, which is the breath of God, has been separated from its source and longs to return to be lost in Him. Since there are different "ways" by which man may reach God, the Sufis are not only tolerant of all religions and philosophies, they themselves have been affected by them. Religious influences from Mithraism, Buddhism, Hinduism, and Christianity and philosophical concepts such as gnosticism (*Erfan*), monism, and pantheism can readily be seen in Sufi literature. The venerable Persian mystic, Attar of Nishapour, who in his old age was massacred by the Mongols in 1222, has a beautiful and allegorical poem called "The Conversation of the Birds", which interestingly enough was the subject matter of a course being taught at Stanford University as recently as in 1997. In this story the birds (humanity) want to go and be with their king (God) whose name is Simorgh. They pass through seven valleys (conditions) of search: love, understanding, detachment, communion, wonder, union and/or extinction. Of the thousand that start out many perish and many even kill each other to save themselves. In the end, only 30 birds (Persian si = 30 and morgh = bird) arrive. When they are ushered through the portals of the king's palace, the veil which has covered their eyes is asunder. They gaze at each other and realize that there are 30 birds (*si morgh*) and that Simorgh (God) is none other than they, the *si morgh*!

Another great mystic was Hafez of Shiraz (d.1389) who must be ranked among the top five poets of Iran. He had Gnostic (*Erfan*) tendencies and like other mystic poets, used wine, roses, and love both as allegory and as aides to a spiritual life. He was accused of agnosticism and heresy by the local critics, but these did not bother him. To him life continued to be supremely joyous, and like the wine which he enjoyed, also bitter. He could see the "Light of God" even in the Magian House of Worship (*Dar kharabat-e Moghan noor-e Khoda mebinam*) and the "Countenance of the Beloved in a cup of wine" (*ma dar pialeh ax-e rokh-e yar dideheem*). He pitied the "witless fellow who could not see that God was with him all the time and was calling for Him from far off."

Perhaps in imitation of the Christian or Buddhist order of monks or both, the Sufis also organized orders, *tarigheh*. They met in their headquarters, *Khaneghah*, under the leadership of an abbot, *peer*, who had attained spiritual insight, discipline, and wisdom. The Christian or the Buddhist monk who wanted to obtain salvation or nirvana found the world transitory and decided that he could not enjoy any part of it and became an ascetic. The majority of the Sufis, however, disavowed the world as a whole, but at the same time enjoyed the parts which were within their reach. Jalal o-Din Roomi(Rumi) (1207-1273) was the founder of the *Molavi* order which flourished in Turkey and Iran. His book of parables and anecdotes, *Masanavi(Mathnawi)*, is one of the most popular books in Persia, and presently its translation is a best seller in the United States. Because his followers played music and danced for the joy of knowing God, they are called "whirling dervishes."

The Safavids 1501-1722

As noted, the Turkish tribes accepted Eslam with great zeal and fanaticism, and were loyal to its institutions. Perhaps because the discipline, devotion, and obedience to the leader practiced in the Sufi orders were similar to the life in the tribes, the Turks were attracted to these orders. Gradually, the coming of the tribesmen added an economic and military dimension to the life of the orders. In addition to their spiritual leader, there were "lay" brothers who took care of the economic needs of the order. There were also warriors who protected the community and fought for the advancement of Eslam. There were quite a number of these orders in Asia Minor and Azarbaijan. As the Ilkhan kings became Shi'i, a number of the Turkish tribes did the same and they came into being Sufi orders which were Shi'i. In the Shi'i orders, however, the leader of the order and the commander of the warriors was usually the same person; consistent with Shi'i tradition, the position of the leader was hereditary.

One of these orders which had a large following among the Turkish tribes was called Safi or Safavi, in honor of the first leader, Sheykh Safi, who died in 1334. Since these warriors had red headgear, they were called *Ghezelbash*, or "Red head". Sheykh Heydar, a direct descent of Safi, was killed in 1490, and left the leadership to his thirteen year old son Esma'il, whose mother was a Greek princess from Trebizon, named Martha. With the help of the devoted Ghezelbash, who comprised seven clans, this remarkable youth revenged his father by defeating the prince of Shirvan, and took Armenia and Azarbaijan. He proclaimed himself king with Tabriz as his capital. In the next fifteen years of almost constant warfare, Esma'il was the master of Iran, from the borders of Syria to the Oxus, and from the Caucasus to the Persian Gulf.

It was apparent that the Safavi dynasty founded by Esma'il was not just another principality established by the adventurous ambition of a warrior. From the very beginning the dynasty was established on two foundations. One of was Shi'i and the other Persia, and Esma'il concentrated more on the first than the second. His hatred of the Sunnis knew no bounds, and his persecution of them was ruthless. The alternative for the majority of the Persians who were Sunnis, at the time, was either convert to Shi'ism or accept death. Conversion must have been rapid, because half a century later Iran was a Shi'i country and gradually became an isolated island surrounded by a sea of Sunni Eslam. While regretting the cruelty of forced conversion, modern Persian historians are generally agreed that the establishment of Shi'i religious hegemony saved Iran from being incorporated into the Ottoman Empire.

The Ottomans, who had extraordinary success in Europe and had sealed the fate of the Byzantine Empire by the capture of Constantinople were eager to go eastward and occupy the traditional lands of Eslam. Indeed, Bayezid II (1481-1512) was in touch with the Uzbek chief, Sheybak Khan, in an attempt to cut the Esma'il's ambitions in the bud. Eventually the Ottomans did concur Arabia, the Fertile Crescent, and North Africa, and they would have extended the empire to Central Asia had it not been for the Safavids. In his letters to Esma'il, Bayezid gave him "fatherly" advice and asked him to refrain from shedding Sunni blood and desecrating Sunni graves and cautioned him to be wary of the Persians because they "are a people who will not obey a king who is not one of them."1 This reference to the fact that Esma'il was not a Persian when he was claiming that he was a descendent of the Sassanian kings, must have cut him to the quick.. When Esma'il defeated and captured the Uzbek leader, he had his skin filled with straw and sent it to Bayezid.

The inevitable contest between Esma'il and the Ottomans, whose new ruler Selim I (1512-1520) was as hot-headed and cruel as Esma'il, took place at the battle of Chalderan in 1514. On his march eastward, Selim destroyed some 40,000 Shi'is in Asia Minor. At the battle of Chalderan, the Ottomans won a resounding victory, but it did not prove conclusive, partly because the Janissaries refused to pursue Esma'il farther east, and partly because richer prizes were awaiting Selim, namely Syria and Egypt. The battle of Chalderan was a contest between the Ottoman artillery and muskets and the Safavid spears, bows, and swords. Furthermore, the Safavids found out that religious fanaticism and courage were no match for the muskets and cannons. Chalderan was also the beginning of a senseless and inconclusive struggle between Iran and Turkey that lasted for nearly 300 years.

From the death of Shah Esma'il in 1524 to the accession of Shah Abbas The Great in 1587, three Safavid shahs turned their attention eastward and carved out an empire which was fast approaching the size of the Sassanian empire. Because Tabriz was too close to the borders and vulnerable to attack and occupation by the Ottomans, the capital was moved to Ghazvin. The Ghezelbash warriors formed the backbone of the state, and their leaders were each given a district as a fief. In return, they provided the Shah with soldiers and with revenue. These leaders had power of life and death over the population and were given the task of converting them to Shi'ism. The proof of conversion was cursing the first three Caliphs as "usurpers". Those who refused were summarily executed.

Even though the Shah as leader of the order was considered supreme, the Ghezelbash leaders who had become rich and powerful tried to interfere in the question of succession. Each supported his own favorite among the sons of the deceased Shah, and all of them preferred to have a weak person on the throne so that they would be able to do what they pleased. During the early Safavid period, we witness a standard struggle between the oligarchy and autocracy and the fighting among the oligarchs themselves for a position of leadership. During the reign of the mild-mannered and ascetic Shah Mohammad Khodabandeh, the Ghezelbash became especially unruly; and in order to ensure that they would have another weak person on the throne, they killed the crown prince, his mother, and most of the Safavid princes. The younger brother of the crown prince, however, was rescued, and a few years later, in 1587, he assumed the throne as Shah Abbas. Under Shah Abbas Iran reached a zenith of its power, and at the same time, the beginning of its culture and political decline. While his predecessors concentrated on forcing all the people to conform to Shi'ism, Shah Abbas emphasized the Persian aspect of his rule. The cultural advance, which had continued through the Mongol period and had experienced a setback by the ruthless imposition of Shi'i dogma on the people, had still some life in it and Shah Abbas kept it alive a little longer. It was his good fortune to be king at a time when the neighboring countries had their own difficulties. The Ottomans were fast declining; the Russians had their "Time of Troubles"; and the Mongols of India had lost their hold on the country. Shah Abbas gained territory at the expense of all three of them, especially Russia and the Ottoman Empire.

One of the first things which he did was to destroy the power of the Ghezelbash. He took land away from them and killed most of their leaders. He still maintained a Ghezelbash corps, but it was mostly ceremonial and the men were armed with antiquated weapons. He built a base of support for himself among the people. In place of the Ghezelbash, he organized two armies, one made up of Christians from Gorjestan (Georgia) and Armenia, and the other made up of Persians. He equipped both armies with modern muskets and artillery. This act of Shah Abbas broke the back of the military Sufism in Iran, which considered its mission to be the conversion or destruction of the Sunnis rather than the advancement of Eslam. Around 1597, when Shah Abbas was fighting the Uzbeks, there came to Iran two young Englishmen, Anthony Sherly and his 18 year old brother, Robert. They had military experience and some of their English companions knew the art of casting cannons. Shah Abbas was attracted to these brothers both as persons and as means of improving his army. He trained and equipped his new forces with the help of the Sherly brothers. They took part in the wars between Iran and Turkey and later were sent by Shah Abbas on diplomatic missions.[2]

Government

In the Safavid period, the same tension that had existed at the time of Saljooghs between the palace, *dargah*, and the chancery, *divan*, continued to exist. The system of land grants was also continued. The expenses of the office of the Grand Vazir (Prime Minister) as well as those of the provincial governor, district supervisor, aided by a county commissioner (*khan*) and his assistant, the local supervisor (*soltan*)3, were all paid from the income of the land assigned to each. It was their job to collect taxes, pay the soldiers in their locality, and send a specific amount to the Shah. They also sent gifts to the king. Some of the provincial officers had friends who were close to the Shah, who in return for appropriate gifts would speak well of them in the presence of the Shah.

The Shi'i nature of the Safavid dynasty created another tension within the government which has continued in Iran to the present. In as much as the hidden Emam was the true ruler of the empire, he had spokesmen who could interpret the law according to the needs of the time. These spokesmen were called *mojtahed*; their opinions were binding on all the Shi'is. This would take all power from the hands of the Shah had there not always been more than one mojtahed at a given time. Sometimes there were four or five who, naturally, did not agree on all questions. This division among them gave a free hand to the Shah or the government to carry out its program. There was more than one spokesman for the hidden Emam because of a lack of any hierarchical position to appoint a mojtahed. In addition to proper academic training, anyone aspiring to be a mojtahed had to have a reputation for piety, wisdom, and common sense. Since always more than one person had the above credentials, the person would be considered a mojtahed by unofficial and popular consensus. Seldom did all the mojtaheds agree on a given question, and the Shah or government could get by with a great deal of innovation and deviation, both of which are anathema in Shi'i and Sunni Eslam alike.

The Safavid kings had a special position and the early shahs of the dynasty tried to maintain it. It has already been stated that the Safavid rulers combined in their persons, as leader of the Safi order, both temporal and religious powers. The shah was called "the most perfect leader." They also claimed that they were descendants of the prophet and tried to extend their power over all the Shi'is as the spokesman for the Emam. They could not, however, do away with the office of the mojtahed but they did not endow the office with any actual political or administrative powers. The Safavids created another office called *sadr*, headed by a religious leader who, with the help of a large bureaucracy, administered all the courts, religious endowments, marriage and divorce, and also the police. The mojtahed was a "chaplain" to the shah and his influence was in direct proportion to the power and personality to the king. After Shah Abbas, when the power of the king declined, the mojtaheds became powerful.

Shah Abbas himself had friendly relationships with the religious leaders and called himself the "the dog of the threshold of Ali." He built a beautiful mausoleum over the tomb of the 8th Emam, Ali al-Reza, in Mashhad and, when it was completed, walked all the way (some 800 miles) from Esfahan on a pilgrimage. The honorary title of *Mashhadi*, given to those who made the pilgrimage became as important as *Haji*, for going to Mecca, and *Karbala'i*. There were other kings, however, like Nader Shah (1736-1747) and Reza Shah (1924-1941) who did not have any use for religious leaders or mojtaheds. Most of the rest of the kings were subservient to them in differing degrees.

Social and Cultural Life

Shah Abbas moved the capital from Ghazvin to Esfahan and built it into such a beautiful city that to this day it delights visitors. Some of the most beautiful mosques and buildings still stand. He encouraged architecture and painting. He did much to revive some of the old festivals of Iran such as the festival of water, of roses, and of lights. He was especially fond of the festival of lights, when he would order fireworks.4 Other pastimes engaged in by the populace were cock, wolf, bull, and ram fights; card games; acrobatics; tightrope walking; and puppet shows. The aristocracy, as usual, played Polo. The brotherhood of men who spent their leisure and physical exercise was perhaps in existence before the Safavids. This brotherhood, which is still in existence, called their place of exercise Zoorkhaneh " *house of strength*" and had a hierarchy with a special code of honor. The drummer would usher in the leader with special beats on the drum and then would sing the adventures of Persian heroes from the *Shahnameh*, as they went through their exercises.

The Safavids, as Shi'is, encouraged the passion plays and the religious processions commemorating the tragic events of Emam Hossain's death at Karbala. In cities all over the country, the processions were the most important social event and districts vied with each other in the excellence of their productions and sometimes actually fought with each other. A major procession involved the cooperation of over a thousand people. Hundreds participated in them in fulfillment of their vows. Some beat their breasts and some beat their bare backs with a cluster of chains, all in unison and to the rhythm of the dirges they chanted. The climax came on the tenth day of Moharram, when a new group joined the procession. They were clad in a white shroud and each held a sword or a machete in his right hand while with his left he clung onto his companion's belt. They marched sideways in two lines facing each other, and inflicting wounds on their own shaved heads. Each of these "machete beaters" (Ghameh Zan) had a friend marching behind him with a stick in his hand. He would bring the stick between the machete and his friend's head if he noticed that the sight of blood and the frenzy of the occasion might cause the participant to inflict fatal wounds on himself.

The shahs, of course, had their harems, which were guarded by black eunuchs. The Safavids took their women with them to wars, and some of these women were very good markspersons and actually participated in battle. In cases of defeat, the eunuchs had orders to kill the women. Prostitutes were brought under strict supervision and were housed in a special quarter of the city called "veil-less." In campaigns, they were allowed to follow the camps and each would be charged a special tax.5 Sometimes there were "women's days" at the bazaars when no men except the shopkeepers would be allowed. There were also "women's evenings" in the boulevard that had been built in Esfahan where the women of the city would promenade up and down the tree-lined streets. It is not difficult to imagine that such occasions were eagerly awaited by the women who otherwise led secluded lives.

Shah Abbas was especially popular with the peasants and the masses. Cruel though he was, the victims of his ruthless rages were the Ghezelbash leaders and members of the officialdom whose liquidation brought respite to the people. He frequented bazaars and in his trips to different sites he walked in the streets and talked with the passersby. He had the habit of inviting himself to people's houses without previous notice and sharing their meals with them. The true and embellished accounts of such activities have become part of the lore of Iran which grandmothers tell their grandchildren to this day. As a popular and powerful shah, he also set style. He popularized shaving and actually ordered men to shave their beards.6 He frequented teahouses where he would listen to poets and storytellers and exchange pleasantries with the people.

Economic Situation

The theory that everything belonged to the shah continued. There was no distinction made between the personal expenses of the shah and the government. The main sources of revenue for the shah and the government were :¹ Taxes levied on each province.² Income from the private domains of the shah.³ Income tax. This included an annual tax of one half of all livestock, one third of all silk and cotton, bridge and road tolls, head tax for non-Moslems, import duties, etc.⁴ Taxes on the sale and cultivation of tobacco. Shah Abbas himself did not like to smoke and no one dared to smoke in his presence, but it was popular and became more so after his death. By the end of the 19th century the cultivation and use of tobacco introduced into Iran probably by the Portuguese, became a factor in international relations and national uprising.

What seems to have been an innovation of Shah Abbas was an officer in charge of fair prices. Every three months or so, the officer of price stabilization met with the leader, *white beard* (Rish sefeed), of each guild and determined a fair price. Until the early years of the 20th century offenders were paraded in the bazaars and sometimes met with some severe punishments.

Contact with the West

One of the most interesting episodes in the history of Iran after the Mongol invasion is its contact with the West. The main reasons were political and economic and had religious and cultural implications as well. All sorts of people from Europe, diplomats, merchants, soldiers, priests, and adventurers, made their way to Iran. As early as the 12th century, the Crusaders had become aware of the differences which existed between Iran and the Arabic speaking parts of the Moslem world. They tried unsuccessfully to involve the rulers of Iran against Syria. When the pagan Mongols invaded Iran, Europeans were eager to seek their friendship in order to counteract the aggressive conduct of Moslems in the Fertile Crescent and also to convert the Mongols to Christianity. Pope Innocent IV sent embassies to the Mongols. The adventurers of Marco Polo did much to encourage traders and adventurers to journey to Iran. By the middle of the 14th century because of the constant wars of expansion waged by the Ottoman sultans, it was Tabriz rather than the blockaded Constantinople that was an important center of commerce.

In the 16th century two factors helped to increase the contact of Iran with the west. One was the avowed anti-Ottoman policy of the Safavids, which coincided with a similar policy on the part of the rulers of Europe. The second was the fact that the 16th century ushered in the age of exploration. Trade routes had shifted from the Mediterranean, and Europeans were seeking other routes. It was not long before the Portuguese were bringing spices from India and had established themselves in the Persian Gulf. In 1508 shah Esma'il signed a treaty with the Portuguese over the trade of the Persian Gulf and mutual military assistance against the Ottomans. Even though the military clauses were never implemented, the Persian Gulf ports of Muskat, Bahrain, and Hormoz became important trade centers. The importance of Hormoz as a world trade mart has been recorded by Milton in his *Paradise Lost*.

Since the cape route had been monopolized by the Portuguese and the Spaniards, the British, for a time, tried the northern route that had been open to them. They made contact with the court of Ivan the Terrible and formed Muscovy Company. In 1561, a representative of this company, Anthony Jenkins, went by way of the Caspian to Ghazvin, the capital of the Safavid Shah Tahmasp I. The dangerous and costly route, the lack of market for English woolens, and the reluctance of the fanatic Tahmasp to have anything to do with infidels, all worked together to persuade the British to give up the project. Shah Abbas' attitude, however, was very different from his predecessors. He used his contact with the Europeans to equip his army with artillery and muskets, to open excellent markets for Persian products, especially silk and to try to subdue the Ottomans. In the first two he was successful.

When Shah Abbas was improving Esfahan, he brought a large number of Armenian families and hostages from their homes in Jolfa and settled them across the Zayandeh Rood (river) from the city. As the "New Jolfa" flourished, more Armenians migrated voluntarily and settled in many parts of Iran. He never failed to impress the European ambassadors and Christian monks with his tolerance towards the Armenians. They were permitted to build their own homes, ride horses, and wear any kind of clothes they pleased, a privilege which non-Moslems did not have before or very long after the Shah Abbas until modern times. The shah had a monopoly of the silk trade, which was one of the most important items of export, and he let the Armenian merchants administer it for him. He gave special privileges to Catholic monks and allowed them to open a mission in Esfahan proper. Indeed, by his remarks he had led some of the Christian monks from Rome to think that he himself was about ready to be converted. He was lavish in his entertainment of foreign visitors and gave the European merchants special privileges.

The shah sent a number of embassies to the capitals of Europe. In 1599 he sent a large embassy accompanied by Anthony Sherly and in 1608 another one accompanied by Robert Sherly. The main purpose of the embassies, which was to launch a simultaneous attack on the Ottomans, was not accomplished. No doubt these contacts provided Shah Abbas with enough information to know that the power of Spain was on the decline. He entered into a trade agreement with the British East India Company in 1616 and by 1622 a joint Anglo-Persian force expelled the Portuguese and Spanish traders from the Persian Gulf. Shah Abbas built a new port on the Persian Gulf, Bandar-e Abbas, and the British did most of their business there with branches in Shiraz and Esfahan.

The Dutch also appeared on the scene in 1581 and were received with enthusiasm. They made a barter arrangement exchanging Dutch merchandise, mainly textiles, for Persian silk and rugs, wool, and brocade. This arrangement was more popular with the Persian merchants, and by the time of Shah Safi (1629-1642), the Dutch had virtual control of the Persian trade. They were exempt from paying import duties but instead they had to buy 600 bales of silk annually.[7] Toward the last decades of the 17th century trade in Persian Gulf began to slacken. This was partly because Europeans had found greener pastures in east Asia and partly because the weak Safavid shahs could not maintain peace and security.

Even though there were brisk and varied economic activities throughout these years, cultural interaction was practically non-existent. The reason is perhaps not hard to find. On the one hand, Shi'i orthodoxy had strengthened its hold ever since the coming of the Safavids and had created such a dogmatic and fanatical shell that it had stultified almost all intellectual investigation or artistic expression. Iran was insulated not only against an intellectual ferment from Europe, but was isolated from contact with the world of Eslam.

On the other hand, the Catholic monks, who represented the European intellectuals in Iran, were similarly closed-minded and were unaffected by and opposed to the Reformation which was going on in Europe. Both sides were convinced that there was nothing they could learn from the other, and they came together without being aware of each other's existence. The intellectual interaction between Iran and the world had to wait until the middle of the 19th century.

Nader Shah

The death of Shah Abbas was a signal for the old enemies of Iran to rise for revenge. The excesses of the Shi'i cruelty against the Sunnis could not be tolerated by the Ottoman sultans, who were caliphs and protectors of all Moslems, especially Sunnis. While the Ottomans were weak they did not have much choice. But when Shah Abbas died and each of his successors proved weaker than the previous one, the Ottomans moved against Iran from the west and encouraged their fellow Sunnis, the Uzbeks and the Afghans, to attack from the east. It took a number of years of warfare, for neither the Ottomans nor the Afghans were strong enough to win a decisive victory. Among the many weak successors of Shah Abbas, Shah Soltan Hossain (1694-1722) was the worst. He was an indecisive and extremely superstitious man and was so much under the influence of the Shi'i clergy that he would not take a drink of water without a *fatva (religious sanction)* from the *mojtahed*. In 1722, the Afghan leader Mahmood invaded Iran and defeated the Persian forces on May 8, 1722 near Esfahan. Shah Soltan Hossain surrendered but his son Tahmasp II, who had fled to Ghazvin, continued the struggle.

Tahmasp himself could not accomplish very much, were it not for the rise of Nader Gholi, a soldier of fortune, a military genius, who was destined to be called the "Napoleon of Iran." Nader was a Turk and belonged to the Afshar tribe loyal to the Safavids. He was an officer in the Persian army and did much to help Tahmasp II push the Afghans back. In the meantime, the victory of the Afghans had whetted the appetite of the Ottomans and the Russians against Iran. The Russians had to withdraw because of the death of Peter the Great in 1725, but the Ottomans continued the attack. The Turks defeated the Persians while Nader was in the east, and Tahmasp signed a treaty in 1732 by giving up 5 cities in the Caucasus. Nader, who was against such a treaty, led a revolt against Tahmasp and chose his infant son Abbas III as king with himself as regent. During the next three years he defeated the Turks, pushed the Russians back, and secured eastern Iran against the Afghans. In 1736 the infant shah died and Nader assumed the throne as Nader Shah Afshar. He was crowned in the plain of Moghan in Azarbaijan, the northwest part of Iran. During the next eleven years, his main work was to retake the territories lost by later Safavids and further to expand the empire. Iran got off its deathbed and set out on a path of conquest. His spectacular campaign was against India. He captured Kabol, Peshawar and Lahore in 1738, and the next year he defeated the Mongol emperor Mohammad Shah and entered Delhi.

Nader Shah might have become an enlightened founder of a dynasty had he not succumbed to the senseless cruelty which had become the habit of kings. When he became shah he did so on the condition that the people of Iran would stop cursing the first three caliphs and would cease molesting the Sunnis. He realized the danger to Iran of needlessly arousing the hostility of the Sunnis. Furthermore, he wanted to break the power of the clergy. There is a difference of opinion about whether Nader Shah was a Sunni or a Shi'i. It seems that he was a free thinker. He gathered the representatives of all religions and told them that since there was only one God there should be only one religion. He ordered the Old and the New Testaments and also the Ghor'an to be translated into Persian. He is reported to have commented that if he had time he would devise a new religion. He certainly wanted to end the strife between the Sunnis and the Shi'is. He made a five-point proposition for unity between the two: 1. That the Shi'i doctrine be recognized as the fifth school of thought in Eslam. 2. That the Shi'is should have special accommodations in Mecca. 3. That every year there should be a special leader of pilgrimage, *Amir al-Haj*, from Iran. 4. That the Ottomans and Persians should exchange prisoners of war. 5. That the Ottomans and Persians should exchange ambassadors.[8]

The Shi'i leaders were greatly perturbed over this news and supported the revolt that was brewing against him. He had become cruel and suspicious. He killed his own son and in the end was assassinated in 1747. Nader's accomplishments were transitory, but they came at an opportune time and gave Iran a continued existence.

The period between the death of Nader Shah and the coronation of Agha Mohammad Khan, the founder of the Ghajar (Qajar) dynasty in 1795, lasted 50 years. The first 12 years were spent in warfare among the many claimants to the vacant throne. The victor was Karim Khan, the head of the Kurdish Zand tribe. For 21 years this kindly man ruled most of Iran without the aid of an executioner, and it seemed that he might save Iran; but his untimely death ended that hope. He never called himself shah, but his title "The Advocate of the Peasants," seems to anticipate the thoughts of the French revolution. He was eager that everyone in his capital, Shiraz, and in the rest of the country live in peace. He was so very different from what was considered the characteristic king that, rather than destroying the son of his bitterest enemy, he kept him as an honored guest in his house. At Karim Khan's death this same man, Agha Mohammad Ghajar, fled Shiraz and after 17 years of warfare crowned himself as Shah of Iran in 1795 at Tehran. During the Ghajar period, Iran was ushered into the 19th century, the era of European imperialism and contact with the West, which practically shattered the isolation of Iran.

ENDNOTES

1. Nasrollah Falsafi, in *Chand Maghale-ye Tarikikhi*, (a few historical essays) (Tehran: The University of Tehran Press, line 1062), p.6.

2. Eghbal, Tarikh-e Mofassal, p.279.

3. In order to belittle the Ottomans, the Safavids gave the title of high Ottoman personages to the low functionaries in their own government. "Sultan," which was the title of the Ottoman emperor, was a very low officer in the Safavid dynasty.

4. Nasrollah Falsafi, *Zendegani-ye Shah Abbas* (*Life of Shah Abbas*), III (Tehran: Ebn Sina),p.168

5. Ibid., vol. 3, p.55

6. Ibid.,Vol.2, p.280

7. Nasrollah Falsafi, *Tarikh-e Ravabet-e Iran va Oroopa dar Doreh-ye Safaviyyeh* (*A history of Irano-European Relations During the Safavid period*) (Tehran: Ebn Sina,1939),p.95.

8. *Reza Zadeh Shafagh, Nader Shah* (Tehran: University of Tehran Press, 1961), p.65.

9. Ibid., p.71.

CHAPTER SEVEN

MODERN AGE, IMPERIALISM, AWAKENING

When the 19th century dawned, Iran was so isolated that it was oblivious to what was happening in the world and so insulated that what little information came through was ignored altogether. If the Safavids had encouraged freedom of thought rather than suffocation of the Persian spirit with religious dogma, and if the brightness of the reign of Shah Abbas had been the beginning of an era of excellence rather than the end of an intellectual ferment which had ushered in the Persian renaissance, then the nearly two centuries of relationship with the countries of Europe would have produced leaders who were at least aware of the tremendous movements that had rejuvenated the western world. But unfortunately the main seed sown by the Safavids was religious fanaticism, and the main crop harvested was superstition and ignorance. Compared to the whole Safavid period, the age of Shah Abbas had the permanency of a beautiful bubble and the Iranian people had only been treated to a spectacle of pomp which had regenerated into effeteness leading to ruinous defeat.[1] Religious fanaticism was so strong that even the attempts of Nader Shah were not able to dislodge it, and the reign of cruelty and lawlessness was so pervasive that the humane rule of Karim Khan Zand was not able to soften it. Even men of letters felt the spirit of restriction. In writing about the poets of his period, Azhar (1711-1781), said that the situation was such that "no one had the heart to read poetry, let alone compose it.[2]

The Ghajar dynasty, which ruled Iran from 1795 to 1924, produced kings who, on the whole, were inept, unimaginative, superstitious, and selfish. The founder of the dynasty, Agha Mohammad Khan, was a eunuch who had been castrated by an enemy of the Ghajars at the age of 5. He grew up to become a conniving, vindictive, cruel, and stingy misanthrope. He was assassinated by his own servants in 1796. His nephew, Fath Ali Shah, whose reign of 36 years coincided with some of the momentous events in the history of modern Iran, was no better. In addition to presiding over the diminution of the country, he is also known for his unusually long beard and a progeny of some 2000 princes and princesses. He had all of his uncle's bad traits and none of his good ones.[3]

From one important historical viewpoint, the modern age opened for Iran at the start of the 19th century. At that time the western powers, already long engaged in expanding rivalries, rapidly intensified them in ruthless of colonial empires throughout Asia. Iran, at the crossroads of east and west, suffered greatly during this prolonged and tumultuous period. It saw a loss of territory and prestige, then repeated exploitations and humiliations. It was also plagued by the social upheavals and economic dislocations which most Asiatic countries experienced during the age of western imperialism. Despite all this Iran survived, it's cloak of sovereignty patched and threadbare but still serviceable.

When the 19th century opened, Iran partially recovered but still weak from many centuries of misrule and internal decay, found itself in peril by two gigantic, spreading empires, Russian and British, both based on the rising strength of the industrial revolution in the West. Historically, its one strength had more or less matched the traditional threat from the West, whether Roman, Byzantine or Ottoman. Now Iran had become the object of open Russian pressure in the north and subtle British encroachment in the south. Squeezed in the middle, Iran was still harassed in the west by the Ottoman Turks and by the perennial nomadics in the east. Two disastrous wars fought with Russia taught Iranians that upon the issues which they faced depended Iran's survival or its destruction. The Anglo-Russian threat, by far the most pernicious of the problems facing Iranian policy makers, sometimes was direct, but often it appeared as the almost random byproduct of the sinister rivalry between the two empires. Whatever the form, Iran's independence was at stake. Iran was too weak to remove the threat, but it gambled its survival in a grim, costly, and humiliating game of diplomacy and concession, and eventually it won. Rather, it did not lose, which was a victory in the age of imperialism.[4]

The Russian Advance

Notwithstanding the decline of its fortunes, Iran was still a power to be reckoned with in west Asia and important enough to be wooed by European rivals. During the first decade of the 19th century European politics were dominated by Napoleon. British animosity toward Napoleon was constant while the Russian attitude fluctuated between friendship and animosity depending upon the situation. On the other hand, Russian and British interests in Iran were constant, while Napoleon's interest in Iran, and in India, for that matter, was only in how far it could be used as a tool to defeat Great Britain or force Russia to come to terms. The rulers of Iran, however, neither cared nor knew how to benefit from this rivalry and shifting of alliances. Indeed, practically every time Iran was caught for having made the wrong alliance. The cornerstone of British policy in west Asia was to safeguard the route to India, while Russian policy was to have access to the Persian Gulf through Iran. It is not certain whether Russia was interested in India, but its supremacy in the Gulf area would certainly threaten Great Britain. Consequently, Great Britain did not want Russia to annex all of Iran, which in the early years of the 19th century included most of Afghanestan.

At the turn of the 19th century Great Britain sent a mission to Iran and persuaded the shah to sign a diplomatic and commercial agreement in which Iran promised to follow an anti-French policy. Commercially, Iran exempted British and Indian merchants from paying taxes and allowed the importation of British broadcloth, iron, steel, and lead without duty. In return Great Britain promised to provide Iran with necessary weapons in case the Afghans or the French attacked Iran. The enemy of Iran was not France but Russia, about whom there was no provision in the treaty simply because at the time Great Britain was friendly toward Russia. To the pleas of Iran for help against Russia, Great Britain lent a deaf ear. In the mean time, France and Russia had one of their periodic quarrels. Accordingly Napoleon sent a mission to Iran in 1805 proposing an alliance against Russia provided Iran would repudiate its treaty with England. The shah, who had become disappointed in the British attitude, agreed to this and the result was the treaty of Finkenstein in May 1807. A large French mission under general Gardanne came to Iran for the purpose of training the Persian army and making cannons and other weapons. The French general concluded a commercial agreement to facilitate the importation of French goods and services into Iran. It is indicative of the vision of the shah to note that in article 6 of this agreement, Iran wants France to send a painter, printer, crystal cutter, china maker, cabinet maker, stone cutter, watch maker, diamond cutter, carriage maker and so on.[5]

All this came to naught, however, because Alexander of Russia and Napoleon became friends albeit temporarily, and signed the treaty of Tilsit in 1807. This freed Russia to carry out its campaign of expansion against Iran. Now it was Napoleon's turn to lend a deaf ear to Iran's request for assistance against Russian aggression. This gave the British an opportunity to send a mission to Iran in 1808 and sign a treaty against France and Russia. The French military officers in the Persian army were replaced by British officers, and evidently the change of military advisors confused the Persian soldiers. The crown prince, Abbas Mirza, who had the reputation of being the most able of the Ghajars, was in command of the Persian army. They did not have the support of the shah, who was reluctant to spend any money for the defense of the country. The major battle was fought in Aslandooz in 1812. Very likely the Persians would have been defeated anyway, but there is no question that they were demoralized when all the British officers withdrew. Once more Russia and Great Britain had become friends and Iran was expendable. Ghaem Magham, one of the two enlightened Prime Ministers of the Ghajar period, accused Great Britain of causing the defeat of the Persian forces.[6]

Iran signed the Treaty of Golestan on October 13, 1813. Iran lost five cities in the Caucasus, gave up the right to maintain a navy on the Caspian, and gave up its claim to Georgia and Daghestan. Perhaps the most damaging provision was Russia's promise to support the claim of Abbas Mirza to the throne. In accepting this support, the crown prince was inviting Russia's interference in the internal affairs of Iran. Not to be outdone, Great Britain also promised its support. From then on every Ghajar crown prince was escorted to the capital by the Russian and British ministers when he came to ascend the throne.

The war, which had lasted some ten years, created staggering financial problems for Iran which in turn weakened the central government. Some of the tribes rose in rebellion. The war was especially hard on the people of Azarbaijan, who had to carry the burden of the war for ten years without any help from any other part of the country. As far as the shah was concerned, the war was in the territory under the care of the crown prince and he had to raise the money for it. After the war, the shah did not help in any program of reconstruction and the people of Azarbaijan were groaning under heavy taxes. The result showed when the war was resumed some twelve years later.

The need for money on the part of Iran and the need of Great Britain to reciprocate the actions of Russia resulted in a new treaty between Great Britain and Iran in 1814. It is referred to as the "Definitive Treaty," or the Tehran Treaty in which Iran promised to break its alliance with any European power at war with Great Britain; to prevent armies hostile to Great

Britain from entering Iran; and to help Great Britain in case the latter is attacked through Afghanestan. On its part Great Britain promised to come to Iran's aid if it was attacked by a European country; not to interfere in the affairs of Iran with Afghanestan; to pay Iran an annual subsidy of 150,000 pounds; and to help Iran settle its boundaries with Russia.

The last item seems to support the contention of Persian historians that the Golestan Treaty had not settled very much and should be regarded as a truce agreement rather than a peace treaty. Furthermore, it could not be expected that the Russian program of expansion was over. In as much as the majority of the population of recently annexed cities was Moslem, there were credible reports of Russian persecution of these Moslems. There is no doubt that the Persians felt humiliated and wanted revenge.[7] The Russians did persuade Abbas Mirza to attack the Ottomans while the latter had their hands full with the Greek rebellion. Perhaps the crown prince succumbed to this temptation because he wanted to regain his prestige which had suffered at the hands of the Russians. The war against turkey was, as usual, inconclusive and ended with Treaty of Erzeroom. This was the last war between the two nations. The struggle had continued ever since the battle of Chalderan in 1514.

The desire for revenge on the part of Iran, the maltreatment of the Moslems, which eventually resulted in the declaration of a "holy war," and the Russian encroachment on Persian territory all brought about the renewal of hostilities in 1825. The Persians were unable to maintain the success they had gained in the early months of the war. The shah's avarice prevented him from appropriating any funds so a good number of the army disbanded because of lack of pay. There was erratic leadership and lack of discipline. Great Britain, who had signed a treaty of friendship with Russia, refused to honor its agreement of 1814 or to come to the aid of Iran on the grounds that Iran was the aggressor. The Russians occupied Tabriz in 1827 and the Persians sued for peace.

The treaty of Turkmanchay in 1828 gave all of the Caucasus to Russia and set the boundary following the Aras River, and then south to include Lankaran and east to Astara on the Caspian. Iran officially accepted the principle of extra territoriality and the payment of an indemnity amounting to 3 million pounds. Furthermore, the commercial agreement set a maximum duty on Russian imported goods at 5% ad valorem. The treaty of Turkmanchay ushered in a new era because for nearly a century Iran became a buffer state between Russia and Great Britain. It was not entirely a colony of either power and yet not free to chart an independent course internationally or internally. For a long time the leaders in Iran were either

"Russophile" or "Anglophile." Later on the "Iranophiles," who brought about Persian revolution, thought that Iran needed a third western power to save them from the Russian and the British.

The British Advance

Crown Prince Abbas Mirza, who was reputedly the most able leader among the Ghajars, died in 1833, just a year before his father Fath Ali Shah. This was unfortunate for not only was Iran deprived of his leadership, but the throne went to his own son, Mohammad Shah, who proved to be as narrow-minded, superstitious and incapable as his grandfather. The young shah entered Tehran with an army commanded by the British general Sir Henry Lindsay Bethune and was accompanied by the Russian and British ministers. Even so, there were some claimants to the throne who foolishly persisted for a time.

Russian desires to control Istanbul and the Straits were so important a part of the "Eastern Question" that the powers of Europe had left Russia alone in its ambitions in Central Asia and regions east of the Caspian Sea. There were no stable relationships between Iran and the different khanates of this region, which was populated by Uzbeks, Tajiks, Turkmans, Afghans, and others. Some were independent at times; some paid tribute to Iran; and some were under the suzerainty of Iran. The Persians considered Harat (Herat) to be the capital of Khorasan and thought that most of Afghanestan was part of Iran. Indeed, judging by the treaties signed by Iran and Great Britain it would seem that Great Britain recognized this fact. After Turkmanchay Treaty, however, the situation had changed drastically. The British policy to defend the approaches to India was still valid but there was a definite change in the British appraisal of Iran. Great Britain was no more willing to let Iran have a free hand in Afghanestan and east of the Caspian. When Mohammad Shah tried to strengthen his hand in Afghanestan, Great Britain intervened contrary to the promise made in the "Definitive Treaty" of 1814.

There was disagreement among the members of the British government in India as to where the line should be established for the defense of India. Some believed that the Indus was the best, which would have left Iran free in Afghanestan. Others, recognizing the Russian interest in that region, felt that they could cooperate much better with the Russians than with the "Mohammedan races of Central Asia and Kabul," which would presumably give Russia a free hand in Afghanestan. There were still others who thought that the defense of India would be made easier by the British supremacy in Afghanestan, which included the Hindu Kosh mountains.8 Apparently the last option won acceptance.

Mohammad Shah spent most of his 13 years in office strengthening his position in Afghanestan, but Great Britain intervened and the shah was forced to retreat. The British believed that Iran was not strong enough to stop the Russians, and they also felt that Ghajar kings had Russian proclivities and might enter into an alliance with them against the British in India. They were probably correct in both. Consequently the history of Iran from Turkmanchay until the turn of the 20th century is the story of the slow but sure advance by Russia from the northeast and by Great Britain from the southeast.

The internal affairs of Iran in these years were reflections of what was going on in foreign affairs. Iran had lost initiative in its relations with Great Britain and Russia and lagged behind in internal reform and reorganization. The very able Abol Ghasem Gha'em Magham, who showed much awareness of the need for reform, was put to death by Mohammad Shah. The new Prime Minister was Haji Mirza Aghassi, whose lewdness, ignorance, fanaticism, and avarice have made him a detestable character in the Ghajar administration.

The question of Afghanestan and more especially Harat remained on Iran's agenda during the early years of Mohammad Shah's successor, Nasser o-Din Shah, who ascended the throne in 1848. Harat was the center of a Persian speaking area with great ties with Iran. The Persian forces occupied the city in 1856, but Great Britain considered the move serious enough to declare war on Iran. While the British column was marching towards Harat, another army went by way of the Persian Gulf. After occupying Booshehr (Bushire), the British took the port of Mohammareh, now called Khorramshahr, at the confluence of Karoon and Shatt-ol-Arab rivers. Later a flotilla sailed off the Karoon and captured Ahvaz. Most of this was accomplished without much resistance on the part of the Persian forces. As the treaty of peace was concluded in Paris in 1857, according to which Iran agreed to evacuate Afghanestan and recognize its independence. Iran also agreed to use the "good offices" of Great Britain in any border disputes with Afghanestan. According to Professor Peter Avery, in 1879 a conservative British government was seriously considering returning Harat to Iran, but in the elections the liberals won and the plan was abandoned.

Most of this was during the Crimean War, which had kept Russia busy. It was not until 1868 that Alexander II had enough stability at home to venture into Central Asia by occupying Bokhara. Two years later the Russians took Khojand (Kokand). In 1884 Russia annexed Marv and thus became master of the region east of the Caspian Sea and all of Central Asia. Iran was forced to accept the Atrak River as the new boundary, thus ceding to Russia the most fertile part on the north bank of the river. In all these advances, Iran sought the aid of Great Britain to stop Russia. Great Britain, however, either could not or would not help. Since India was secured through British control of the affairs of Afghanestan, it did not really matter to them if the Russians controlled the territory east of the Caspian and Central Asia.

In the same way that the British virtually gave Russia a free hand in northeastern Iran, the Russians reciprocated by looking the other way when Britain annexed territories south of Afghanestan to the Persian Gulf. The British did not use military campaigns to gain their ends although the threat was always present. From 1870 to 1903 there were boundary disputes in Afghanestan and minor revolts in Baloochestan (Baluchistan). In all the disputes and uprisings Britain offered its good offices to settle them. There were the Mokran Boundary Commission of 1871, the Sistan Arbitration Commission of 1872, the Perso-Baloochestan Commission of 1892, and the Second Sistan Commission of 1903. When all of this was over, the western boundaries of British India had somehow expanded considerably at the expense of Iran! In annexing the territory west of the Caspian Sea, Russia had cut Azarbaijan in two, calling its half "Russian Azarbaijan." In the same way Great Britain cut Baloochestan in two, calling its half "British Baloochestan."

Economic Imperialism

By the beginning of the 20th century the annexation phase of Anglo-Russian Imperialism had come to an end. Neither country allowed the other to annex any more Persian territories. While it is true that if it were not for the presence of Great Britain, Russia would have annexed all of Iran, it is equally true that if it were not for the presence of Russia, Great Britain would have controlled Iran. It was the fate of the country to be a buffer state in which Russia and Great Britain wielded economic and political power without having any responsibility for the welfare of the people.

Long before the end of the 19th century, however, what is known as economic imperialism had started. It lasted for about 50 years from 1870 to 1921. When Great Britain assumed full responsibility for India after the well-known "Mutiny" in 1857, speedy communication between London and Delhi became of utmost importance. In 1863 the Overland Telegraph Convention was signed in Istanbul, connecting London to Baghdad. A year later the Shah agreed to have the line extended to Kermanshah, Hamadan, Tehran, and Booshehr. The

Indo-European Telegraph Company, formed in 1870 operated the communication between London and Delhi through Iran with several branch lines in the country itself. There is no question that the telegraph lines connected the different cities and made the governing of the provinces from the capital easier. Furthermore, it ended the isolation of Iran and put her in close touch with the capitals of Europe. Nevertheless, it opened the way to many more concessions granted to Great Britain and Russia, which eventually put the resources of the country under foreign control. It can readily be seen that some of these concessions were nothing but evil exploitations of the people, while there were others that were profitable to both sides. Unfortunately, the good was more than offset by the superior attitude of the foreign managers which, at best, were suffocatingly paternalistic, and at worse, destructively humiliating. It must also be said that all concessions were granted by the members of the ruling class, from the shah down, with the sole purpose of advancing their own selfish interests.

In 1872, Baron Julius de Reuter, a naturalized British citizen, received a 70 year concession for a gigantic monopoly for the building of railroads, exploitation of mines, establishment of a bank, building of water works, regulation of rivers, and so forth. The Shah was insistent that negotiations be kept secret. Before signing Nasser o-Din shah went through the motions of asking the opinions of his ministers. They all assured him that if he placed his "most blessed name to the concessions, this one stroke of his pen will vouch- safe to the people of this land and more benefit than they have received from all the kings of Iran over thousands of years."[9] It is important to note that this concession was granted without knowledge or pressure from the British government. The greed of the shah and his ministers made them give away the resources of the country, and their appalling ignorance of the European business scene made them do it for a miserably low sum. "The pretty phrases about benefiting the country by bringing the fruit of European progress to Iran and the pretense had concern for the well-being of the people made the actions of the corrupt ruler and his equally corrupt ministers still more offensive by adding hypocrisy to treasonable greed."[10] Fortunately for Iran, the Russians were against the concession, as the shah found out when he made his first trip to Europe soon after signing it. The British government was not in favor either and so it was canceled.

When Nasser o-Din Shah made his second trip to Europe, he was impressed with the smart uniforms and riding ability of the Russian Cossack detachments. He expressed the wish that he would like to organize a similar force in Iran. The Russian government was delighted at the idea and offered to send an officer to help the shah in the project. The Persian army, it will be recalled, was trained by the French and the British, followed by Italians and Austrians. When it came to the Russian turn, the British tried to stop it. But the shah was adamant and refused to approve the British project to develop the lower Karoon for navigation. The British acquiesced and, as a result, they had their Karoon River concession while the Russians trained a Persian Cossack brigade, which was commanded by Russian officers and was the only organized force in Iran until 1921.

Baron de Reuter who had not stopped his efforts to salvage something out of his ill-fated concession, was given a new concession for the establishment of a bank, to be called the Imperial Bank of Persia, with the right to issue bank notes. In order to give the appearance of impartiality, a concession was given to the Russians to open the Banque D' Escompte de Perse. The Imperial Bank printed money with each bill carrying the name of the city in which it would be used. Individuals traveling from city to city had to pay a commission to exchange their money for the bill which would be accepted in that city. Not only were the profits on this scheme astronomical, but Persians were given the feeling that they were traveling in a foreign country.

By far the most notorious concession and the most far reaching was the Tobacco Regie of 1890. This concession was also negotiated secretly by the shah and a certain Major Gerald F. Talbot with the good offices of the British minister in Tehran, Sir Henry Drummond Wolff. The concession gave the British company a monopoly for the production, sale, and export of all tobacco in Iran. The shah was to receive an annual payment of 15,000 British Pounds while the promoters of the company in England claimed in their advertisement for the sale of the shares that they expected a profit of 500,000 Pounds per annum. While the aborted Reuter concession of 1872 dealt with the undeveloped wealth of the country, the tobacco concession of 1890 affected the lives of thousands of growers, merchants, and users of tobacco. The vehement, well-coordinated, and general opposition to this concession surprised everyone, especially the shah. The opposition was somewhat slow in forming, but when it was organized it acted with such a fury that it forced the shah and the British government to retreat.

Among the leaders of the opposition were the merchants, who stood to lose their income; the Shi'i clergy who were afraid that hundreds of foreign employees scattered all over the country would undermine Eslamic beliefs and practices; and a small band of "Europeanized" liberals. They were followed by peasants who were led to believe that they would suffer and by hundreds and thousands of smokers who could not see the necessity of buying from a foreign company the tobacco which they themselves had grown. All of these groups were encouraged one way or another by the Russians.[11] The shah, who was not used to such large-scale opposition, responded by imprisoning the opponents of the concession. The struggle continued until December 1891, when the leading Shi'i Mojtahed, Haji Mirza Hassan Shirazi, issued the following fatva from his residence in Samereh (Samarra), Iraq: "In the name of God the Compassionate and the Merciful. Today the use of tanbakoo and tutoon in any form is tantamount to war against the Emam of the Age; may God hasten his advent."

Obedience to the ban was universal. Dr. Feuvrier, the French physician of the shah reported, "Suddenly, with perfect accord, all the tobacco merchants have closed their shops, all the *ghalyans (waterpipes)* have been put aside, and no one smokes any longer, either in the cities or in the shah's entourage or even in the women's apartments."12 The shah was forced to cancel the concession, but the cancellation cost Iran 500,000 Pounds in damages. This sum was borrowed from the Imperial Bank at 6% interest. The loan was to be paid in forty years and the customs duties of the Persian Gulf were placed as collateral. This was a first loan and there were many more to follow. Eventually most of the resources were mortgaged to the British and Russian creditors. An eyewitness Persian author reported "not withstanding this loss, Iran has come through herself and is on its way to awakening. From the settlement of the Regie concession, the nation of Iran has learned that it is possible to stand in front of the king and demand one's rights."[13]

On Friday, May 1, 1896 Nasser o-Din Shah was assassinated by Mirza Reza of Kerman, a disciple of the notorious Pan Eslamist agitator Sayyed Jamal e-Din Afghani, who had been ousted from Iran by the late shah in 1891.

The crown prince, Mozaffar o-Din, arrived from Tabriz accompanied by the British and Russian ministers. He was an amiable man of 43, ineffective and uninterested in the affairs of government. He was also sick and felt that he should go to Europe for a cure. With no money in the treasury, search for ready money became the main preoccupation of the shah. The Russian bank offered a loan of 2,400,000 Pounds at 5% against the customs receipts of the whole country except the Persian Gulf. It was recalled that Iran already owed 500,000 Pounds to the British. Since the Russians wanted to be the sole creditors, one condition was that the British loan be paid out of it. After payment of the British debt, discounts, commissions, and other obligations, just enough was left to pay for His Majesty's trip to Europe in 1900!

Almost as soon as he returned from the European tour, he made plans to go again. His father had been to Europe three times, but he had been there only once and was still sickly. Russia again came forth with a loan of over 1,000,000 Pounds at 4%. In return Iran gave a concession for the

Russians to build a road from Jolfa, on the Russo-Persian border to Tabriz, Ghazvin, and Tehran. Another condition of the loan was a revision of the tariff regulation. The Belgian customs advisor to the shah, Joseph Naus, has usually been derided for working against the interest of Iran, but evidence does not support this accusation. The shah wanted money and Naus revised the tariff and produced more revenue.[14] It was the shah and his court who were working against the interests of Iran. All that can be said is that Naus' "solution" favored the Russians, who had given the loan, rather than the British, who had refused.

Great Britain, however, did not have to wait too long to be of service to the shah, for he returned home penniless and needed more money. This time the British offered a loan of 300,000 Pounds at 5% payable in 20 years from the receipts of the Caspian fisheries. There were more loans and the competition between the British and Russian banks was fierce to the point of being ridiculous.[15] The backbreaking loans, the rivalry between the Russophile Persians and the equally corrupt Anglophile compatriots, the concern of the merchants for their own future, the fear of the clergy for the future of Eslam, and the general awakening caused by contact with the west culminated in the demand for an *Edalat Khaneh* "House of Justice." This meant different things to different groups. To the common man the important word was "justice." To the clergy it meant the establishment of Shi'i theocracy, while to the Europeanized Persian it meant constitution. Whatever it was, the disinterested shah granted it, with a little pressure in a royal script of August 5, 1906, that limited the power of the monarchy and ordered the establishment of an assembly, called the Majless, as well as the creation of a constitution.

Background of the Revolution

In order to understand better the awakening of Iran and the revolutionary movement that was a symbol of it, one should take three points into consideration. The first is the Persians' consciousness of their identity. This identity was started during the Achaemenid period and has continued with different degrees of intensity until the present. During the Eslamic period it manifested itself religiously in such movements as the "Black Robes," "White Robes," "Red Robes," "Brethren of Purity," and the Twelver Shi'i and Esma'ili Shi'i. Sometimes it had manifested itself politically and in the Barmakids, Saffarids, Samanids, and others. It has also appeared culturally as in the Shu'ubiyeh movement, in poets like Ferdosi, in scientists and philosophers like Avicenna and Razi, and on to the Mongol period when the Persian culture became fully independent. Perhaps it was the strength of this consciousness and the sense of belonging which enabled the Persians to absorb their conquerors and Persianize them.

The second point is the fact that creativity and intellectual and spiritual advance is possible in a society where there is intellectual and religious freedom. This is true about any people, but you have seen in these pages the creativity of the Achaemenids when there was tolerance as compared with the period of cultural stagnation during the last part of the Sassanids when religion and state joined in the imposing dogma upon the people. In the Eslamic period during the Omayyads, who were more interested in Arab superiority than in imposing Eslam, there was freedom for the intellectually curious to translate the known knowledge of the world into Arabic and the religiously sensitive to discuss Eslam in the context of the Greek and Persian religious thought. The Abbasids, however, who had come to power on a religious platform, so to speak, introduced religious inquisition in Eslam, executed writers and accused philosophers and scientists of heresy. Fortunately, their power did not last very long. As they became weak and unable to impose any dogma, we witnessed the "Golden Age" of culture which, in the case of Iran especially, continued throughout the Mongol period, when there were no dogmas or inhibitions to amount to much. It was again during the Safavid period when Shi'i heterodoxy became the state religion and was imposed upon the people that we witnessed a cultural retrogression.

The third point is the isolation of Iran, which is the inevitable result of the religious and political dictatorship during the Safavid period. Not withstanding the extensive political and commercial relationships between Iran and various European countries, there was no intellectual or spiritual interaction. Iran was even separated from the rest of the Moslem world. It was considered to be *in* the world of Eslam but was certainly not *of* it. As the power of the clergy increased, the isolation of Iran became more complete. The various movements in 19th century Iran can be understood in the light of this isolation; Babism certainly dealt a severe blow to the spiritual authority of the clergy. The Pan Eslamism of Afghani was an attempt to destroy the wall which separated the Shi'i from the rest of the Moslems. The purpose of the Europeanized constitutionalists was definitely to raze the wall that isolated Iran from the rest of the world. In all this the identity with the past was used to arouse the populous and only when the walls crumbled and religious dogmas weakened did the resurgence of a new Iran become a possibility.

Bahaism

Babism (pronounced bobism) or Babi-Bahaism was an indigenous reform movement in Shi'i Eslam with no influence from abroad. It grew out of the Shi'i tradition and remained so until Bahaism carried it abroad and made it a "world faith." According to the Shaykhi sect, the absent twelfth Emam, who shall someday appear, is in touch with the believers through one person, who is called the Bab (pronounced as Bob) or gate. The leader of this group, Mirza Ali Mohammad of Shiraz, claimed to be the Bab in 1844. Later, in his book, *Bayan*, in which mystic and esoteric terms abound, he refers to himself as the Emam himself, or the "Point of Revelation," or the "Point of Explanation," and speaks of "Him whom God shall Manifest." In so far as the date 1844 was one thousand years after the 12th Emam, the new movement was considered the beginning of a new dispensation with a new calendar, laws and so forth.

The fact that Mirza Ali Mohammad gained a ready following from all walks of life in many parts of the country is indicative of the disappointment of the people in the life and message of the clergy and in conditions in general. Typical of most Eslamic movements, the Babis, as they were called, took up arms and set out to establish the new kingdom. The shah was against it and the clergy preached against it, but the movement grew. Soon after the execution of the Bab in 1850, the abortive attempt of two of his followers to assassinate Nasser o-Din Shah reopened the wrath of the government against them. The severe persecution which ensued and the courage with which the Babis endured it helped their cause tremendously.

The designated successor of the Bab was a man named Yahya, with the title of *Sobh-e Azal*, the "Morning of Eternity." His half brother, Hossain Ali, must have also been close to the Bab, for he had the title "Bahaollah", the "Splendor of God." Both brothers were exiled to the Ottoman Empire. In 1866 Bahaollah claimed that he was "Him whom God shall Manifest," whose coming was foretold by the Bab. Yahya, however, did not accept his brother's claim, and the ensuing struggle between the two and their followers caused the Ottoman government to separate them. Sobh-e Azal was sent to Cypress and Bahaollah to Acre in Palestine.

It appears that Sobh-e Azal wanted to keep the movement limited within the bounds established by the founder, while Bahaollah wanted to broaden it in scope. Bahaollah won and the movement was changed from Babism to Bahaism. The Babis were active in the social and political government in Iran while the Bahais kept aloof. It cannot be said that Bahaism, as a faith, spearheaded the modernization of Iran, or had anything to do with the constitutional movement. Nevertheless, the movement created a ferment and the Bahais were more receptive to new ideas even though they were not interested in propagating them.

The Shi'i clergy certainly accused them of every innovation with which they disagreed and all modern concepts were attributed to them. Babi-Bahai movement shook the foundations of Shi'i orthodoxy. A large number of Jews and Zoroastrians became Bahais and as such broke the religious barriers which existed.

Pan-Eslamism

As a religio-political movement, Pan-Eslamism was not popular in Shi'i Iran. It is ironic, therefore, that the most famous Pan-Eslamist of the 19th century should be a Persian by the name of Jamal e-Din Afghani (1839-1897). The activities of most of his life do not belong to the history of Iran, but his writings and his correspondence with a number of Persians contributed a great deal to breaking the wall of isolation around Iran. He was controversial, and possessed a remarkable personal magnetism. His life was so tumultuous, his writings so incendiary, and his ideals so inconsistent that the last word has not been written about him.[16]

He claimed to be from Afghanestan even though he was a Persian known as Asadabadi. He paraded as a Sunni, though he was a Shi'i. He is considered a forerunner of the Persian revolution[17] though he might not have supported it had he lived. He does not seem to have had any scruples and was willing to appear in any guise that would gain him his end of appearing "to the Shi'i olama as a pious Shi'i, interested in preserving the existing faith against the infidel Shah; to his followers as an excoriator of the backward clergy; to a mass Eslamic audience as a defender of Eslam against Western inspired materialism; and to western audience as a defender of science and philosophy against religion."[18] Some historians dismiss him as a paranoiac political agitator, and his claims for freedom and progress as only means to his main purpose which was Pan-Eslamism. Still it should be noted that some of the influential Persians of the 19th century were impressed by him; some of the Shi'i clergy were goaded by him into action; and Persians, to this day, quote his writings.

The Pan Eslamic group in Iran was very small. One of its leaders was Shaykh Ahmad Roohi, a poet from Kerman. His poetry denouncing Nasser o-Din Shah and praising Abdol Hamid as a "Sultan of Eslam" leaves no doubt as to Afghani's plan for the union of Eslam and Iran's position in such a union. As has been noted, one of his disciples killed Nasser o-Din Shah. Pan-Eslamism, like Bahaism, was not a major factor in the awakening of Iran, but it served to pierce the veil of isolation behind which Iran had been kept.

Contacts with the West

In the 19th century Iran stepped in a long and slow process which culminated in the ending of the isolation of this country. Perhaps it was the crown prince Abbas Mirza's bitter defeat at the hands of the Russians that induced him to send seven students to England between 1811 and 1815 to "study something of use to me, themselves and their country."[19] So far as is known, these were the first Persian students to study abroad. Of these seven, one died; the rest returned a physician, gunsmith, engineer, chemist, artillery man, and teacher-printer. The last one went to Oxford and his memoirs described life in England, which he called the "country of freedom," compared it with Iran, and blamed the Moslem clergy for the backwardness of Iran.[20] In 1845 five more students were dispatched to study in Paris. Throughout the century more students were sent and they came back not only with technical knowledge but with observations on the life and culture of Europe.

The person, however, who laid the foundation of modernization was Mirza Taghi Khan Amir Kabir, the astute Grand Vazir of Nasser o-Din Shah. He was the son of a cook and a protégé of Gha'em Magham, the able and ill-fated vazir under Mohammad Shah. He was the chief officer to Nasser o-Din, when the latter was crown prince residing in Tabriz. In that position he had occasion to go to Turkey and observe the "Tanzimat" reforms in that country. He also went to Russia and knew the language well enough to absorb what he saw and heard. When Nasser o-Din was crowned in 1848, Amir Kabir, who was the new shah's brother-in-law, became the grand vazir. This was a very auspicious beginning, if only it had been allowed to continue. However, during his three short years in office, he did more than any other individual to push Iran towards modernization.

This remarkable man, whose capacity for work seemed unlimited, did not leave a single stone unturned, and made his presence felt in every facet of government. He established a newspaper that published articles on a wide range of subjects from parliamentary government in Europe to the headhunters of Borneo, and from building of railroads and opening of mines to planting American cotton in Iran.[21] He reorganized the court system, the army and postal service. He built jute, sugar and textile factories. Perhaps his greatest accomplishment was the establishment of the Dar ol-Fonoon, "Polytechnic Institute," with departments in medicine, mining and military science. It had a press of its own for publishing scientific and technical works, and employed European instructors.*

Both the reforms and the energetic way that Amir Kabir was carrying them out aroused the opposition of many groups and individuals. Among his enemies were the Shi'i clergy, about whom he had remarked to the British Consul, "the Ottoman government was able to regain its authority only after breaking the power of the clergy."[22] In 1849, it was rumored that the shrine of Saheb ol-Amr in Tabriz had performed a miracle and that the city should be exempt from paying taxes. The British consul, to encourage the idea, sent a gift of a chandelier to the shrine. Amir Kabir arrested the leaders of the clergy, including the Sheykh ol-Eslam, and had the British consul recalled home. "Never again did the shrine perform a miracle." [23]

The clergy found a powerful ally in the person of the Queen Mother, who had great influence over her son and was a mortal enemy of her own son-in-law. Amir Kabir was dismissed in 1851 and a year later, he was executed by the shah's order, in Kashan. About the only person who had stood by him until the end was his devoted wife, the shah's only sister. It is said that the shah "never forgave himself for the role he had played."[24]

Another person who must be mentioned as a forerunner of the Westernization of Iran is Mirza Malkom Khan (1833-1908). He was the son of an Armenian from Esfahan, whose stormy life can easily fill a volume, and was in and out of favor with Nasser o-Din Shah. A good portion of his life was spent as the shah's representative abroad. During the years when the granting of concessions was popular, as Persian Ambassador in London, he persuaded the shah to sign a concession for a national lottery system. Later the shah changed his mind and cancelled the concession and recalled him. Keeping this secret, Malkom sold his worthless concession to a British company for 40,000 Pounds. There was a scandal and Malkom Khan, who was dismissed from service, stayed in Europe and edited a Persian paper which he called *Ghanoon, 'Law.'* This paper was smuggled into Iran and became very influential and a thorn in flesh of Nasser o-Din Shah.

Malkom Khan, who had studied extensively in the west, was influenced by Auguste Conte and John Stuart Mill. He translated part of the latter's book, *On Liberty*, into Persian. He wrote on all subjects such as the need of a new alphabet, distribution of land, revision of law, Westernization, and so on [25] His main message was the rule of law, and his style of writing did very much to end the bombastic style prevalent during the

Ghajar period. He also introduced Free Masonry, *Faramoosh-Khaneh*, 'House of Forgetfulness' into Iran.

Malkom Khan was a humanist at heart and one of the most interesting results of his work is the organization of humanist societies in Iran. At one time they had over 300 very influential members, most of whom became active in the Persian constitutional movement. The Persian humanist (*Adamiyat*) societies were on the whole theistic. The members were called "brothers," and new members were received with a special ceremony and had to sign the following pledge: "O Creator of the world, I confess that thou has bestowed upon me the nobility of the humanity. In return for such a glorious gift of God, not withstanding my former shortcomings, I now stand before thee and swear by Thy Truth and Almighty Power, that I shall try with all my strength to uphold the honor of this position, as long as I live. If I ever fail in my undertaking, may I be cut out from Thy grace and compassion both in this world and in the next." [26]

Other Influences

Newspapers also played a great role in the Westernization of Iran. Most of the papers were published in 'Diaspora,' to borrow the apt phrase from Professor Avery. Besides Ghanoon which was published in London, there was *Akhtar*, published in Istanbul, *Habl ol-Matin* in Calcutta, and *Sorayya* in Cairo. The publication of books helped in destroying the walls of isolation in Iran. Mirza Yousef Khan Mostashar ol-Doleh, who was in and out of the government foreign service and died in prison, wrote two books on the two subjects which he considered to be essential to progress. One was *Ketabche-Ye Banafsh* (The Purple Handbook) in 1877 on railroads, and the other volume was called *Yek Kalameh* (One Word) in 1878, concerning law and constitution.[27] Two authors who wrote popular books on the necessity of social change, were both merchants from Azarbaijan. One was Abdol Rahman Talebof, whose popular book *Ahmad* is a dialogue between father and son on the causes of Iran's backwardness. The other author was Zayn-ol-Abedin Maragheyi, whose *Travels of Ebraihm Bey* is the story of a young Persian residing in Cairo who went to see what Iran was like. The effect of these two books on the general population cannot be exaggerated.

As previously stated, about the only school opened by the government in the entire 19th century was the Polytechnic in 1851. But liberal merchants of Azarbaijan, Guilan, and other provinces opened private schools along western lines. These were modeled after the schools which had been established by the American, British, and French missionaries.

The Constitutional Revolution

The Persian revolution is perhaps unique among the revolutions of the 20th century Middle East in a few points. First, it was not a military revolution. The Cossack brigade, which was the only effective military unit in the country, was not aware of it. Secondly, no one person had charge of it. The revolution was directed, somewhat haphazardly, by the merchants, the Europeanized liberals, and the moderate clergy. Thirdly, the Persian revolutionists did not have to fight to get a constitution and a parliament. Rather, they were forced to fight in order to defend what they already had achieved. Finally, it is indicative of the nature of the Persian culture to note that the Persian constitution granted in 1906 is the oldest constitution in all of Asia.

It has been mentioned that Mozaffar o-Din Shah had mortgaged the future of the country for his two trips abroad. He had negotiated a loan of 300,000 Pounds with the British; but that did not seem to be enough, for he was negotiating a joint Anglo-Russian loan of 400,000 Pounds. As a result of Naus's effort to increase the revenue, the price of sugar had been raised. On December 11, 1905, a group of merchants called a strike and closed the bazaar. When the government retaliated by flogging the merchants, some 2000 merchants and clergyman, headed by two moderate Mojataheds, Sayyed Mohammad Tabataba'i and Sayyed Abdollah Behbahani, took sanctuary at the shrine of Shah-Abdol-Azim, and asked for a "House of Justice."

The shah was perhaps willing to acquiesce but his advisors persuaded him to make a halfhearted promise and dragged on the affair until the summer of 1906. In July, a large number of the clergy and the followers took sanctuary in Ghome (Qom), 60 miles south of Tehran. Not to be outdone, some 13,000 Westernizers, merchants and others took sanctuary in the grounds of the British Legation in Tehran. Taking sanctuary, bast, has been an honored tradition in Iran, but never before had anyone gone in a foreign Legation. This was of course done with the British consent. It was then that the Shah granted the constitution.

It was impossible that, in such an important transition, the two rival powers, Great Britain and Russia, would not intervene. The Russian Tzar, who had been forced to grant a constitution to his own people and was disbanding the Duma as soon as it was elected, did not want such a thing to occur in Iran. Since Russia was against the constitution, Great Britain was for it. Their support of the Constitutionalists was dictated purely by self-interest and did not have anything to do with the ideology of freedom or democracy.

The young revolutionary movement experienced two severe blows in 1907. The first was the death of the shah, on January 8, 1907, and accession of his son Mohammad Ali, who was known to be a Russian puppet and against the revolution. From the beginning he started to undermine the work of the Majless, and in this he was encouraged by the Russians. The reactionary activity of the shah was challenged in two ways. One was by the "people of the pen." Ever since the granting of the constitution and its corollary freedoms, the number of newspapers had increased by the month. They attacked and lampooned the Shah and the reactionaries in poetry, prose, satire, humor and cartoons. Songs were written on revolutionary topics and troubadours used to sing these, instead of love songs, at weddings and other gatherings.

The other means was the appearance of the Anjomans, 'Councils'. More than anything else, it proved that the revolution was not the sole monopoly of the clergy or of the European educated elite. It had a wider base among the people. There were literally hundreds of these all over the country and each had from half a dozen to one hundred members. Some opened schools, some had discussion sessions, others conducted literacy classes, and still others wrote pamphlets. There were some anjomans who volunteered to help the deputies in their work. There were also terrorist anjomans. Even the women, secluded as they were, had their anjomans. There was no central group to direct these activities.

One of the first acts of the new shah was to recall the reactionary Amin ol-Soltan from Europe and make him Prime Minister. On August 31, 1907, as the Prime Minister was leaving the Majless, he was shot dead by a terrorist, who immediately committed suicide. On the assassin's body was found a paper with the inscription "Abbas Agha, moneychanger, member of Azarbaijan, member of the anjoman, national Fada'i, ['devotee'] #41." On the same date the Majless heard its second bad news of the year, namely the signing of the Anglo-Russian convention. This dealt with Iran, Afghanestan and Tibet, and was directed against Germany. It divided Iran into three sections, the territory north of the line from Kermanshah to Yazd to the Afghan border south of Mashhad, was designated as a Russian sphere. The territory east of the line from Birjand to the Persian Gulf, west of Bandar-e Abbas was the British sphere. The rest was not designated, which probably meant that it was for both. This very uneven division shows that Great Britain was still obsessed with the defense of India.

Persian reaction was one of dismay turned into anger against Great Britain. It was often Great Britain "the mother of parliaments," that the revolutionaries had depended; and now that they had their backs to the wall, Great Britain not only had violated the independence of Iran but also had betrayed the revolution by joining with the opposition.

The revolutionaries, however, did not have time to brood over this, for the shah was closing in on them. No doubt encouraged by the Anglo-Russian convention the shah ordered Colonel Liakhov, commander of the Cossacks, to bombard the Majless. A large number of the revolutionaries were arrested, their leaders were executed, and the rest went into hiding or fled the country. It seemed that the revolution was over, and it would have been if it had not had support among the rank and file of the population. Overnight, three centers rallied to the defense of the constitution: Tabriz, under the leadership of Sattar Khan and Bagher Khan; Rasht under the leadership of Sardar Mohi and the Armenian Dashnak nationalist, Yefrem Khan; and the Bakhtyari tribe in Esfahan.

Tabriz was besieged for nine months by the Shah's and Russian troops. Everyone seems to have joined in the defense of the city, including Howard Baskerville (Princeton, 1907) a young teacher in the American Mission School, who resigned his post to join the revolutionaries. He was killed on April 12, 1909, when he led a sortie to bring food for the starving population. The determined resistance of the Tabrizis gave time to the Bakhtyaris in Esfahan and a volunteer army from Rasht to move toward Tehran. They took the capital on July 13, 1909, and deposed the shah. The seize of Tabriz was lifted and the Constitutionalists were in power again. During all this time when so much atrocity was committed by the shah and the Russians, Great Britain did not raise her voice in protest. Oil was discovered in the "neutral zone" of Iran in 1908, and in order to prevent the Russians from coming to the south where the oil was, they left Russians free to do as they pleased in the northwest.[28] Upon the good offices of Russia and Great Britain the revolutionaries agreed to exile the ex-shah with a pension, and chose his young son Ahmad as the new shah.

When the second Majless convened on November 15, 1909, it was confronted with two major problems, both of which had arisen during the first session. One was the ideological differences among the deputies, and the other a desperate need for money. Two distinct political factions had emerged, one revolutionary and the other evolutionary. The former or the "Social Democrats" wanted separation of temporal and religious powers, compulsory military service, land distribution, compulsory education, and so on. Most of the European educated, middle-class merchants and young writers belonged to this group. The second faction called the "Social Moderates" included the moderate clergy, and some of the landlords and nobility who were simply against the excesses of the ex-shah. The Europeanized nationalists wanted a constitutional government, *Mashrooteh,* based on laws legislated by the elected representatives of the people. The clergy desired *Mashroo'eh,* or the rule of Moslem *Shari'a* as interpreted by the *Mojtaheds.* Neither side was strong enough to subdue the other, and the compromise is apparent in the Supplement to the Constitution. Article II of this document required that a committee of Mojtaheds be present in the Majless with veto power over any legislation which they considered to be against Moslem law.[29] The fact that this article was never implemented shows that to the secular nationalists it was only a window dressing.

The bankruptcy of the country however, knew no ideological boundary. The Majless felt the need of a financial adviser from abroad; in the light of all that had happened, the United States was a natural choice. Morgan Schuster, together with a number of assistants, arrived in May 1911 as Treasurer General and was invested with extensive powers. At the same time a French lawyer, Adolphe Perni, was employed to draw up a new penal code, which he completed by 1912. The fact that the Mojtaheds accepted such arrangements showed not only their lack of power but also the inadequacy of the religious law.[30]

In as much as the Majless gave full support to every plan proposed by Shuster, the Russians sent an ultimatum on November 29 for his dismissal. A second ultimatum followed, which asked Iran to promise not to employ any foreign advisors without the consent of Russia and Great Britain. This was followed by a third in which Iran was asked to pay indemnity for the troops that Russia had dispatched to enforce the first ultimatum. The British not only supported all these Russian moves but brought up Indian troops ready to occupy south Iran.

The Majless sent cables appealing for aid from the parliaments of the world. This was the revolution's darkest hour and yet it proved to be its finest. The cabinet, headed by the Bakhtyari chieftain Samsam ol-Saltaneh, was in favor of dismissing Shuster and presented a resolution to this effect on December 1, 1911. It was a few hours before the 48 hours fixed by Russia ran out. One deputy arose and said: "It may be the will of Allah that our liberty and our sovereignty shall be taken from us by a force, but let us not sign them away with our own hand."[31] Others spoke in the same vein, a roll-call vote was taken and the Majless rejected the Russo-British ultimatum with only a few abstentions. The people outside were ecstatic, Russian and British goods were boycotted, and hundreds volunteered for resistance. Pressure was brought to bear for the Majless to reconsider. When it was rumored that the they might yield, a group of women representing their own anjomans, went to the Majless, some with revolvers under their veils, and told the Speaker that they would "kill their own husbands and sons, and leave behind their own dead bodies if the deputies wavered in their duty to uphold the liberty and dignity of the Persian people and nation." [32]

The deputies held, and on December 24 the cabinet closed the Majless by force and dismissed Schuster. Thus came to an end the first phase of the Persian Revolution. It had failed because of the Anglo-Russian interference, because of the rift among the Constitutionalists, and also because of the lack of unity and experience. It had also succeeded. The constitution remained as a living symbol of their efforts, to which even the strongest dictator was obliged to pay lip service. It had succeeded because it inaugurated a period of freedom in which new poetry and prose flourished, new ideas were formulated, and songs of freedom were heard in the midst of the deprivation of war.

Cultural Life

The new poetry and prose showed a marked departure from the bombastic and flamboyant style prevalent in the early Ghajar period. Some of the same persons responsible for the modernization of Iran were also pioneers in the reform of Persian literature. Ministers like Gha'em Magham Farahani (1779-1835) and MirzaTaghi Khan Amir Kabir (d.1852) began using more lucid Persian in their official reports and communications. Until recently their writings were used as models of good Persian in the high schools of the country. The simplification of Persian literature thus begun was advanced by the prolific pamphleteer Malkom Khan (1833-1908), who introduced the European style of writing, which became a model for the 20th century Persian writers. Malkom Khan and his contemporary reformer, the playwright Mirza Fath Ali Akhoondzadeh, were pioneers in the ranks of those unsuccessful individuals who have attempted to reform or change the Persian script.

Other writers began to express their social and political reformist ideas in the form of European style novels such as Ahmad, by Talebof, and Travels of Ibrahim Bey, by Maragheyi. A work that received belated literary distinction is the Persian translation of the delightful book, the *Adventures of Haji Baba of Esfahan*, by James Morier, which appeared in England in 1824. [33] The translator, Mirza Habib Esfahani, combined colloquial

Persian with the classical so skillfully that the result has been compared favorably with the Sa'di's *Golestan*.[34]

The revolution of 1905, however, ushered in a period of literary creativity the significance of which has not been fully studied. This "literature of revolt," as it has been called, appeared in poetry and prose in over eighty newspapers, which sprouted like mushrooms all over the country. Even the naming of the distinguished poets and writers of the time would make too long a list. What is important, however, is the fresh content and the new form of prose and poetry of this period. Among the poets may be mentioned Abolghasem Aref Ghazvini (1883-1934), who became the songster of the revolution. He wrote more ballads than any other poet of the time. These did not deal with love and roses, as is usually the case, but with the burning political and social questions of the period. They were sung at parties and at wedding feasts all over the country.

Another writer of note was Ali Akbar Dehkhoda (1879-1956), whose column *Charand o Parand* (Balderdash) in the revolutionary newspaper *Soor-e Esrafil* was very popular. He wrote in colloquial Persian and by the use of popular expressions and idioms injected a new vitality into the Persian language. Later in life he eschewed politics and devoted his time to the compilation of an ambitious encyclopedic dictionary of the Persian language.

Perhaps the most active and talented writer was the poet laureate, Mohammad Taghi Bahar (1886-1951), whose life spanned the revolutionary period through the hectic era after the Second World War. He was prominently active throughout, intermittently as editor, member of Parliament, minister, and university professor.

Music, frowned upon in Eslam, did not enjoy periods of development in Iran. During the revolutionary period, however, it was brought into the service of social and political change. Musicians like Darvish, Shahnazi, Shokri, and others cooperated with poets in the compilation of ballads. Musical plays with political motivation were introduced. The most talented in this field was the son of Haj Sayyed Abol-Ghasem Kordestani, Mirzadeh Eshghi (1893-1924), who wrote a popular nationalistic opera but whose tragic assassination put an end to such activity. What is important to note, however, is that the melodies used were all Persian, with practically no influence from abroad.

As very aptly pointed out by the Cambridge History of Iran, volume 7: however adverse their circumstances may be, Iranians never lose sight of the great assets they have in their language, and are ever adept at putting it to use.

ENDNOTES

1. Avery, *Modern Iran* (New York: Praeger, 1965), p.18.

2. Browne, *A Literary History*, IV, p.282.

3. Nafisi, *Tarikh-e Ejtema'I*, p.75.

4. Farmayan, The Foreign Policy of Iran — A Historical Analysis 559B.C.-A.D. 1971, p.16.

5. Nafisi, *Tarikh-e Ejtema'I*, p.118.

6. Ali Akbar Bina, Tarikh-e Siyasi va Diplomasi-ye Iran (Political and Diplomatic History of Iran) (Tehran: University of Tehran Press, 1959), p. 171.

7. Ibid., p.187.

8. Avery, *Modern Iran*, p.37.

9. Ebrahim Teymoori, Asr-e Bikhabari ya Tarikh-e Emtiyazat dar Iran (*The Uninformed Period or a History of Concessions in Iran*) (Tehran: Eghbal va shoraka, 1954), p.107.

10. Firuz Kazemzadeh, *Russia and Britain in Persia, 1864-1914* (New Haven: Yale University Press, 1968), p.108.

11. Nikki R. Keddie, Religion and Rebellion in Iran, the Iranian Tobacco Protest of 1891-1892 (London: Frank Cass, 1966), p.65.

12. Quoted by E.G. Browne, *The Persian Revolution, 1905-1909* (Cambridge University Press, 1910), p.52.

13. Nezam ol-Eslam Kermani, *Tarikh-e-Bidari-ye Iranian (History of Persian Awakening)* (Tehran: Bonyad-e Farhang, 1966), p.13.

14. See Marvin L. Entner, *Russo-Persian Commercial Relations, 1828-1914* (Gainesville, Florida: University of Florida Press 1965).

15. Kazemzadeh, Russia and Britain, p.45

16. Nikki R. Keddie, An Eslamic Response to Imperialism: Political and Religious Writings of Sayyed Jamal al-Din "al-Afghani" (Berkeley: University of California 1968.)

17. C.f. Brown, *Persian Revolution*, p.14.

18. Keddie, *Eslamic Response*, p. 45.

19. 19.Hafez F. Farmayan, "The Forces of Modernization in Nineteenth Century Iran," in William Polk and Richard Chambers, eds., *Beginnings of Modernization in the Middle East, The Nineteenth Century* (University of Chicago Press, 1968), p.120.

20. Ibid., p.123.

21. Fereydoon Adamiyat, *Fekr-e Azadi (The Thought of Freedom)* (Tehran: Sokhan, 1961), p.46.

22. Ibid., p.50.

23. Ibid., p.51.

24. Farmayan, "Forces of Modernization,"p.127.

25. Adamiat lists 26 pamphelets,pp.101-2

26. Ibid., p.222.

27. Farmayan, "Forces of Modernization," p.139.

28. See. Avery, *Modern Iran*, p.134.

29. For the full text see Brown, *Persian Revolution*, Appendix AOIV, p.372.

30. Banani, Modernization of Iran, p.68.

31. Morgan Schuster, *The Strangling of Persia* (New York: The Century Company, 1912), p.182.

32. Ibid., p.198.

33. There is a controversy as to whether Morier wrote the book or a Persian author using Morier's name.

34. Mohammad Taghi Bahar, Sabk Shenasi (Understanding Style). Vol. III (University of Tehran Press, 1958), p.366.

CHAPTER EIGHT

THE RESURGENCE OF IRAN

The young Ahmad Shah Ghajar, having reached the age of 18, was crowned in July 1914. No one expected that the world would be engulfed by a war, and certainly no Persian thought that he was witnessing the coronation of the last Ghajar king. Everyone seemed to be happy, especially the Constitutionalists, because the coronation brought the Constitution to mind and the Constitution demanded elections for the third session of the Majless, which had been closed since the ousting of Schuster in 1911.

The third Majless still had the two factions of Liberal-Radicals and Conservative-Moderates. The World War, however, had changed the situation drastically. Iran had declared neutrality, but did not have the power to enforce it, with the result that it became the battlefield of hot war between the Ottomans and the Russians, and the scene of a "cloak and dagger" war between the British and the Germans. Great Britain formed a Persian militia in the south, called the South Persia Rifles (SPR), and it was kept fairly busy quelling tribal uprisings caused by the German agents Niedermayer and Wasmuss.[1] There was brigandage and highway robbery, tribal raids on certain areas, and insecurity throughout the country.

The Soviet Republic of Guilan

The third Majless was conspicuous in not having many sessions. In as much as Great Britain and Russia were on the same side, most of the Persians and especially the liberals felt that Iran would be divided between them. Consequently, their sympathies were on the side of the Central Powers, and a number of them made the long trek to Istanbul. Some went to Germany, among them the fiery deputy Hassan Taghizadeh, who published the popular magazine *Kaveh* until 1921. Those who remained tried to bring about the defeat of the allies by helping the Germans.[2] There were also a number of liberals who took matters into their own hands and set up revolutionary governments in Azarbaijan, Guilan and Kordestan. The most important of these was the movement which was started in Guilan by a former theological student, Mirza Koochak Khan. He was a nationalist who, together with his following, had vowed not to shave or cut his hair until the foreign troops had withdrawn from Iran. Living as they did in the jungles of Guilan, they were called *Jangali*. Later when the German and Ottoman officers came to train the Jangalis, some undertones of Pan-Eslamism crept into the ideology.

The October revolution of the Bolsheviks in Russia changed the situation in Iran. It gave a new life to the Persian nationalists. In the Russian revolution they did not see the triumph of an ideology but the breaking of an alliance with Great Britain that, in their minds, would have certainly divided and destroyed Iran. In a speech that one of these nationalists, the poet laureate Bahar, made in Tehran a few weeks after the revolution, he said: "Two enemies had a rope around the neck of the man and were pulling from both sides. The poor fellow was struggling for his life. Suddenly one of the enemies let the rope loose and said, 'You helpless fellow, I am your brother,' and the man was saved. The man who let loose the noose around our neck is Lenin!"[3]

Immediately after the war, Iran was occupied by British troops on their way toward Baku and the Caucasus to help the "Whites" in the civil war against the Bolsheviks[Reds]. Mirza Koochack Khan, like most of the Persian nationalists, was quite ambivalent toward communism, but his deputy Ehsanollah Khan was quite enthusiastic and wanted to set the Jangali revolt on the basis of class struggle. On the other hand, there was this argument in the Central Committee in Moscow as to whether Iran was "ready" for revolution. Nevertheless, the fortunes of the civil war gave the Bolsheviks the upper hand in the Caucasus; they got in touch with Mirza Koochak Khan and eventually landed troops in Guilan. A Soviet Republic of Guilan was established in 1920 with Rasht as the capital. The combined Soviet-Jangali forces drove the Persian government troops to near Ghazvin. There was a rift, however, among the leaders of the Jangalis. At the same time the soviet government decided to give up the Guilan project and enter into negotiations with the Persian government. The Russian troops were withdrawn to the port of Anzali, and the government troops under the command of Colonel

Reza Khan defeated the Jangalis. Koochak Khan fled into the mountains and died of exposure.

Students of communism have wondered why the Soviet Union gave up Guilan and with it perhaps Azarbaijan and the whole northern littoral. Professor Zabih in his authoritative study finds it still difficult to interpret the events. "The Soviet habit of fitting historical data into changing ideological interpretations has clouded not only the facts themselves but also the background of the event."[4] As stated, there was disagreement among the members of the Central Committee and especially the Baku congress of 1920, whether Iran was ready for Marxism. There was also disagreement as to how to approach the intense nationalism prevalent in Iran. Furthermore, there was still idealism among some of the old Bolsheviks to be against an accession as an act of imperialism. It is also significant to note that the Russians had just emerged from seven years of international and civil war, and were not strong enough to maintain an occupying force in Iran. It is also possible that they made a mistake. In any case the Russo-Persian relations took a turn from hostility to friendship.[5]

The Anglo-Persian Agreement

On the whole, the liberal nationalists of Iran looked with favor on the Bolshevik revolution, not so much as an ideology to follow but as a tool to be used to save Iran from the "clutches" of Great Britain. The moderates, however, among whom were a large number of landlords and clergy, looked at the Revolution from a different point of view. Some of them saw in the Revolution an opportunity for Iran to regain territories lost to Russia during the previous century. They reasoned that Russia had become extremely weak through war, revolution, civil war and famine. Furthermore, they were trying to maintain a regime which was hated by the rest of the world. Consequently, the Persian government sent a delegation to Paris Peace Conference with instructions to ask, among other things, for the return of territories both east and west of the Caspian Sea, contiguous with Iran. They were not admitted to the conference because of British opposition and nothing came of their demands.

The vast majority of the moderates who were in control of the Persian government looked upon the Bolshevik revolution as a disaster. They were afraid of it for themselves and for the country. Any contamination with it might wrest from them their lands, their privileges, and their birthrights. Great Britain, to be sure, was not popular among the people but it was much better than Russia, especially a communist Russia. Even though British troops were in the country, the government was having trouble with Guilan in the hands of Koochak Khan, Azarbaijan under Khiabani, and central Iran pillaged by brigands, Nayeb Hossain-e Kashi and his son Mashallah Khan. The situation would have been worse without the British troops. Furthermore, Great Britain was paying the penniless Persian government a monthly stipend of 225,000 pounds.[6] Everything considered, it was rather natural for a landowning prime minister like Vosoogh o-Doleh, a Foreign Minister like Prince Firooz, and associates to come to the conclusion that it would be to the best interests of Iran to come under the protection of Great Britain, at least for a while.

The Russian revolution had changed the situation for Great Britain also. It had rendered the Anglo-Russian convention of 1907 obsolete, and had also created a vacuum which, if filled with Great Britain, would control the land and sea approaches to India as well as the oil wells of Iran. It had been a dream of foreign secretary Lord Curzon to create a "chain of vassal states stretching from the Mediterranean to the Pamirs" in which Iran was the "most vital link." In 1919, the veteran British diplomat, Sir Percy Cox, who was minister in Tehran was given the task of implementing the above policy.

The agreement was concluded in secret between Great Britain and Premier Vosoogh. According to the agreement Great Britain would provide advisors with "adequate power" at the expense of Iran for as many Persian departments as considered necessary. Great Britain would also train and equip an army at Persian expense. A loan of 2 million Pounds at 7% was arranged to pay for the above and the pledge was to be "all the revenues and customs receipts" of Iran. Furthermore, "the purpose behind it" was, to put it in Professor Avery's words, "if not the only voice, Britain's was to be so far as external powers were concerned, the supreme voice in Iranian affairs. Also, it was designed to ensure that Iran should prosper, but prosper in tutelage to Great Britain."[7]

The above agreement can be best understood in the light of the interpretation given in the above paragraphs. Whether there was any bribe involved can not ,of course, be ascertained. It is doubtful, however, whether there is a Persian historian who thinks that there was not. Ahmad Shah was against the agreement and refused to sign it or even endorse it when he visited England in November of 1919, saying "Let those who receive money endorse it; I shall never endorse it."[8]

According to the constitution, the agreement had to be ratified by the Majless to be binding. The British, who should have known better, showed their contempt for the document by not waiting for this. Prime Minister Vosoogh did everything in his power to rig the election of the Fourth Majless, and the British were so sure of themselves that three chief advisers were dispatched to Iran. Mr. Armitage-Smith was sent for finance, General Dicskon for the Army, and Sir Herbert Smith for customs. When the arrangement was announced in Paris, world reaction was immediate and negative. The United States was especially opposed, partly because of the Wilsonian antipathy to secret agreements and partly because the American oil companies who hoped to enter Iran were rightly apprehensive that the agreement would give Britain a virtual monopoly in Iran. The agreement was abandoned, Vosoogh o-Doleh resigned, and the way was made clear for one of the most important events in the creation of contemporary Iran.

The Iran-Soviet Treaty of 1921

After the resignation of Vosoogh, the new Prime Minster, Moshir o-Doleh showed an entirely different attitude toward the Soviet Union. He took advantage of the friendly gestures of the Soviet government and tried to put the relations between the two countries on the basis of trust. His opposition to the Anglo-Persian agreement and his liberal attitude toward the Soviet Union did as much as anything else to persuade the Russians to withdraw their support of the Azarbaijan and Guilan separatists. The treaty of 1921 was a direct result of the policy of reconciliation followed by Moshir o-Doleh.[9] It was also the implementation of the declaration of the Soviet Union canceling all debts and credits existing within the Tsarist government and the other countries. As debtors in Europe the Bolsheviks appeared as "thieves", and as creditors in Asia they were considered most generous. The Bolsheviks took care to put this treaty, as well as others which they concluded with Turkey and other countries in Asia, in the context of anti-imperialism and in contrast to the Anglo-Persian agreement of 1919.

By this treaty, which had 26 articles, the Soviet Union relinquished all Russian claims to assets, concessions, and property to Iran. On its part Iran promised not to cede any of these to a third power but to "retain them for the benefit of the Persian people." The treaty, however, retained some vestiges of Tsarist imperialism and made provisions for future Russian proletarian imperialism. The Caspian fishery concession of 1867, for example, and the tariff regulation of 1902 remained unchanged. In 1927 a new

Iran-Soviet Fisheries Company was organized with a concession to operate for 25 years. The tariff, which was extremely favorable to Russia, remained intact and Persian trade suffered.

It was Article Six of the Treaty which caused Iran trouble in later years. It stipulated that if a third power attempted to "use Persian territory as a base of operation against Russia, Russia shall have the right to advance her troops into the Persian interior." Almost immediately the Soviet Union used this article not to withdraw its troop as long as remnants of the British army were still in Iran. It was also used as an excuse for invading Iran in September 1941, and at other times to object to Iran's security agreements with non-communist countries. Even though the treaty as a whole was beneficial to Iran, the realization was not lost on a number of deputies of the fifth Majless, which ratified it, that the old Anglo-Russian rivalry in Iran would continue with the only difference that Russia had a different tool to work with, namely communist ideology.

The Coup d'Etat

It could not be expected of Great Britain, which had been dealt such a great blow in the cancellation of the notorious 1919 agreement and which had sustained such a great loss of prestige, to sit on its hands and not do anything to recoup the losses. By the same token, no modern historian should be expected to do so when interpreting the events before the coup. Reading through the mass of material on the background of the coup is as confusing (and also fascinating) as reading half a dozen detective stories at the same time. Perhaps the view that Great Britain planned every move and controlled every event is an exaggeration, but it is equally unrealistic to think that Great Britain had given Iran up, especially when she knew about the Russo-Persian negotiations, and had let events take their course, come what may.[10] It is very reasonable to think, however, that having failed to have its own nationals in every department of Iran to safeguard British interests and to keep the Soviet Union at bay, the next best thing would be to create a strong central government which would be friendly toward Great Britain and fearful of Russia.

There is ample evidence that there was a good deal of talk about a coup d'etat in those days. The very influential deputy and cleric, Modarress, reported that Reza Khan had invited him to help put an end to this chaos because, said Reza Khan, "I'm afraid Iran will become Bolshevik."[11] Mr. Smart of the British Legation talked with Malek ol-Sho'ara Bahar, the prominent member of the liberal faction of the Majless, about the necessity of "creating a strong government." They agreed on this but, "in the choice of the individuals who carry this out, our taste did not coincide," says Bahar; "all my difficulty was in this matter. We agreed to talk again but afterwards it became clear that had there been further talks the opportunity [for the coup] would have been missed."[12]

There's also ample evidence that Sayyed Ziya o-Din Tabataba'i, one of the two actors in the coup d'etat, was a gifted young editor of Ra'd, "Thunder." It is agreed that this paper was consistently pro-British and supported the 1919 agreement. He was suspect among liberals and was a member of the *Poolad Anjoman*, which was originally founded by the British in Esfahan. There was a good deal of coming and going between Sayyed Zia and the members of the British Legation, during the days before the coup d'etat. On the very night of the coup d'etat, the shah and the prime minister heard that a Cossack contingent was approaching Tehran, and sent a party to Shahabad, a short distance from Tehran, in the middle of the night to see what they were up to. It is significant to note that the two representatives of the British Legation accompanied this party. The cat was finally let out of the bag, twenty years later, in World War II when the British information services issued the statement that, "it was the British who made possible Reza Shah's rise to power."[13]

To say that Sayyed Zia or Reza Khan was aided by Great Britain is not to conclude, as unfortunately many Persians do conclude, that they were traitors to the best interests of Iran. In the 20th century no country, even the superpowers, have complete independence of action. Most certainly in the chaotic years after the First World War Iran was not in a position to act independently. No one could have done anything without the aid of Great Britain or Russia or some other power. Sayyed Zia, in his lifelong pro-British attitude, was not any less of a nationalist than Bahar who, without being a communist, thought that cooperation with the Soviet Union was vital to Iran's interests.

The second main actor in the coup d'etat was Colonel Reza Khan, a man diametrically opposite to Sayyed Zia in background, education, temperament, and lifestyle. He was a man with little education who at the age of fifteen had joined the Cossack brigade and through his courage and initiative had risen to a position of command. His long association with Russian officers had turned him against them, and perhaps against all Russians. When the October revolution left the Russian officers of the Persian Cossacks stranded, it was Reza Kahn who wrested power from them. He was a nationalist but unlike Sayyed Zia, his lifelong military experience led him to think of the salvation of Iran in military terms. Because of his harsh experience under Russian commanders, he was generally anti-foreign and especially anti-Russian and certainly anti-Bolshevik.

Reza Khan in command of the Cossack forces fighting against Koochak Khan in Guilan had come in close proximity with the chaotic situation in the government and had been convinced that something must be done about it. It was evident that he needed a partner who knew his way around in politics, who could make speeches, and do many other things for which he himself was not as yet prepared. On the other hand, Sayyed Zia was rightly convinced that he would not be able to stage a coup without military support. In as much as they did not know each other, it is not at all surprising that the British Legation, who knew them both, put them in touch with each other and let them work out their plans. So far as we know, Sayyed Zia went to Reza's headquarters in Ghazvin twice, which was not enough for them to get to know each other, let alone plan a coup d'etat. This lack of planning became evident after they came to power.

The entrance of Zia and Reza at the head of some 2500 Cossacks into Tehran at the early hours of Sunday, February 21, 1921, was rather uneventful. A few machine gun and rifle shots were perhaps more for effect than necessity. Since there was no planning, the cabinet was not formed until the end of the week, with Zia as Prime Minister. Reza was given a new title, *Sardar-e Sepah*, commander in chief of the armed forces, but no cabinet post. The main activity during that week was the indiscriminate arresting of people from the ages of 14 to 80 and from known reactionaries to famous radicals. Even in this, there was no previous planning. Sometimes Reza would free a person whom Zia had ordered arrested and vice versa. For example, on Thursday of that week, Zia called the poet Bahar and asked him to be editor of the *Iran* newspaper. That same evening Reza arrested him, most likely because he was a known liberal.[14]

In any case the government of Sayyed Zia did not last more than three months. On April 25, 1921, Reza Khan became Minister of War in the cabinet while holding his command of the armed forces, and on May 24, Zia was forced to leave the country. The immediate issues were the taking over of gendarmes by the Minister of War and dismissing the British military advisor in the Cossack brigade, both of which were opposed by Zia. The difference between the two was wider than this. Reza Khan was a man of temperament and the power to carry out his purpose. On the other hand, Zia did not have the temperament and did not know how to gain power when he had the opportunity. In the words of Bahar, Zia "was not enough of a communist to kill everyone, not enough of a fascist to cooperate with the nobility, not decisive enough to silence the communists. He did not have a political party so that he could give positions of responsibility to fellow members and dismiss the rest. Neither was he a member of a tribe to be able to subdue others with its help. According to his own statement, he had not even planned ahead and did not have a hundred friends to count on to prevent Sardar-e Sepah from pulling the rug from under his feet in three months."[15]

As soon as Sayyed Zia was ousted, the prisoners were released and Ghavam o-Saltaneh, the brother of Vosoogh, became Prime Minister, and it seemed that the old order was back again. But there was a significant difference and that was the person and power of Reza Khan. In many ways, he was to the Persian Revolution what Napoleon was to the French Revolution. As a person who was definitely anti-Bolshevik and anti other radical ideas, he was the darling of the landed gentry until he began to liquidate some of them. As a leader who carried out some of the goals of the Revolution and limited the power of the clergy, he was acceptable to the liberals even though he was not using democratic methods. To the masses he was the God-sent deliverer because he used the reorganized army (no more called Cossacks) to subdue rebellion, to disarm the tribes, and to bring every corner of the country under the authority of the central government. His methods were ruthless, but the villages and roads were safe from brigands; and for the first time in a century, well-laden caravans could travel in all parts of the country without fear of molestation. All of this needed money, and thanks to oil and a reorganization of the country's finances, money was available. During Ghavam's premiership, Iran employed Dr. Arthur Millspaugh of the United States to be financial advisor. He and his party arrived in 1922 and served Iran for five years.

The Rise of Reza Khan

In October 1923, Reza Khan became Prime Minister. For the first time since the revolution, not only a military man was a Prime Minister, but all the provinces had military governors or men under the influence of the commanders of the area. The Fifth Majless was elected in a military dominated atmosphere. It proved to be a very important session and also the last Majless until 1942 in which deputies dared to speak their minds. Soon after Reza Khan became Prime Minster, Ahmad Shah, contrary to all advice, decided to go on another trip to Europe, a practice which had become endemic in the Ghajar family. Reza Khan faced the Fifth Majless in which there were three factions: reformers who approved of Reza Khan; socialists who approved of him but hoped to influence him in line with democracy; and the "minority," headed by the cleric Modarres who opposed Reza Khan. The rest were " independent."

Reza Khan, however, had prepared his strategy well. In a very short time, he had organized a strong army, had created a central authority, and had appeased the clergy, had gained control of the cabinet, and had manipulated the Majless. The climax of Reza Khan's popularity came when he established a central government's authority over the oil-producing province of Khoozestan. Shaykh Khaz'al was the semi-autonomous ruler of that province with special agreements with Great Britain. Reza Khan moved against him in spite of Great Britain's opposition. Shaykh Khaz'al surrendered unconditionally and Reza Khan had a triumphal entry back into Tehran.

It was after the triumphal entry that the talk of a republic got started. The newspapers began to criticize the shah as the whole Ghajar dynasty. On the whole, the supporters of a republic were liberals, moderates and the military. The clerics and their followers were against it. This was the time when Turkey had proclaimed a republic and had abolished the caliphate. Certainly, this influenced both the opponents and proponents of the idea for opposite reasons. The *Iranshahr*, a magazine which was published in Germany and was safe from censorship, in it's February 15, 1924 issue, discussed the idea and was all for it; but at the same time it doubted whether Iran was ready to "do anything with a republican form of government when we have not benefited from a constitutional monarchy." The movement for a republic had progressed so fast that the same magazine in it's March 22, 1924, issue thanked Reza Khan for bringing about a republic and devoted a good many pages to it and expressed a wish in a poem that, "As today Iran has been freed from having a king, tomorrow she may escape the evils of the clergy."

It was not only the clergy and the merchants of the bazaars who were against the republic, but the ultra liberals were also against it, mainly because it was led by a "dictator Cossack." The talented poet and dramatist, Eshghi, used to lampoon Reza Khan and his "synthetic republic" in his paper, *Twentieth Century*. Reza Khan was shrewd enough to see the handwriting on the wall. He had a hasty conference with the chief clergy in Ghome and issued a statement saying that he and the clergy had decided to ask the people "to stop mention of the republic and instead spend their energies helping me to ... strengthen the foundations of Eslam and the independence of the country."

The talk of a republic died down but not the criticism of Ahmad Shah. Even though the shah dismissed Reza Khan as Prime Minster, the Majless did not pay any attention to his request to nominate another person. On October 31, 1925, the Majless deposed the Ghajar dynasty and called for a constitutional assembly to choose a new king. Only four deputies had the courage to oppose the resolution. Not one of them defended the Ghajars, but they thought that such a move was against the constitution. In the light of future events, it is interesting to note that Dr. Mosaddegh argued that it was a shame to promote an active Prime Minister like Reza Khan to the inactive position of a shah. If, as shah, he became active, then he would be a dictator and if not, then the country would have lost an active Prime Minster. Of the four, Dr. Mosaddegh was under arrest and banishment until he was pardoned at the intercession of the new crown prince. The second one, Mirza Yahya Dolatabadi left public life, and Taghizadeh and Ala served the new Shah in important posts. The constitutional assembly met and amended the constitution on December 12, 1925, and proclaimed Reza Khan as Reza Shah Pahlavi.

The Pahlavi Reforms

Very much like Shah Abbas, Reza Shah was popular among the masses, mainly because he had brought them security. His ruthlessness was directed against the leaders of the tribes and nobles rather than the peasants. He was a nationalist reformer, who unlike Kemal Ataturk, did not have a philosophy to back it up and make it a continuous process. His lack of formal education made him impatient with philosophy and ideology and his personal temperament as a loner precluded any discussion of issues in a political party. He was more interested in the industrialization for the power of the state than for the good of the people; more in independence from foreign rule than for freedom of thought and initiative on the part of the people. He sent scores of students to Europe for study but would not allow them to express themselves when they returned. He was an indefatigable worker, and like Peter the Great of Russia, did not think that anyone could do anything as well as he. Even if he did not start that way, the constant nauseating flattery of newspapers, members of the Majless, and others made him think he was the paragon of knowledge and wisdom. Perhaps it was this rationalization that made him acquire so much land on the ground that he would develop the land for the good of the state. Either by instinct or osmosis, he had grasped the central message of western nationalism, namely that whatever is good for the state is good for the people, rather than the other way around.

There were great improvements, however, during the rule of Reza Shah. He built roads, constructed wireless service and took over the operation of the Telegraph Company from the British. In communication, his greatest achievement was the construction of the railroad from the Caspian Sea to the Persian Gulf. He was rightly proud of the fact that it had been financed by a special tax on sugar and tea with no foreign loans. He abolished extra territoriality, established a national bank, and took over from the British the privilege of issuing bank notes. He curbed the power of the clergy and took away the control of religious endowments from their hands. Eslamic laws were partially set aside and Eslamic education was abandoned in public schools. The Eslamic lunar calendar was replaced by the old and much more precise Persian Zoroastrian solar calendar with Persian names for the months of the year. He discouraged religious processions and passion plays in the month of Moharram, frowned upon the giving of the call to prayer and made it difficult for Moslems to go to Mecca.

He opened schools for men and women and inaugurated adult education. He abolished all titles and required that everyone should choose a family name. Like Ataturk, he forced Persian men to abandon their Persian hats and attire in favor of European ones and he made women abandon the veil. He established a Persian academy whose task it was to rid the Persian language of Arabic words. He built cement, sugar, and textile factories; he built state monopolies and subjected all commerce to a strict state control.

In the opinion of all nationalists, liberals or moderates, all of the above reforms were considered to be the *sine qua non* of Westernization. These had to be done in order for Iran to be a nation among nations. At the same time, it was evident that none of these would have been done, certainly not in this century, if force had not been used. This had been the greatest dilemma for all developing nations. In order to silence the critics of reform all criticism was banned and newspapers, one by one, went out of business and the handpicked members of the Majless eulogized the shah.

The creative enthusiasm that had been ignited during the revolution period died down during extreme censorship. Political criticism gave way to moralizing and social reform was concentrated on the position of women, which was the vogue of the day. Poets chose the conventional subjects of the bygone past and prose writers experimented with European style novels.

This was the period of founding of the University of Tehran, the first in modern times, and the importation of western music, architecture, and cinema. It was also the time when the increasing number of students returning home from abroad experienced that phenomenon that later came to be known as "culture shock."

Persian Oil

No history of Iran is complete without an account of oil, and the story of oil in Iran is replete with crises. By 1933 Reza Shah had virtually wiped out all the remnants of the old economic imperialism except the oil concession. He decided to challenge it for both nationalistic and economic reasons. This was the period of world economic depression and oil royalties had depreciated.

The presence of oil in the Middle East was long known. Noah's Ark was prepared for sailing by the use of pitch, and the Zoroastrians of Iran built their fire temples around ignited natural gas. In the infamous concession given to Baron de Reuter in 1872, oil was one of the items mentioned. William Knox D'Arcy, whose name has been immortalized in connection with Persian oil, was an Australian oil prospector. He heard about the possible presence of oil in Iran through his friend Sir Henry Drummond Wolff, the former British Minister in Iran. Wolff, in turn, had heard it from a Persian customs official by the name of Ketabchi Khan, who had read an article on the subject by a French archaeologist in Iran.

D'Arcy sent his representatives to Iran in 1901 and after receiving a favorable report applied for a concession from Mozaffar o-din Shah. The Ghajar shah would not do anything without permission from the Russians. With proper inducement, the grand vazir, Amin o-Soltan, told the British minister to write him a letter in Persian and describe the terms of the concession and he would then send a letter to the Russian Legation for comment. He then explained to the British Minister, no doubt with a wink, that he knew that the Persian interpreter of the Russian Legation was going to be away on vacation and the letter would not be read until his return. In the mean time he would tell the shah that no objection had been received from the Russian Legation. All this happened and the shah signed the concession.[16]

The term of the concession was for 60 years, after which all machinery, buildings, and installations were referred to Iran without compensation. The area of the concession was all of Iran except for five northern provinces. The Persian government was to receive 20,000 Pounds in paid up shares, plus an annual royalty of 16% of the net profit. The exploration of oil continued for seven long years without result. When they were about to abandon the whole project, oil was discovered near Masjed-e Soleyman on May 26, 1908. A year later the Anglo-Persian Oil Company was formed with a capital of two million Pounds. At this time the Persian Revolution was two years old. The members of the first Majless discussed the oil concession, but it is evident that the deputies were not aware of its importance.

In the same way that the British Legation had helped D'Arcy get the concession, it also helped the company to arrange with the Bakhtyari chieftains for the lease of the land and with Shaykh Khaz'al, who claimed jurisdiction over the area. At the beginning of the First World War, the British Navy started to use oil. In order to obtain it at a low price and to prevent other countries from having a share in the rich deposits, in May 1914, the British Admiralty bought enough shares in the company to become its controlling partner. Later the House of Commons approved the project, and the British government became the concessionaire instead of the Anglo-Persian Oil Company. From that date until the nationalization of Persian Oil in 1951, the British Navy bought oil from the company at a special price. It was never revealed what this price was, nor whether the Navy paid anything at all. Inasmuch as the Persians were never allowed to examine the books, it has remained a well-kept secret.

In keeping with the rivalry that existed between Great Britain and Russia over concessions, it was inevitable that Russia would clamor for a concession in the north. The Russo-Japanese war followed by the Russian Revolution of 1905 and the fact that it had a good deal of oil in Baku, prevented Russia from seeking a concession. In 1916 a Russian entrepreneur, A.M. Khoshtaria, got a concession from Vosoogh for oil in the north. The terms of the agreement were similar to D'Arcy's except that it was for seventy years. The most significant difference was the fact that for the concession to be valid it had to be ratified by the Majless. Majless never ratified it and the Persians considered the matter closed.

As stated before, during the long period of Anglo-Russian rivalry, a group of Persians had considered Persian salvation to depend upon the introduction of a third power into the scene. Ghavam, the successor of Sayyed Zia as Prime Minister, belonged to this school. He was instrumental in bringing the American financial Mission and he was also instrumental in trying to give a concession for the northern oil to the Americans. The Americans, of course, were very eager to have a concession.

An agreement was signed between the Persian government and the standard Oil Company on November 22, 1921. Both the Russians and the British protested. The Russians protested on the basis of Article 13 of the recently signed treaty, which stated that Iran should not consider concession, which they had given up. The British, however, objected on the grounds that they had bought the concession from Khohstaria and had organized the North Persia Oil Company. Iran's answer to both was the same, namely that Khoshtaria's concession was null and void because it had never been ratified by the Majless.

Great Britain had the upper hand not in logic, but in the right of way. The APOC had exclusive rights of oil transportation in the Persian Gulf area and would not allow anyone to pipe oil to any port on the Persian Gulf. Consequently, the Americans and the British formed a partnership for the northern oil with the Americans having the controlling vote. The Persians, however, did not agree to have the British in the north and the case was dropped.

The Majless, adamant about keeping the British out of the north, passed a law permitting the government to negotiate with "any independent and responsible American company." In 1923, the Sinclair Oil Company became interested in the project. Sinclair had the advantage over Standard in that it had extensive arrangements with the Soviet Union for the marketing of Baku oil and had the Russians' blessing in the Iran project. In March, 1924, the Majless ratified the Sinclair concession and the company's representative came to Tehran to sign the agreement. From then on, the story is stranger than fiction. A wing of the Majless was burnt, reportedly by arsonists. One of the numerous water fountains in Tehran was said to have performed a miracle and throngs of people, encouraged by the clergy, went there to see the place or be cured or both. In the midst of all this, Major Imbrie, the swashbuckling Vice Consul of the United States, decided to go and photograph the miracle- performing fountain. This he did at the instigation, and in the company of, an American employee of the Anglo Persian Oil Company and against the advice of American and Persian friends. He was murdered by the mob, but his companion was not harmed. At about the same time, thousands of miles away in the United States, Sinclair was involved in the Teapot Dome scandal. Somehow the news wires of the world and imaginative reporters put all these events together and made a very exciting international intrigue out of it.

The Persian government executed three of the ring leaders of the murder, paid $60,000 to Imbrie's widow, and $110,000 to the United States government for the expense of sending a battleship to take the body of the slain Vice Consul home. The American government promised to set aside a sum to use as a scholarship for Persians studying in the United States.

The question of the northern oil did not come up again until after the Second World War.

In the mean time, the profits of the Anglo Persian Oil Company were increasing in meteoric proportions. By 1933, the company was producing upwards of seventy million tons of crude oil and the large refinery in Abadan had a capacity of more than five million tons annually. In the course of years there were problems between the Persian government and the company, some of which were solved and the rest swept under the rug. Up until 1930 most of the administrative staff of the company were recruited from among the Englishmen who were in the service of their government in India. They brought with them their paternalistic and superior attitudes and dealt with the Persians as they had dealt with the Indians. Indeed, a good number of unskilled and semi-skilled laborers were from India. The accounts of the company were in Indian Rupees and the laborers were paid in that currency. The administration of the company was in the hands of people like "Sir Charles Greenway whose purpose was exploitation of the Persians and their oil and who tried, in every way possible, to make the maximum profit while giving only a minimum to Iran."[17]

With the rise of a nationalistic government in Iran under Reza Shah, it could not be expected that the old order would be allowed to continue. In 1928 the Shah and a large number of Persian officials went to Khoozestan for the opening of the main highway which had been constructed. The company invited him to visit the oil installations. He refused to go but sent a message to the president of the company through Mostafa Fateh in which he repeated more than once that, "Iran can not anymore endure that the huge profits of oil should go into the pocket of foreigners and Iran be deprived of it."[18] Mr. Fateh was for a long time the senior Persian officer in the APOC.

The warning was given and negotiations dragged on until 1931 when, because of the depression, the royalties decreased by a little over three million Pounds. Iran refused to receive the royalty and members of the Majless talked about revision of the D'Arcy agreement. On November 27, 1933, Taghizadeh, the Minister of Finance, informed the company that the Persian government considered the D'Arcy agreement null and void because it was signed prior to the establishment of a constitutional government. It also said that Iran was willing to negotiate a new agreement.

Great Britain appealed to the League Nations and World Court, but the matter was settled by the intervention of the Shah himself.

The impatience of the Shah, and the idea that only he could get things done made him take the matter out of the hands of four able Persians who were negotiating with the company. In 1949, Taghizadeh, one of the four members, in a long speech to the Majless, explained the situation and how the all- powerful Shah had silenced them and had brought the matter to a close by signing a new concession. The new agreement contained two advantages for Iran which proved to be superficial. One was a reduction of the area of the concession to only 100,000 square miles. The company had already gathered considerable geological data and knew in which area oil could be found and saw that these were within the area left to it. Secondly, the royalty was arranged in such a way as to guarantee a fixed income for Iran. This was good for times of depression, but in times of prosperity all that Iran got was 20% of dividends distributed to ordinary stockholders. On the other hand, the company gained tremendously by being exempt from paying taxes and by prolonging the duration of a concession to sixty years from 1933. These were tremendous losses for Iran.

Relations with Neighbors

In his struggle for independence from Russia and Great Britain, the Shah had to be friendly to Iran's neighbors, a number of whom were involved in a similar struggle. The closest neighbors of Iran, other than the Soviet Union and the British government in India, were Afghanestan, Iraq, and Turkey. The problems with Afghanestan centered around the waters of the Hirmand River and some minor border dispute. Both governments agreed in 1934 to accept the arbitration of a neutral power. The fact that this power was Turkey showed that a new era had dawned and Iran was not using the good offices of a European power. The arbitration was accepted even though Iran was not too pleased. The Hirmand River problem was solved by the signature of an agreement in 1938 which made it possible for both countries to use the waters for irrigation purposes.[19]

The problems with Iraq were more serious partly because of the proximity of oil lands and mostly because Iraq's treaty with Great Britain did not give her complete independence of action. The problems were, first, the problem of Kurdish people, second, the status of Persian citizens in Iraq, and third, the Shatt ol-Arab River. The latter was the most important problem between the two countries. It was the cause of eruption of the other two problems. The River formed the boundary between the two countries. Iran claimed that the boundaries should be the main channel, *Thalweg*, of the river while Iraq wanted its boundary to include the whole width of the river to the bank on the Persian side. The dispute in the end was "solved" by a compromise in 1937.

Both Turkey and Iran had changed enough to see the futility of the Preso-Ottoman wars. These two antagonists, who had fought each other as equals, had respect for each other in peace. The first conclusive boundary treaty was signed on January 23, 1932, and ended centuries of dispute. At the same time a treaty of friendship was signed. Reza Shah paid a state visit to Turkey in 1934 and laid the foundation for expansion of economic ties.

The crowning achievement of Reza Shah in Iran's policy with its neighbors was the Sa'dabad pact on July 8, 1937. It was a non-aggression agreement among Afghanestan, Iran, Iraq, and Turkey. For the first time in modern times these countries arrived at a pact without European tutelage.

Reza Shah and Germany

The rise of Hitler and his anti-communism appealed to Reza Shah. In Germany, he saw an effective third power to free Iran from the Anglo-Russian domination. Commercially and culturally relations with the Third Reich increased by the month. To make his administration more effective, Reza Shah brought advisors from Germany. A council for the "Nurture of Thought," *Parvaresh-e Afkar*, was formed, and when the students were not marching or singing martial songs, they were listening to speeches on 'God, Shah, and Country.'

When the Second World War started, Iran declared its neutrality. But the declaration was no more effective then than it had been during the First World War. When Germany attacked Russia, Iran became the only route to which lend-lease material could be sent to the Soviet Union. Furthermore, there were score of Germans in Iran in the vast commercial and cultural activities which had been going on for some time. It was assumed that a large number, if not all, of these were political agents. The allies demanded that Iran expel the Germans. But the Shah procrastinated. Many theories have been advanced as to why the Shah did not acquiesce to the demands. Some blame the Shah himself; other accuse his counselors; still others blame the Germans; and Mohammad Reza Shah Pahlavi, his son, blames the Allies. Yet, one must add to the above theories the fact that Reza

Shah was anti-Russian; and there were few men in 1941 who did not think that the Germans were going to win. A man in Reza Shah's position would procrastinate or await the results. It is also likely that the Russians and the British did not want him around because they knew they could not work with him.

The British and the Russians attacked Iran simultaneously at dawn on August 24, 1941. By August 27, the Persian military strength had been dissipated. The Prime Minister resigned and the new premier, the veteran Mohammad Forooghi accepted the allied terms. Reza Shah abdicated in favor of his son, Mohammad Reza, and was taken under British custody to the island of Mauritius. Later he was transformed to Johannesburg, where he died on July 26, 1944.

ENDNOTES

1. For an interesting account of German espionage, see Avery, *Modern Iran*, pp.191-93; also Christopher Sykes, *Wasmuss, the German Lawrence* (London: Longmans, 1936)

2. See Movarrekh ol-Doleh Sepehr, *Iran dar Jang-e Bozorg (Iran in the Great War, 1914-1918)* (Tehran: Bank-e Melli Press, 1957). The author was the Persian secretary in the German Legation and was actively involved.

3. Bahar, *Political Parties*, p.27.

4. Sepehr Zabih, *The Communist Movement in Iran* (Berkeley: University of California Press, 1966), p.13.

5. See George Lenczowski, *Russia and the West in Iran, 1918-1948* (Ithaca: Cornell University Press, 1949), pp. 59-60.

6. Joseph Upton, *History of Modern Iran, an Interpretation* (Cambridge University Press 1961), p.41.

7. Avery, *Modern Iran*, pp.204-5.

8. Bahar, *Political Parties*, pp.36-38.

9. Roohollah Ramezani, *The Foreign Policy of Iran, 1500-1941* (Char-lottesville: University of Virginia Press, 1966), p.167.

10. Cf. Avery, *Modern Iran* pp.226-31.

11. Bahar, *Political Parties*, p.61.

12. Ibid., p.63.

13. Avery, *Modern Iran*, p.20.

14. Bahar, *Political Parties*, p.90.

15. Ibid. p.94.

16. Mostafa Fateh, *Panjah Sal Naft* (Fifty Years of Oil) (Tehran: Chehr Press, 1956).

17. Ibid., pp.279-80.

18. Ibid., p.286.

19. Ramezani, Foreign Policy of Iran, pp.206-9.

CHAPTER NINE

THE STRUGGLE FOR POWER

Reza Shah's abdication and his departure from Iran let loose the pent up feelings of the whole nation. People in all walks of life started doing what they were not supposed to and gave up what they had been doing, just because they were tired of acting or not acting at the command of one person. For twenty years, the whole nation had been gradually forced to think, to speak, and to wear that which had been decreed. Now that the source of power had disintegrated, the people reacted and went all the way back to what had been.

Newspapers that had been suppressed started publishing as though nothing had happened. The members of the Majless, the same handpicked eulogists of his ex-majesty, started abusing him and putting all the blame on him. They started wrangling among themselves and acted as though the people had elected them. Even the Allies were not immune from this. The Russians occupied the north and the British the south, as they had done before the First World War, and they both rushed their troops to Tehran. To ease the sting of "occupation" Great Britain and Russia concluded a Tripartite Treaty with Iran on January 29, 1942, stating that the presence of their troops in the country did not constitute occupation. They also agreed to evacuate their troops from Iran within six months after the end of the hostilities.

The Persians, who were rightly afraid of the resumption of the old Anglo- Russian rivalry in Iran, rejoiced when American service troops came to Iran in great numbers to facilitate the transportation of lend-lease material. The constant interference of Great Britain and Russia in the internal affairs of Iran reminded the Persians of old days. The Persians, therefore, were happy for a third power to come in, and proposed an agreement with the United States along the lines of the Tripartite Treaty. Unfortunately, the Americans refused and preferred to come into Iran on the coattails, so to speak, of Great Britain. Later events proved this to be a mistake, for the Persians came to identify the Americans with the British, which justifiably or not, was not meant to be a compliment. Throughout the war one could read in the newspapers and hear in conversations the statement "The Allies and Russia," always lumping the United States and Great Britain and separating the two from Russia. In a short time all the real and imaginary sins of Great Britain was transferred to the United States.

Great Britain and Russia, who were fighting the war for democracy and freedom, missed their opportunity to help the Persians create such a government. They could not very well suppress the mushrooming press and the feverish activity in the formation of political parties. The affairs of government remained in old hands, for the Allies were more interested in winning the war than in establishing democracy and preferred to do business with the known and tried older men than with the hotheaded young nationalists who were clamoring to be heeded.

Once again, Ahmad Ghavam became Prime Minister. He, it will be remembered, was a believer in the concept of introducing a third power in the affairs of Iran. It was he who, as Prime Minister, twenty years earlier, had arranged for employing an American financial mission headed by Dr. Millspaugh. So, he started where he had left off, and asked the same Dr. Millspaugh to come again in 1943 and resume his old position. Millspaugh also acted as though nothing had happened in Iran during the 16 years that he had been absent, and got himself into all sorts of difficulties. He was forced to resign in 1945 and came home to write his memoirs.

The younger men, however, would not be denied. During the twenty years of the Pahlavi era, a new generation of Persians had gone through a significant social change. Education at home and abroad, construction of railroads, and industrialization under Reza Shah had created a middle class that had provided the entrepreneurs and contractors of the new era. They were slowly replacing the bazaar in trade and were represented in the army and in many new institutions created by Reza Shah. The industrialization, limited though it was, had created a new labor force which had reached the unprecedented figure of over half a million in 1942.[1] The old titles had been abolished and a number of title holders had left public office. Some of their sons, and a larger number of the sons of people who did not belong to the nobility, A'yan, came back from Europe with the new title of Doctor and *Mohandes* 'Engineer', and expected to determine the destiny of the country.

The Toodeh Party

All of these were involved in feverish political activity. They organized political parties and received permits to publish two or three newspapers so that if one was suppressed they could publish another one. Most of these political parties did not have a national base, but represented either interest groups or personal ambition. The one glaring exception was the Toodeh party, which was organized by some of the 53 young men who had been tried on the charge of communist activity. Their leader, Dr. Erani, had died in prison and the rest were freed after the abdication of Reza Shah. They formed the *Toodeh 'Masses'*, which became, by far, the best-organized political party in the country.

The Toodeh was admittedly Marxist, but either because of the presence or the number of nationalists in the group, or because of the realities of Soviet diplomacy, they claimed that they were not communists, thereby minimizing their dependence upon the Soviet Union. They were organized along communist lines with the central executive committee, a platform of labor legislation, social insurance, trade unionism, free education, distribution of land, rights of minorities, disarmament of tribes, and the like. At no time did they ask for the nationalization of property. They had cells, *Hozeh,* among workers, women, peasants, and students, and a branch in every section of the country. They were strongest in the north that was occupied by the Soviet forces. They edited a number of newspapers, held conferences, mass meetings, and were able to organize the workers in the textile mills of Esfahan and the oil fields in the south. Their slogan was "Bread, Health and Education for all."

Meanwhile, the presence of the thousands of foreign troops handling war supplies to Russia necessitated more currency than the country had. According to Mohammad Reza Shah, the Allies forced the Persian government to print large amounts of currency.[2] This, coupled with the fact that there was very little import, created a rocketing inflation. Contractors and entrepreneurs supplying the Allies with their needs became wealthy. Land prices and house rentals went up, and it got so that shopkeepers and grocers would hoard their goods to sell them to foreigners at prices which the Persians could not afford. Furthermore, the Persian army, following the attack by Great Britain and Russia, had become so disorganized that when thousands of soldiers were discharged no one apparently thought of collecting the weapons. These were either sold to the tribes, who rose against the central government, or were used by the ex-soldiers to pillage the countryside. Added to all this, the poor crops caused near famine, and Persians, even in Tehran, had to stand in long lines to buy bread. It is quite evident that under such circumstances, the program of change and reform put forward by the Toodeh Party would have great appeal. In the election of 1943, they won eight seats from the north.

The National Will Party

The British, who were alarmed at the rapid growth of the pro-Soviet Toodeh Party, countered with moves of their own. In addition to the landed gentry, one of the most conservative groups was the clergy, who Reza Shah had pushed to the background and who were becoming prominent after his abdication. Based on the naive belief that religion, especially organized, will stop communism the British encouraged the Shi'i clergy. Travel abroad, which was hard to come by in war times, was open to thousands of Persian pilgrims to Mecca. Ayatollah Ghomi who had been exiled by Reza Shah, came back and was welcomed by Premier Soheyli. The theological school connected with Sepahsalr Mosque became a faculty of the Tehran University, and the government radio started its daily broadcasts with recitations from the Ghora'n. The clergy were against communism, but they were also against westernization, which meant that they were against most of the reforms approved by the majority of the noncommunist educated class.[3] The Society for the Propagation of Eslam was formed with branches in different cities of the country, and through the publication of magazines and books it tried to inculcate the tenets of Eslam. This group continued its work until 1953 and then gradually went out of the picture. It is revealing of the nature of their emphasis to note that of all their publications only one dealt with the problem of science and religion.[4]

Another important anti-Communist activity was built around the person of Sayyed (pronounced *say yed*) Ziya Tabataba'i, the co-leader of the coup d'etat of 1921. He came back from his exile in Palestine wearing a hat that was similar to the one that he had worn when he left Iran. He was elected to the Majless in 1943 and a year later he organized a right wing, pro-British, and anti-Communist party called *Eradeh-ye Melli*, 'National Will'.

It is interesting to note that the National Will had an organization similar to the Toodeh. Its cells were called *Halgheh,* circle, and were composed of nine men and a chief. Every nine circles formed a "Little Parliament," which sent its representatives to the national meeting, which was called the "Great Parliament." Zia himself headed its executive committee and the magnificence of the Party headquarters came to indicate that money was not one of its problems. The platform of the party dealt with justice, health, division of state domains, industrialization, and so forth. The special policies advocated by the party were "strong defenses of the political and economic independence of Iran; friendly treatment of the tribes, defense of Eslam, introduction of religious teaching into the school program, and a foreign policy of eternal neutrality for Iran, following the Swiss pattern"[5]

While it is true that the Soviet Union and Great Britain supported the Toodeh and the National Will parties respectively, it would be grossly misleading to think that these parties existed because of outside support. Each one represented the needs, ambitions, and interests of certain segments of the population within the country. The National Will had the support of elements from the clergy, bazaar merchants, landlords, and the tribes, while the Toodeh had the support of elements from labor, intelligencia, white collar workers, professionals, and students. Of course, there were people from every one of the above segments who were independent nationalists and afraid of the domination by the Soviet Union or Great Britain. The young Shah was against the Toodeh Party, but it cannot be said that he was altogether with the National Will or they with him. The bulk of the army was loyal to the Shah. On the whole, it can be said that most of the political parties considered the Shah's position above political wrangling and did not take him into account.

The Northern Oil

By 1945 the two parties were at each other with hammers and tongs. At one time or another the Toodeh party had an aggregate of 39 newspapers disseminating its message while the National Will had over 27. The rivalry between these two parties had all the earmarks of developing into a genuine two party system divided among ideological, social, and economic lines. But 1945 was also the year in which the war ended; and the Soviet Union refused to evacuate Iran on March 2, 1946, the date set by the Allies. It was also in 1945 that a group of communists launched a separatist movement in Azarbaijan and the Kords (Kurds) demanded autonomy. All of these events are related to each other and to the fact that the Soviet Union wanted a concession for the exploitation of oil in the northern provinces. So did the United States, but in all the confusion that ensued the American desire was forgotten and the attention of the world together with the anxiety of the Persians were directed to the Irano-Soviet relations of 1946.

While the war was still raging in 1944, some British but principally American companies had been talking with the Persian government about oil concessions in the north. When Premier Sa'ed reported this to the Majless in August 1944, there were expressions of caution and opposition on the part of some deputies. In September, however, Sergei Kavtaradze, the Assistant People's Commissar for Foreign Affairs of the Soviet Union, came to Iran at the head of a delegation and asked for concession of northern oil. The result of the negotiation was the announcement of the Persian government to the effect that no oil concessions would be given to any country until after the war. This brought a direct attack on the government by the Soviet representative. The Toodeh party, which had opposed the giving of concessions to anyone, came out in favor of a concession to the Soviet Union. It organized demonstrations in Tehran and some northern cities and caused Sa'ed to resign. It was during this tense period that Dr. Mohammad Mosaddegh, a leading independent deputy, offered a bill which made it a criminal act on the part of any government or minister to negotiate or grant oil concession to any foreign government without the previous permission of the Majless. The Soviet official went home with another harsh statement, but the matter was closed for the time being.

The Azarbaijan Affair

When World War II was over and the British and American groups prepared to withdraw from Iran by March 2, 1946, it became increasingly clear that the Soviet Union did not have any intention of doing so. Iran, like many countries of the world, has and does still have its regional problems. The problem facing Iran is somewhat more acute, partly because in some of these regions some of the people speak in a different dialect, and partly because the central government has not usually been attentive to their needs. This regional interest began to cause a rift in the ranks of the Toodeh party toward the end of summer of 1945.

More of an activist than a theoretician, and more of a provincial than a Persian nationalist, Ja'far Pishehvari, started agitating for a separate

Azarbaijan. He had been active in the establishment of the Guilan Autonomous Republic of 1920 and had lived in exile during Reza Shah's period. He asked that the people of Azarbaijan live within the constitutional democracy of Iran but with the right of self-government. He also demanded that Azari-Turkish be the official language of the province in order to "develop our national culture and education." By December 1945, the Toodeh party of Azarbaijan had been replaced by a new party, called "Demokrat," which deposed the governor of Azarbaijan and took matters into its own hands.

When a contingent of the Persian Army was sent to Azarbaijan to deal with the insurrection, it was stopped by the Red Army from advancing into the province. In February 1946, Ghazi Mohammad was declared the President of the People's Republic of Kordestan. Soon the two autonomous regions signed a treaty of alliance and mutual defense. All of this shook the Central Committee of the Toodeh party as well as the rest of the nation. Khalil Maleki, the brilliant theoretician of the party proposed a resolution refusing to recognize the new party. The Soviet embassy, however, intervened and the Toodeh was made to congratulate the Demokrat Party.[6] Later on, Maleki repudiated Toodeh's subservience to Moscow and formed a socialist party called the Third Force.

For a while there was the unusual phenomenon of two communist parties in Iran, the Toodeh and the Demokrat, not counting the "Peoples Republic of Kordestan." In a penetrating article Mr. Abrahamian describes that these two parties " were separated from each other by contrasting social bases, conflicting interests, and at times, crashing interests."[7] The leaders of the Toodeh were intellectuals believing in class struggle while organizers of the Demokrat were activists believing in communalism. The fact remains, however, that both of these parties were manipulated by the Soviet Union for its own end. In 1946 the Red Army was the only foreign force in Iran. It was effectively protecting the two insurrectionist provinces, and it had another party with members in the Majless to do its bidding. The Soviet Union felt that Iran did not have any other recourse but to comply with its demands.

In January 1946 the Cabinet had changed and, once more, Ghavam was the Prime Minister. A week before his appointment on January 19, Iran had formally requested the Security Council of the United Nations to stop the Soviet Union interference in the internal affairs of Iran. This was the first important case presented to the fledgling organization and all it did was to ask the opposing parties to negotiate and report the result. It was evident that the United Nations could not do very much in a dispute where a strong power was involved. Nevertheless, Iran's case got world publicity and in the early days after the war the Soviet Union was more sensitive to world opinion.

The new Prime Minister went to Moscow in March and in his talks with Stalin he realized the Soviet Union was after oil. He told the Russians that he could not do anything as long as the Red Army was in Iran. He returned home empty- handed, but negotiations dragged on both in Tehran and in the Security Council. On April 4, 1946, a draft agreement was signed between Iran and the Soviet Union. According to this, the Red Army agreed to evacuate Iran by May 9th, and in return Iran agreed to the formation to an Irano-Soviet Oil Company for the exploitation of oil in the northern provinces of Iran. The term was to be for 25 years and Iran was to receive 51% of the profit.[8] It also recognized the Azarbaijan incident to be an internal affair, and Iran promised to solve it peacefully "with due consideration for the legitimate grievances of the people."[9] The Oil Concession, however, to be legal had to be ratified by the fifteenth Majless, which was yet to be elected.

Ghavam instructed Ambassador Hossain Ala in Washington to withdraw Iran's case from the security counsel. This able and sincere nationalist, feeling that Ghavam had perhaps sold out to the Russians, refused to comply and kept Iran's case on the agenda. This brought upon his head the wrath of the Toodeh and Azarbaijan Demokrat parties who were rejoicing at the success of their cause. Both were at the peak of their power. The Toodeh party was raising its argument on what was later called "positive neutrality"; that is since Iran has given the oil concession to the British in the south, it could give one to the Russians in the north. Indeed, the Toodeh party went a step farther and claimed that the entire northern region of Iran was essential to the security of the Soviet Union. This sounded very much like the proletarian version of the old capitalistic "sphere of influence." To this the Toodeh deputy in the Majless had the oft-repeated answer: "The Soviet government can not and will not advocate colonialism, for Russia is a classless society where no exploitation of many by man or by state takes place. Such a society is incapable of pursuing colonial policies. We should know our neighbor in order to formulate a correct policy towards its government."[10] In a few months he had occasion to know the neighbor better and would find out that a kick in the back does not hurt any less when it was delivered by a worker rather than by a capitalist.

The Ghavam government recognized the Azarbaijan regime, and on June 13, 1946, signed an agreement to this effect accepting a number of items on their platform. In May, the Red Army evacuated Iran and later Ghavam formed a coalition Cabinet in which he invited three Toodeh members to participate. Then, in preparation for the election, he formed a new political party called Iran-e Demokrat, which turned out to be a coalition of all political parties including the Toodeh. It had an extensive organization and a uniform "Guard of National Salvation." For good measure, he arrested the anti-Communist Sayyed Zia and disbanded the National Will Party. In December 1946, the Persian Army took possession of Azarbaijan and Kordestan and severely punished the Communist rebels. Pishevari and some of the leaders of the movement escaped to Russia. The Soviet Union, whose declared policy was to help all "national liberation movements" in all parts of the world, betrayed the one which it had helped organize and abandoned the movement for the sake of the oil concession.

The fifteenth Majless was opened in August of 1947. Ghavam was still Premier and his party had the majority. He presented the Irano-Soviet Oil Agreement for ratification, and on October 22, 1947 the Majless defeated it only with two dissenting votes. Ghavam resigned, his party was disbanded, and the Toodeh Party was discredited. In the absence of further evidence, it is difficult to evaluate the role of Ghavam in this affair. It is possible to say that he was clever enough to beat Stalin at his own game and save the province of Azarbaijan from becoming part of the Soviet Republic of Azarbaijan. It is also possible to think that Ghavam did not believe that the oil concession in the north would be determined to the interests of Iran and that it would be a cheap price to pay for saving Azarbaijan. An Irano-Soviet Fisheries Company had been in operation for quite some time, and it had not threatened the independence of Iran.

Mosaddegh and Oil Nationalization

The nationalization of oil, which drained the Persians economically and emotionally, must be understood in the context of the time in which it occurred. The vast expansion of the oil industry after the war had made a revision of the Anglo-Iranian Oil Agreement necessary. Furthermore, the success of the Seven-Year development plan depended upon oil royalties. Added to these was the emotional involvement of the Persians in the recent Azarbaijan crisis and the defeat of the Irano-Soviet Oil Concession. Lack of sensitivity on the part of the British to the changing situation in Iran contributed to the intensity of the crisis. It was hard for Great Britain to accept its reduced position in the world scene. Great Britain was getting a bad press in Iran, so much that "a British agreement to indemnify Iran with over 5 million Sterling Pounds for use of the railways during the war and a gift in July 1949 of two frigates to the Persian Navy did not have the effect of reducing anti- British feeling."[11]

The picture will not be complete without mentioning that in the new Majless, which convened in 1950, eight of its members had formed a coalition by the name of National Front. It was basically a union of the liberal nationalists and the clergy. What appeared to be the common denominator was their goal to uproot the last vestige of economic imperialism, namely the Anglo- Iranian Oil Company. Imperialism to the liberal nationalists meant specifically Russian or British. In their minds the United States and other foreign countries had not been contaminated with the evils of imperialism so far as Iran was concerned. Imperialism, however, to the Shi'i clergy meant all foreign influence and domination. As Ayatollah Kashani, the clerical member of National Front said, "Eslam warns its adherents not to submit to foreign yoke". [12] This yoke embodied not only political and economic exploitation but all types of westernization dear to the heart of the liberal nationalists. It was precisely the same goal that had brought the two groups together in 1905 and precisely the same disagreement in interpretation that had pulled them apart. The National Front did disintegrate within two years, but at the moment they were joined together under the leadership of Dr. Mohammad Mosaddegh, a distinguished lawyer, a man who had a reputation for honesty and patriotism.

The story of the nationalism of oil is too long, complicated, and controversial to be related here. It seems that throughout the controversy solutions were advanced a little too late, with the results that the provisions of solutions were not considered to be enough. In 1949, while all negotiations were in progress, the Shah went to the United States hoping to get help for the seven-year plan, but he returned home empty-handed.

The oil negotiation, which had resulted in a tentative agreement called the Supplemental Oil Agreement (also referred to as "Gass-Golshayan"), was not in time for the Fifteenth Majless. The Sixteenth Majless, which after some difficulties came into being, was dominated by the small band of the National Front. The Supplemental Oil Agreement was sent to a committee headed by Dr. Mosaddegh for study and recommendation. In the mean time, the Shah, in continuation of his reform policies, appointed the enlightened young General Razmara as Prime Minister in June 1950. Throughout the rest of that year Razmara reorganized the administration by replacing the officials who were either inept or had a reputation for corruption with younger men. The Soviet Union arranged a $20 million trade agreement with Iran, but the response of the United States was a $25 million loan from the Export-Import Bank.

The National Front members first began to talk about the nationalization of the oil industry, a concept which had been popular in those days by the programs of nationalization carried out in Great Britain. Lack of sensitivity on the part of the British and lack of response on the part of the United States lead the National Front to say that it was beneath the dignity of the nation to send its King begging when it had all the required money for the Seven-Year Plan in oil revenues. This fell on receptive ears in the Majless and outside. The Oil Committee headed by Mosaddegh rejected the Supplementary Oil Agreement and espoused the principle of "negative neutralism." This was in belated response to the Toodeh party's "positive neutralism," which argued that since Iran had given an oil concession to Great Britain, it should give one to the Soviet Union. The National Front's "negative neutralism" reasoned that since Iran had refused to give an oil concession to the Soviet Union, it should take it away from Great Britain.

After the rejection of the Supplementary Oil Agreement, negotiation had started again but was not getting anywhere. It was announced in January that the Arabian American Oil Company had offered the Saudi Arabian government a 50-50 profit-sharing plan. The news strengthened the hands of the National Front. By the time the AIOC consented to do as the Americans had done, it was too late. Prime Minister Razmara, who had expressed himself against the practicality of nationalism, was assassinated in Sepahsalar Mosque by a member of the Devotees of Eslam. It was reported that a religious Fatva, issued by Kashani encouraged the murderer in the act. The assassin stated, "If I have rendered a humble service, it was for the Almighty in order to deliver the deprived Moslem people of Iran from a foreign serfdom. My only desire is to follow the doctrine of Ghor'an." The fact that Majless voted to exonerate the assassin gives credence to the involvement of Kashani in the affair.[13]

On March 15, 1951, a week after the murder of Razmara, the Majless passed a nine-point enabling law nationalizing the oil industry. Hossain Ala, who was in charge of the government after the assassination, supported nationalism and replied to the protest of Great Britain that this was an internal matter and that the British government had no right to interfere. Events occurred swiftly from then on. On April 15 the British closed the Abadan oil refinery and on April 28, Mosaddegh became Prime Minister. There was wild enthusiasm in Iran, consternation in England, and disbelief in the rest of the world. There were charges and counter-charges. From the British point of view Iran did not have the right to act unilaterally, while the Persians thought that the principles of nationalism superseded any prior agreement. The British accepted the principle of nationalism but thought that the appropriation of the company was against the 1933 agreement. The Persians, on the other hand, said that since they had provided in the nine-point law the payment of compensation to the company, the question of appropriation was not involved. They had done to the oil company what the British government had done to the steel industry in Great Britain. Perhaps the most important question was Iran's contention that this was an internal affair between the Persian government and a company and not the business of the British government to interfere.

Great Britain took the case to United Nations and Dr. Mosaddegh represented Iran's case. The Security Council referred the question to the World Court and the Court decided in favor of Iran, stating that the problem was an internal question and outside the jurisdiction of the World Court or of the United Nations.

This, however, did not solve the problem. Several alternative proposals were advanced and even though all of them accepted the principle of nationalization, they failed to bring about a solution. Great Britain overreacted and, for a time, forgot that this was not the nineteenth century. Neither they nor the other western countries understood the depth of the feelings of the population in this matter. The Persians had an opportunity to show their support in the tobacco protest of 1890, the constitutional movement of 1905, the crisis of the dismissal of Morgan Shuster in 1911, the change of destiny in 1924, and the oil nationalization of 1951. Without doubt the popular support for nationalization was broader and deeper than any of the rest. The British reaction was gunboat diplomacy when they sent the cruiser *"Mauritius"* to the Persian Gulf, when they froze Persian assets, when they seized a few tankers taking Persian oil, and when they persuaded the United States to withhold aid to Iran. Furthermore, Great Britain looked at the company as a purely business venture. In all the plans that they submitted, they not only wanted compensation for the assets of the company, which the Persians acknowledged, but they wanted payment for all profits they would have made until 1993. Also the British sincerely felt that they had done Persians a great service by developing the oil industry and did not understand why the Persians were not appreciative. The fact that their huge profits in some years reached 150 percent did not matter. What was important in their minds was that the Persians would not have had any oil income at all were it not for the British effort.

On the other hand, the Persians could not forget that they were refused the inspection of the company books; that the company was not replacing foreign technicians with Persians fast enough; and that the company was not willing to give them a larger share of the profits. But what made the reaching of any solution difficult was the fact that Dr. Mosaddegh and his advisors looked at the nationalization of oil with romantic nationalism mixed with a great deal of naiveté. He apparently felt that all he had to do was to nationalize the oil and customers would flock to buy the Persian oil. The fact that Iran didn't have a single oil tanker did not bother him. He should have known that European countries that were buying Persian oil would tap the vast oil resources of Kuwait and Saudi Arabia. He was too much of a romanticist to think that the Arab countries would refuse to help a brother Moslem nation against the Christians of the West. Egypt gave Dr. Mosaddegh a rousing welcome when he stopped there on his return from the United Nations, but Egypt had no oil. An excellent description of the oil industry in the world was prepared for Dr. Mosaddegh and he was shown several charts explaining the inter-relatedness of the large oil companies of Europe and United States and the control they exercised on shipping and marketing. Even if Great Britain had not challenged nationalization, Iran had to depend upon the major companies to market the oil .

At the base of Dr. Mosaddegh's inability or unwillingness to reach an agreement were at least two factors. The first was his personal hatred of the British, which he allowed to cloud his judgment. Among all the proposals made, perhaps the plan presented by the World Bank was the best. It adhered to all the points of the nationalization law but Mosaddegh rejected it because the Ward Bank, as a neutral world organization, wanted the freedom to employ British personnel in its operation.

The other factor was the fact that Dr. Mosaddegh was not a revolutionary. To him the nationalization of the oil industry was an end and not just the means to carry on the reforms. He was reluctant to inaugurate internal reforms for fear of offending the other members of the coalition. Professor Cottam believes that the great mistake of Mosaddegh was that he did not comprehend "that immensity of his popular support gave him a freedom of action that no Iranian statesman had ever enjoyed."[14] Nevertheless, Dr. Mosaddegh's name will go down in history as the charismatic leader who, in spite of the fact that he did not offer a constructive program, moved the Persians to the depth. During the two years of Mosaddegh's regime, the Persians were cooperative, their officials were less corrupt, and they took more interest in the affairs of the nation because they believed a new day had dawned.

As the crisis dragged on, the internal situation worsened, and disagreement developed among the members of the National Front. The election of the Seventeenth Majless was freer than many elections held before, and therein lay Mosaddegh's difficulties. The members refused to go along with him. He demanded more power and as more and more of his friends left him, he had to rely upon the underground Toodeh Party for support. His communication with the Shah, which was not too good, broke altogether. On August 13, 1953 the Shah dismissed Mosaddegh, and appointed General Fazlollah Zahedi, but Mosaddegh had the officer who had brought the message arrested. Three days later the Shah fled Iran. On August 22, following a successful coup d'etat engineered by the U.S. Central Intelligence Agency the Shah returned to Iran. The Shah himself tactfully admits this engineered plan when he says "I do not deny that payments could in some cases conceivably have been made But it takes much more than money to impel people to do what Iran's loyal citizens did during those days."[15]

The fact that almost immediately President Eisenhower put $25 million at the disposal of the penniless government, an aid he had refused to Mosaddegh, shows that the United States was pleased at the latter's fall.

The Shah returned to Iran with a new resolve. For 12 years he had reigned; now he wanted to rule. From that time on the political, economic, social, educational, and cultural life of Iran became closely connected with the person of the Shah. Iran faced grave problems. One of them was economic, the other was international; but the most important of them was the alienation of the educated youth and the resentment they felt against the United States for intervening in Iran's internal affairs.

The Post-Mosaddegh Era and Economic Recovery

One of the most important steps for the economic recovery was the solution of the oil controversy. Agreement was reached and passed by the Majless on October 21, 1954. It accepted the principle of nationalization and recognized the National Iranian Oil Company. A consortium was formed to operate the oil fields and the refinery in Abadan. There were eight companies in the consortium. The Anglo-Iranian Oil Company, whose name was changed to British Petroleum, held 40% of the shares; five major American companies held 35% while nine minor American Companies held 5%; the Dutch Bataafse Petroleum Maatschappij N.V. held 14%; and Compagnie Francaise des Petroles held the remaining 6%. The consortium was incorporated in the Netherlands but its permanent headquarters was in Iran. The president of the consortium was Dutch.

It was arranged that Iran pay the former AIOC the sum of $25 million in ten years without interest. In addition, the other members of the consortium agreed to pay the British company 10% per barrel of crude oil and other products exported from Iran until $510 million had been paid. The British company did not lose much, but for the Persians the agreement was not as good as some of the plans Dr. Mosaddegh had rejected. In later years the National Oil Company made separate agreements with other companies.

The second means of economic reform was planning. The first Seven-Year Plan was a complete failure, mostly because of the oil crisis. A second Seven-Year Plan was started in September 1955. As part of the plan, an economic bureau was formed made up of well-trained Persians supported by foreign advisors. Its job was to study the program of the Plan Organization and make recommendations.

The third means of economic recovery was Point Four Program which was first mentioned in President Truman's inaugural address on January 20, 1949, and implemented in Iran in 1952.

ENDNOTES

1. Zabih, Communist Movement, p.72.

2. Mission for my country, p.76.

3. George Lenczowski, *Russia and the West in Iran*, 1918-1948 (Ithaca: Cornell University Press, 1948), pp.239-42

4. For details see Yahya Armajani's "Eslamic Literature in Post War Iran," in R.B. Winder and James Kritzeck, eds., The Word of Eslam (New York): St. Martins Press, 1960).

5. Lenczowski, *Russia and the West*, p.244.

6. Ervand Abrahamian "Communism and Communalism in Iran, "*International Journal of Middle East Studies*, 1, no.4, p.311.

7. Ibid., p.316.

8. Lenczowski, Russia and the West, p.300.

9. Zabih, *Communist Movement*, p.108.

10. Ibid., p.93.

11. Avery, *Modern Iran*, p. 413.

12. Quoted by R. W. Cottam, *Nationalism in Iran* (Pittsburgh University Press, 1964), p. 152.

13. Ibid., p. 150 ff.

14. Cottam, *Nationalism in Iran*, p. 270.

15. Mission for My Country, p. 106.

PART III

CHAPTER TEN

IRAN'S CONTRIBUTION
TO THE WORLD

Today's civilization is the product of the genius and contributions of many nations. Some nations lived for a span of time, contributed to the world and vanished completely from the face of the earth. Others stopped making any new contributions after a period of time, while some started very early and still continue contributing to the modern civilization.

Iran is one of the few ancient civilizations that have survived the onslaught of time and circumstance. Owing to its vitality, Iran, which has been continuously contributing to the enrichment of civilization through the millennia, is still adding to the advancement of modern civilization in new ways.

Dr. Arthur C. Milspaugh astutely states in his book *"The American Task"* that: "...very little attention has been given to the contributions of Persia itself to civilization. Persia either created or appropriated and improved much of the best in the science and art of the ancient world." It is only appropriate that Iran be properly introduced to the West, and its magnificent and prodigious contributions to the present world civilization be recognized. It is hoped that this book in general, and this chapter in particular, will succeed in introducing Iran afresh to the cognizance of the world and especially the American people. It should be noted that the destruction that Alexander of Macedonia inflicted upon Iran in 330 B.C. erased a tremendous amount of knowledge, history, science and philosophy from the Achaemenid era and previous millennia. It is said that he took a copy of everything that was in writing –including a copy of the Zoroastrian Holy Book, Avesta which was written on 12,000 cow skins —

ordered them translated into Greek and then had them burnt. Arab invaders committed the same crime about a thousand years later.

Rebuilding World's History

In a recent interview with the Cultural Heritage Agency of Iran, Jean Perrot, one of world's greatest archeologists said:

Actually the excavations in Jiroft [in the province of Kerman] could have made the first chapter of my book, a chapter that could have focused on the evolution of human thought in the third millennium BC, when he entered the era later called history.

This threshold of history found in Jiroft is what is lost in the evolution course of the Mesopotamian civilization and is not that notable in that of Egypt. There are so many objects dating to this time found in the Halilrood Area, which can fill the gap in the formation and development course of the Jiroft civilization.

Therefore, one can say that Jiroft is the capital of today's world archeology, because it allows the archeologists to correct or even rebuild the ideas they had on how people lived during that time of history.

The part of history that was to day hidden in the strata of Iran's plateau is essential to rebuilding the base of world's history.

Agriculture

Iran has helped the development of agriculture in two ways: first by controlling the forces of nature and domesticating animals and plants existing in the wild state in the plateau, and secondly by inventing ways and means of procuring water and diverting it to the places where it was needed. According to Professor Ernest Hertzfeld and Sir Arthur Keith, the Caspians i.e. the original inhabitants of the plateau of Iran, were the original agriculturists and that their knowledge of agriculture spread from the Caspian plateau to the three adjoining alluvial plains which later became the site of early urban civilizations. This theory was later corroborated by later excavations in Iran. The oldest human settlement to be identified on the plain is at Sialk near the city of Kashan, south of Tehran. Among the tools used by these early settlers, that were all of stone, one could distinguish flint knife-blades and sickle-blades. Per Professor Girshman , stock-breeding and cultivation of land followed, and in the fourth millennium B.C. man already used the plough and was cultivating wheat and barley.[1] Charred grains found at the excavated Neolithic village of Geoy Tepe (tappeh) near Lake Oroomieh in the northwestern part of Iran prove that wheat must have been grown there more than 5000 years ago.

Alfalfa: Alfalfa was cultivated in Media and the Achaemenians carried its seed to other countries including Greece as a source of fodder for their cavalry horses. In Greece it was called Medic grass. Professor Girshman states that from Greece it was introduced to other parts of Europe.

According to *Les Plantes dans L'Antiquite*, the earliest mention of alfalfa is in a Babylonian text about 700 B.C. where it appears under Its Persian name *"Aspasti"* (horse fodder) on a list drawn up by the Gardner of King Marduk.

Fig: Dr. B. Laufer states in Sino-Iranica that it is clear that this plant was introduced from Persia and India into China not earlier than the T'ang period.

Grape Vine and Wine : The laboratory analysis of a 4,500 year old clay pot excavated in the northwestern part of Iran showed that it was used for storing wine. To date, this is the oldest wine container found.

The grape-vine, which is indigenous to Iran, was introduced to China by Can K'ien in 128 B.C. at the time of the Chinese Emperor Wu (140-87 B.C.). The introduction of the vine from Iran to China is well attested. The word for wine the Chinese envoy carried with him to his country was *budo*, which apparently came from the Persian *badeh*.

Robert Byron claims that "etymologists dispute as to whether sherry derives its name from Xerez [in Spain] or Shiraz. Some believe that Xerez is the same word as Sherez or Shiraz which was taken to Spain by Moslems."

Jasmine: According to Pei-hu-lu, the Chinese writer, this flower which in Chinese is called ye-sie-mi, was brought from Persia. The Persian word Yasaman is accepted by French and in English is called Jasmine, thereby showing the origin and habitat of this flower.

Rose: Clement Hurat and Louis Delaporte in their book *"L'Iran Antique"* state that the name of rose in Indo-European and Aramean and Arab languages shows its origin to be Iran because in all these languages the word for it is derived from Zand *"Varedha"*, the perfect plant. In Persian *"Vard"* means the rose. In Syria the rose is called Vard Juri. The whole district of Jur, or Firoozabad, in the province of Fars in Iran was noted for its *atr* (scent) of red roses. Fars included in its Kharaj (to the Caliph of Baghdad) 30,000 bottles of the essence of rose. Rose was introduced to Spain in the 7th century A.D.; hence it was propagated all over Europe.

Sesame: Per Professor Girshman Sesame seed was introduced by the Achaemenians to Egypt and later by the Seleucids to Europe.[2]

Spinach: A. de Candolle believes that it was in Persia where the spinach was first raised as a vegetable. The Spaniards, who spread it throughout Europe, received it through Arabs from Iran. Additional evidence is afforded by the very name of the plant which is of Persian origin. Its name in Persian is *aspanah*, aspanag or asfinaj; Arabic isfenah or isbenah. Hence Medieval Latin Spinachium, Spanish espinoca, Italian spinaci The Chinese name for it means "Persian vegetable".

Tulip: It is believed in Holland that tulip was originally brought from the foothills of Alborz mozuntain in Iran and was cultivated and developed there.

In Webster's third New International Dictionary the following plants are attributed to Persia: Persian apple, Persian berry, Persian clover, Persian buttercup, Persian daisy, Persian dates, Persian lilac, Persian melon, Persian rose, Persian orange, Persian violet, Persian wheat.

Aside from above, The Oxford Universal Dictionary on Historical Principles, Third Edition, has the following:

Persian blinds; Persian Cat; Persian drill, a hand drill operated by the movement of a nut backward and forward on the thread of a revolving screw which carries the drill; Persian earth = Indian red; Persian insect powder, an insecticide made of the flowers of pyrethrum roseum; Persian morocco, a kind of leather made from the skin of a hairy sheep called the Persian goat.

Irrigation: As mentioned in *Avesta*, the Zoroastrian Holy Book, conserving water and irrigation was considered a good deed. The Achaemenian kings granted exemption from land tax for five generations to any person who made a tract of desert land cultivable by utilizing an irrigation system. Herodotus, the Greek historian, describes how Cyrus the Great ordered a dam to be built in the northeastern Iran: There is a plain in Asia which is shut in on all sides by a mountain range, and in this mountain range there are five openings.... A mighty river called Aces, flows from the hills enclosing the plain and this stream, formerly splitting into five channels, ran through the five openings of the hills...the Great King blocked up all the passage between the hills with dykes and flood gates.... Then the plain within the hills became a sea for the river kept rising...Then the king ordered the flood gates to be opened towards the country whose need is greatest....

The Most Ancient Arch Dam of the World- According to M. Goblot the oldest arch dam of the world was built in Kebar near Ghome (Qum) during the Mongol period. This dam is 55 meters long and 26 meters high and only 5 meters thick and the remains of its curves is 38 meters. [3]

The Most Extraordinary Method to Develop Ground Water- The *Kahreez* or *Ghanat* (Qanat) system, which was invented by the people of the plateau of Iran, has been named by water and irrigation experts as the most extraordinary method of developing and obtaining ground water. Kahreezes or ghanats are underground channels dug into the alluvial fans raising from the valleys toward the slopes of the mountains. A head-well or a gallery of them tap the aquifer at a depth between 50 and 300 feet and, by using less slope for the conduit tunnel than that of the surface of the fan, water is eventually led to the open. The length of the Kahreez between the city of Mahan to the city of Kerman is 18.3 miles!

Kahreez system introduced by the Iranians went as far as the Chinese settlements of East Turkestan, and to North Africa, Spain and Sicily in Roman times. Persian general Scylax by order of Darius I, introduced this method of irrigation to the Egyptians. From then on, the Egyptians were no longer hostile to the conquerors and built a temple of Ammon, and conferred the title of Pharaoh on Darius.

Persian Wheel or *Charkhab* (water-wheel) was invented in the west of Iran during the Parthian period.4 The wheels which are thirty to forty feet in diameter, are normally placed on the edge of rivers in the hilly country. The water pressure on the blades which have been devised in these wheels, forces thee wheel to move continually. Water sacks that are secured to the edge of the wheel at short intervals, are arranged in a way that after each submersion of the wheel, they come up full and discharge their contents into a trough as they reach the top of the circuit, thereby providing constant flow of water without any effort on the part of the owner. These water-wheels are in use in India and Pakistan and are called the "Persian Wheel."

Windmills are agreed by most modern authors of the history of technology to be invented by the Persians. They are extensively used in eastern parts of Iran where, in summer time, winds blow constantly for up to 120 days. Sir Arnold Wilson in his book *"Persia"* states that the windmill, like the water-wheel was probably introduced to Europe from Persia.

Persians as Creators of Paradise: The Persians' love for flowers, trees and gardens has been well-documented throughout the history of Iran. Trees and forests were respected and even some forests were considered as sacred. There is mention of one such forest in the story of Gilgamesh, who trying to find Khunbaba killed him in the Holy Forest. It is also recounted that Nebukadnisar, to please his wife who was a Median princess, decided to build a hanging garden in Babylonia in exact likeness to Median gardens. The Persian name for garden was *Paradaeza* and this word traveled into European languages through the book of Xenophon called *Oeconomicus*, in the form of Paradise in English, Paradis in French and Firdous in Arabic.

Early Environmentalists: From ancient times, Persians have shown great respect for flowers, plants and trees. From times unknown to present day, Persians have advocated planting trees, and there is even a special *Derakht Kari* (tree planting) day when thousands of trees are plated throughout the country. Ancient trees still do exist in Iran. The oldest is believed to be a 4000-year-old cedar in the province of Yazd. Another sign of the significance of trees in Persian culture is evidenced in the ruins of Persepolis- the 2,500- year-old Achaemenid palace- where numerous flowers and cypress trees are found in the bas-reliefs throughout the palace.

Crafts and Industries

Pottery and Ceramics: Professor Pope states in the *Masterpieces of Iranian Art*: "In light of the data recently discovered it has been proved that agriculture and perhaps the crafts attached to it i.e. pottery making and weaving originated in Iranian plateau. From several essential points, the civilization in this area began 500 years before Egypt, 1,000 years before India and 7,000 years before China."

Professor Girshman corroborates this theory by stating that between 15,000 and 10,000 B.C. prehistoric men lived on the Iranian plateau. He mentions that in 1949 traces of human remains were found in the Bakhti-yari Mountains. These men used a coarse, poorly baked pottery.

As soon as man settled in the plain, as in the case of Sialk near the city of Kashan, a new red ware with black patches on the surface caused by accidents of firing in a primitive kiln (furnace) was added. A further step was now made in the art of the potter, namely the introduction of painted pottery. Gordon Childe in his book, *Man Makes Himself*, writes that the potters' craft, even in its crudest and most generalized form was already complex. It involved an appreciation of a number of distinct processes, the application of a whole constellation of discoveries. Profes-sor Girshman opinionates that from this period, pre-historic Iran revealed in its pottery an art as lively and spontaneous as that of the earlier bone carvings. He adds: "Nowhere else is a parallel craftsmanship known, which suggests that the plateau was the original home of painted pottery. No other pottery has furnished at so early a date evidence of such vigorous realism passing so rapidly into an abstract style. This was achieved for the first time, about 4,000 B.C. by the pre-historic potter of Iran alone."

World's First Animation: According to Cultural Heritage News Agency, an animated piece on an earthen goblet that belongs to 5000 years ago was found in Burnt City (Shahr-e Sookhteh) in Sistan-Baluchestan province, southeastern Iran. On this ancient piece that can be called the first animation of the world, the artist has portrayed a goat that jumps toward a tree and eats its leaves.

The images on this cream-colored goblet, with a diameter of 8 cm and height of 10 cm, show movement in an intricate way that is an unprece-dented discovery. Archeologists have managed to make an animated piece on the basis of these images in the form of a 20-second film.

Glazed Pottery: About 2,000 B.C. a black shiny lusterware appeared in Tappeh Hessar and after that in Sialk. This is the first luster ceramic yet found anywhere.

Metallurgy: The discovery of 400 tons of metal waste alongside melt-ing furnaces, casting moulds and pieces of earthenware around Arisman village- about 50 miles away from the archeological mound of Sialk in central Iran- confirms Iranians to be the first in metal works. A joint committee of experts from Germany's Meintz University, Berlin Archeological Institute, Bochom Mineralogy Museum, Freiburg University and Iran's Geological Organization and Cultural Heritage Organization studied the discoveries of this archeological site from 1997 through 2001. The preliminary studies showed that the site was comprised of 3 different ages from the second half of the 5th. millennium to the first millennium B.C. Other archeological evidence also confirm that the plateau of Iran is the site of the world's oldest metallurgy.

In the 3rd. century A.D. Chinese smiths produced laminated steel. Chinese chronicle Ke-ku-ya states that Sassanian steel was imported from Persia.

Brass (zinc and copper alloy) was known in Achaemenid period. The Greek writer Zosimos, born 400 B.C., calls it *the yellow of Persian alloy* and names a Persian, Papaknidos, as its inventor. The Chinese Chronicle Sui-shi (617 A.D.) says brass came from Sassanian Persia. In the Chinese book of Ko-Ku-yao-lun it is mentioned that the Persians were the first to mine zinc and to alloy brass. The Persian physician, Avicenna (980-1037 A.D.) knew the method of smelting brass from copper and calamine (tutya) and stated that the process spread from Iran to India and China.

Tutty (Persian Tutya), spelter, litharge, the green of salt or zangar, borax, Tincal, Saltpeter, Sal-ammoniac, tin, and many more have their roots in Iran.

Seal: The seal was invented to mark ownership. It used to be impressed on the lump of clay. The oldest forms of marking ownership are seen in the form of primitive seals found in Sialk. Early seals were conical in the shape of a button made of bone and provided with a loop. Geometric decoration used in the early seals was supplemented later by representations of human beings and plants and symbols whose inspirations, no doubt came from the painted decoration on pottery, and like the decoration, may possibly have had the significance of writing.

Textile Industry: Textile in Iran can be traced back to the beginning of the Neolithic times. Professor Pope believes that textile industry originated on the Iranian plateau. Excavations in the early 1950's in a cave near the Caspian Sea produced evidence of woven sheep's wool and goat hair, dated by the carbon 14 method to about 6,500 B.C.

From 4th or possibly 5th millennium B.C. traces of skillful fine plain linen cloth and signs of tablet weaving at the end of the 4th or early in the 3rd millennium B.C. were recovered by the French Mission at Susa (Shoosh). Pierre

Amiet in his book, *Elam*, states that tablet weaving in the Susian civilization is proved by the discovery of a miniature weaving tablet in the foundation deposits of one of the Susa temples. Also a seal tablet belonging to the second half of the 4th millennium B.C. shows a weaving loom.

In Hassanlu, in northwestern Iran, wool has been identified by Harold Burnham of the Royal Ontario Museum by a microscopic examination of shreds of burned textile.

It cannot be determined at what period the weavers achieved methods of weaving patterns into the material. But ample references in literature, patterns found on the costumes of the King's Guards from Susa and a design on trouser leg of an engraved figure on a gold plaque found in Oxus treasure now in the British Museum, show the existence of inwoven designs in Persian cloths during and prior to the Achaemenid times.

Hans E. Wulff states that the Persian craftsman's contributions to progress within a craft can nowhere be better demonstrated than in the development of the textile industry.

Persian Rug: The world's oldest rug or pile carpet was found at Pazyryk in the Altai Mountain in Central Asia in a royal tomb. This piled wool carpet, 189x200 centimeters in size and made of an extremely fine texture having 520 knots per square inch, belongs to the 5th century B.C. The burial place had been under a perpetual ice cover which helped the preservation of the texture and color of the rug.

"All the iconographic details, as well as the technique employed, display evidence of Persian craftsmanship. This is the oldest known pile carpet. The portrayal of the riders on the fourth and 'widest band' is of particular interest: the headgear is typical of Achaemenid warriors...Scythians, Bactrians and Saka, etc. were portrayed in such headgear on the reliefs at Persepolis. The horse trappings are also typically Achaemenid...."[5] Professor R. Frye writes: "Perhaps the most spectacular discoveries in recent times in this area were made at the Kurgans of Pazyryk in the Gorno-Altai region of southern Siberia where rich, frozen tombs were uncovered. The oldest known carpet in the world with Achaemenian motifs...."

Architecture

According to Professor Arthur Pope (Persian Architecture), Iran has a continuous history of architecture from at least 5,000 B.C. to the present, and characteristic examples of this architecture are distributed over a vast area from Syria to North India and the borders of China, from the Caucasus to Zanzibar. Depending on the climate, three different types of architecture have been developed in Iran. In rainy areas slanting roofs covered with shrubs or tiles are common. In less rainy areas where wood is available, flat or gabled roofs according to the area to be spanned and columned houses with verandas are popular. In arid areas houses with domes or vault can be seen. Columnar style was in fashion from earliest times which was later reflected in the stone columns in Persepolis, Zoroastrian temples in Sassanid era, and later, in mosques and Moslems. Domed or vaulted buildings are of comparable antiquity. The huge Sassanian monument-palace of Teesphoon (Ctesphon) may be considered the archetype of this style. Its vault spans 75 feet, the widest brick vault in the world, and is 90 feet high and 150 feet deep.

Per Professor Pope, the two developed side by side, one stimulating and satisfying the passion for height and tenderness, the other similarly gratifying an admiration for huge tri-dimensional form as an effective expression of power. In medieval times the two trends blended and co-coordinated to form a masterpiece i.e. the dome of the Masjed-e- Jaame' of Esfahan. Pope states: "This work of art, powerful in spirit, subtle in mathematics, impeccable in mechanics, in every adjunct it is worthy of the conception."

First Bricks: Professor Girshman very clearly shows the gradual evolution of molded and baked bricks in different layers of Sialk- near Kashan- and by doing so proves beyond the shadow of a doubt that brick was first made in Iran.

First Building Model: A clay structure discovered in Shahrood, in Mazandaran province, is considered the world's first building model/maquette. The 2x3x3 ft. structure is about 7,000 years old.

First Modern Sewage System: There is a consensus among all scholars of the palace of Persepolis that the sewage system of this palace is the first modern sewage system ever designed in the world, and amazing as it may sound, after the passage of 2,500 years it is still functional.

Influence of Iran on the Architecture of Greece: De Angelis d'Ossat, Professor of architectural history at the University of Rome, states that after the wars between Iran and Greece, Iranian influence on Greek architecture increased measurably. Among the most important marks of this influence are the double colonnades supporting the porches surrounding buildings, the appearance of animal motifs on column capitals (such as those at the Temple of Delos), use of double portal entries, increase in the height of columns, the use of various capital styles in the same structure and the use of four-column modules in the interior of buildings. The Temple of Apollo, which was built at Phigalia in 420 B.C. shortly after the war between Iran and Greece, shows many traces of the Achaemenian influence.

Iran, the Origin of the First Christian Architecture: M.A. Choisy in his *'Histoire de l'Architecture'* prints a map on which he shows that the point of origin of the first Christian architecture is Iran. He declares: "the starting point of this movement could not be neither the Latin countries, nor the purely Greek regions, because the 4th A.D. was a time of complete decadence of the Roman Empire. Most of the Latin provinces had nothing new to offer but an out-of-date civilization which was on the wane. Only one nation was guarding amid all this turmoil and general enfeeblement a vigorous upsurge of vitality based on the souvenirs of ancient grandeur and superiority and that nation was Iran." He further states that Iran was the center from which emanated three rays leading via (1) Asia Minor and Constantinople, (2) Armenia and Transcaucasian regions, and (3) Syria and the southern coast of Mediterranean Sea, towards Europe and Africa to introduce Iranian architecture and arts and crafts to these regions.

Influence of Iran on the Architecture of Byzantinum: One school of authorities led by Dr. Strzygowski, assert in the *'Origin of Christian Church Art'* that practically all the essential features of domical and vaulted construction, as well as the development of the cruciform plan, which constitute the very essence of the Byzantine style were first evolved in Iran. Dr. Hertzfeld, too, believes that there can be no doubt about Cruciform's eminently Iranian character. Dr. Talbot Rice, in his book *'The Legacy of Persia'*, although considering Strzygowski's opinion exaggerated, states: "the role of Persia was nevertheless a vital one, and the elliptical arch, the use of niches for the external adornment of buildings, the squinch to effect the transition from the square plan of a base to the circle of a dome, and probably also the extension of the square plan by additions at the sides into one of Greek cross form, were all thought of in Iran before they were elaborated elsewhere."

During the Eslamic period when Saljooghs reigned over Iran and Anatolia, a fresh link was forged between Iran and the Byzantinum. An example of this link can be found in the fact that a section of the Great Palace at

Constantinople which was built under the Saljoogh influence was known as the *Persicus domus* and it was said to be completely Persian in appearance.

Iran's Influence on the Architecture of France: Per Choisy's opinion Persian art and architecture penetrated France both from Europe and through the Rhone valley. The churches of Tournus and the cathedral of du Puy are indeed Persian edifices. Also, in the region of Rhone valley and the area confined between the rivers Loire and Garonne, one can see domes that are essentially Persian. These domes are built on squinches, a Persian invention.

Iran's Influence on the Architecture of Italy: The idea of a double roof with a void in between, according to Coisy, is Iranian. The double roofing in the dome of St. Marie de Fleurs is an example. The oldest Persian application of a double dome still in existence is seen in the Mausoleum of Oljaytu in Soltanieh, near the city of Zanjan, which dates back to the 14th century. However, the knowledge and expertise used in the construction of this dome, shows that this type of double must have been in style for a long time. Choisy further states that there is no doubt that the architects of Florence and Bologne have conceived the domes of their cathedrals in imitation of a Persian type.

The Origin of Gothic Feature: In a report addressed to the 5th International Congress of Iranian Art and Archeology held in Tehran in 1968, Dr. David Stronach presented a slide from Shahr-e Komis, a Parthian fort belonging at least to the last years of pre-Christian era, depicting very distinct pointed arches. According to the report printed in volume VI of the Journal of the British Institute of Persian Studies in 1968, the fort may belong to periods even prior to the Parthian occupation. This type of arch was carried to Europe through Armenia and Syria and became one of the most important features of the Gothic architecture.

Iran's Influence on the Architecture of India: The influence of Iranian architecture on India, especially in the Eslamic period, is great. Dr. Rice asserts that the art of early Delhi sultanate followed that of Iran, and Bahmani art turned for its inspiration completely to Iran, so much so, that it must be regarded as an integral offshoot of Iran. The Jame' Masjed at Gulbarga (1367) is Persian in spirit and the work of the Persian architect Rafi' Ghazvini.

With the invasion of India by the Mongols another and more powerful wave of Persian influence reached India. This especially became very strong after Homayoun's forced flight to the court of Shah Tahmasp in Iran and his return with the help of the Persian army to re-capture his kingdom. He brought with him to India many Persian artists, craftsmen and architects. Homayoun's famous tomb at Delhi was built by Mirak Ghyath, a Persian architect on the orders of Homayoun's widow. This tomb is the earliest example of a double dome built in India.

The sultans of Deccan, like their Bahmani predecessors, proved to be mighty builders. The Ebrahim Rauza or the tomb of Ebrahim II of Bijapour is said to have been built in 1627 by the Persian architect Malek Sandal.

Taj Mahal: Taj Mahal is the love monument raised by Shah Jahan as the tomb of his queen Arjomand Banoo better known as Momtaz Mahal. The design of Taj Mahal is based on the tomb of Khan Khanan, which was itself a modified version of the famous tomb of Homayoun, both modeled on Persian art. Craftsmen were engaged from many countries for the creation of this magnificent edifice, but there is substantial agreement among writers that the chief master builder, who co-coordinated the center work was Ostad Isa Shirazi assisted by his son, Mohammad Shirazi, both from Persia. H. Goetz holds that Taj Mahal is a Safavid art. And M. Grousset believes that Taj Mahal is the soul of Iran incarnated in the body of India. Dr. Davar from Ahmadabad Arts College in India believes that Taj Mahal is a monument wherein once again and, it is to be hoped, for many centuries to come, Iran and India join hands, in the realm of art and beauty.

Transportation

The Wheel: Will Durant, in his famous work, *'The History of Civilization'* states that the wheel was first used for transport in Elam, in Iran. By about 2,000 B.C. wheeled vehicles were in use from the Indian valley to the Syrian coast. But Gordon Childe states that in Egypt no wheeled vehicles were in use before 1,600 B.C.

Roads: According to Professor Girshman, Iranians in Achaemenid times had developed a method of road building that consisted of paving the softer parts of the road, and even of making artificial ruts for wheeled vehicles. The Greek historian, Herodotus, states that the Persian Royal Road anticipated the Roman road by several centuries.

Post and couriers: Herodotus attributes the creation of post and couriers to the Achaemenid Persians and states: The entire plan is a Persian innovation. He goes on by giving a detailed description of the operation.

Caravan: Caravan and Caravansarai (rest station) were originated by Iranians to promote trade. Both of these terms are pure Persian and clearly indicate the origin of this method of transport. The caravan master, who was called *Caravan-salar*, was entrusted with merchandise . Each caravan-salar had a number of armed men in his employ to protect the caravan from brigands and marauders.

Finance

First Banks: As discussed earlier, during the Achaemenian period private banks were established. The most famous was *Bank of Egibi* which carried on the business of pawn-brokers floating loans and accepting deposits. Its capital was invested in house property, fields, cattle, and in the boats that carried the merchandise. Current accounts were operated and checks were in use. *Bank of Murashshu and Sons* was founded later in Nippur. It held leases, dug canals and sold water to the farmers, secured monopolies, such as brewing or fisheries which were farmed out at a profit.

Per Professor Girshman, Greeks followed the example of these banks and similar institutions appeared there, particularly in the temples of Delos, Olympia and Delphia. He adds: "how many financiers and bankers know, for example, that the word *'check'* or the word *avaliser'* come from the Pahlavi language and were invented by the Iranian banking institutions of this remote age? The Christian traders of Syria borrowed the bill from Iran, and introduced it into the West."

Taxes: Girshman also states that during the same period, the State levied dues on estates, farms, gardens, flocks and mines. There was a land tax as well as a tax on industrial production; there were also port dues, taxes on international trade, and on sales. The money thus levied was partly spent by the satraps to govern the provinces under their government and the rest was sent to the Treasury. These funds were used to meet the expenses of the Royal Court, the Central Administration, and the Army. The government dug subterranean canals (Ghanats), built dams, drained the marshes, built cities, roads, bridges, carvansarais. They were indeed the forerunners in the art of fiscal policy of the present day world.

World's First Labor Laws

One of the most interesting discoveries of ancient Iran is the system of wages established for laborers throughout the empire. The numerous tablets found in the treasury at Persepolis, and translated by Professor George G. Cameron, reveal an amazing array of regulations concerning wages, work, modes of payment, labor exchange, and the like. In these treasury tablets, which are really pay sheets for the building of Persepolis, it is quite evident that payment for different classes of workers such as skilled and unskilled laborers, women and children, were strictly regulated. They even had a severance pay and unemployment benefit where a laborer would receive about three months of wages and benefits upon his or her termination. These documents can safely be considered as the world's first labor laws.

Fashion

Pants and long coats: the trousers that we wear today as well as the long coats that was customary until very recently in Europe is a Persian heritage. None of the nations of the old world except Iranians wore trousers and long tunics coming to the knee. The pants that were called in old Persian Sharval (modern Persian Shalvar) were accepted later by the Greeks with its name in the form of Saraballa, in Latin Sarabara. It was accepted by Arabs and was called Serbal and Serval, in Spanish it is called Ceroulas and in Hungary it is called Schalwary and in Turkish Sharval.

Xenophon writes in *The Persian Expedition* that Alexander liked very much the expensive tunics and the embroidered trousers of the Persians. The attire of the Greeks was a simple piece of cloth as it came out of the weaving frame, and the clothing of men and women were not much different from one another. In fact reliefs, statues and vase paintings clearly show that some Greeks even went to war completely naked. The book of Genesis says: "they were indeed like Adam and Eve before they ate of the forbidden fruit, because at that time they were both naked and unashamed. But later, they came in contact with the people of the East and their eyes were opened and they knew that they were naked and they were ashamed."

Gloves: Xenophon in his *Cyropaedia* speaks of Iranians covering their hands with thick leather and their fingers in frames thereby explaining how he came to know for the first time what Iranians used in order to protect their hands against cold and frosty winds. This shows that the Greeks did not know what gloves were. Excavations in Ziwieh in Iran have produced a kind of a glove used as adornment belonging to the 7th century B.C.

Persian costumes in the East and West: In *'The Legacy of Iran'* we read that the Byzantine imperial costume...was introduced from Iran by Diocletian before the adoption of Christianity; and that the love of bright colors, rich materials, elaborate costumes of the Byzantine civilization is entirely due to Persian influence.

Professor Von Le Coq in his book 'Buried *Treasures of Chinese Turkestan'* states: "The main decoration, the quiver, and coat of mail were adopted by the Chinese of the T'ang period. Thus China has also to thank Iran for these things appertaining to material civilization."

Regarding Europe, Professor Von Le Coq remarks: " If we look up in Chaucer, the Nebelungenlied, or in Wolfram von Eschenbach and Walther von der Vogelweide, the material that were worn by the European Knights and their ladies, we find that they were Persian or Turkish production. But if the materials are Eastern, it is not impossible that the cut was no less so. In fact, these articles of clothing came to Europe ready cut out."

In Act III of Shakespeare's King Lear we read: "...you will say they are Persian attire...."

It is said that Charles II (1660-1685) was so impressed by the Persian costumes that for a certain period the official dress of the Court of England was an imitation of Persian costumes.

Just after the conquest of Iran, Arabs started wearing Persian costumes. In *The Legacy of Iran* we read: Ebn-e Qotaiba of Marv (885 A.D.) quotes a tradition from Omar [the second caliph of Eslam] saying: "Wear loincloth, cloak and sandals (i.e. Arab attire). Throw away top boots, girths and stirrups and mount your horse at abound. Let luxury and Persian costume go and never wear silk."

In Spain, at the court of Abd-al-Rahman II of Cordova (822-52 A.D.), a Persian singer named Zaryab made Persian clothes and style the fashion in Spanish Court.

Percival Spear in *'A History of India'* states that when the Mongols went to India, they wore Turkistani dress that was much influenced by Persian refinement. Akbar affected and adopted later Safavid [of Persia] costumes.

Games and Sports

Among recent treasures found in the Halilrood area of the Kerman province are five ancient game boards which indicate that people of the area enjoyed playing games some five thousand years ago. Three of these game boards look like eagles, one looks like a scorpion with human head, and the other is a flat board. All have 12 or 18 holes with similar sizes.

Polo (Chowgan) is an ancient Persian game. Iranians call it Chowgan (chow to be pronounced like tow, and gan like gun). The oldest mention of this game is in Ferdosi's Shahnameh (composed about 1,000 years ago) where the game played between Siyavash and his Persian retinue in one side and Afrasiyab, the Tooranian King and his brother Garsivaz, on the other is described in the form of poetry. There are also very fine details about the game being played between Shirin and her dames d'honours with Khosro Parviz, the Persian emperor, and his courtiers. In Shahnameh we also find an account of children playing Polo with mallet and ball, on foot, early in Sassanian period. This is similar to many games that were, later on, introduced to Europe in which mallets and balls were used. It is also very interesting to note that in some areas of France, there is a game played on foot with mallets and hard wood balls called "Chicane" a name that is strikingly close to Chowgan.

Omar Khayyam, the Persian mathematician, philosopher and poet, utilizes Chowgan to express his philosophy. A loose translation rendered by Fitzgerald goes:

"The Ball no Question makes of Ayes and Noes,
But Right and Left as strikes the Player goes;
And He that toss'd Thee down into the field,
He knows about it all-He knows- He knows."

Throughout the Iranian history there are many mentions of kings and grenadiers playing polo. And many Europeans have written their accounts of Shah Abbas Safavi either playing polo or watching the game from the balcony of the Ali Ghapoo palace, in Esfahan, while drinking snow-chilled Shiraz wine with his courtiers.

Polo was carried to India by the Mongol rulers. The Mongol emperor Akbar, is said to have judged the suitability of a candidate for the position of the Minister of State by observing his behavior on the polo field.

Later, the British army officers assigned to India brought polo to England from where it was propagated throughout the world.

Horse and Chariot racing: Horse racing has been a pastime in vogue in Iran from the beginning of history. In volume III of *Cyropaedia*, Xenophon gives a detailed account of how Cyrus the Great arranged a race between the cavalry of each nation and their charioteers: He marked out a goal, and a course half a mile in length, and bade the cavalry and the chariots match their horses against each other, tribe by tribe. He himself raced among his Persians and won with ease, for he was far the best horseman there. The winner among Medes was Artabazus.... The Syrian race was won by their chieftain. The Armenian byTigranes....

Xenophon adds that Cyrus arranged chariot races after the horse races, again, tribe by tribe, and to all winners Cyrus gave goblets of price and ox.

According to Herodotus, the Greek historian, when Xerxes arrived in Thessaly, he matched his own horses against the Thessalian horses which he had heard were the best in Greece; but the Greek horses were left far behind in the race.

Backgammon (Nard): There is a story in *'Book of Mazkian Chatrang'* written in Pahlavi language to the effect that the game of chess was introduced to Iran by Dabshlim, the king of India, during the time of Khosro Anooshiravan. The Indian emissary was carrying a letter in which it was stated that "as you are our King of kings so your scientists and philosophers must be superior to ours. If it is so, they will not be in difficulty in finding the rules of the game of chess that I am hereby sending to you by my confidential messenger. If your scientists do not find the secret of the rules of this game, then we expect you to pay us annual tribute instead of us to you." Bozogmehr, the vazir of Anooshiravan, discovered the rules. Then, he sent the game of *Vinardeshir*, which he had invented, to the king of India, but no one in India could understand how the game was supposed to be played.

But in the book called *'Karnamak of Ardeshir Papakan'* which is about Ardeshir, the founder of the Sassanid dynasty and which must have been written long before Anooshiravan, there is evidence that both chess (Chatrang) and Vinardeshir were known during the early part of the reign of Ardeshir. Therefore, it seems that the above story should not be taken seriously.

Backgammon or *nard* was invented in Iran and was named after Ardeshir, the founder of the Sassanid dynasty, its original name being "Vinardeshir."

Although the Book of Mazkian Chatranng is considered to be fiction rather than historical fact, the part which explains the reason for inventing backgammon and what it represents is quite interesting:

I have made something in the name of Ardeshir the Great and have named it Vinardeshir. Its board is the symbol of the earth, its pieces that are 30 as a whole are symbol of 30 days of the month. 15 pieces are black and 15 others with which the opponent plays are white and are the symbols of nights and days. Dices are the symbols of rotation of the planets and sphere (at that time, they believed that planets and stars turned around the earth). The numbers on the dice have each their proper connotations. One is the symbol of *Ormazd*, the sole God of the Universe. Two is the symbol of the earth and the sky. Three is the symbol of [the Zoroastrian motto] Good Thought, Good Deed, and Good Talk. Four is the symbol of the four [basic] Elements and also the 4 corners of the world. Five symbolizes the five Lights: the Sun, the Moon, the Star, the Fire, and lightening. And six is the symbol of the six Gahanbars [Zoroastrian feasts].

Emblems and Signs

Eagle with Stretched Wings and Legs: The emblem of the Achaemenid kings was an eagle with stretched wings and legs. The eagle was adopted by Alexander's heirs and later was used in the emblems of Rome and many European countries such as Prussia, Russia, Poland, and France (during the reign of Napoleon). The Persian eagle sign found in Persepolis with its stretched wings, and two stretched legs holding some objects, have striking similarities with the present emblem of the United States. This, once again, brings to mind former Supreme Court Justice William O. Douglas' statement that "Persians are spiritually close kin to Americans."

The Cross was the sign of the Persian Prophet Mithra and used by the people of the plateau of Iran. This sign was later adopted by Christians with many other ceremonies and rites of Mithraism.

Swastika that became well known as the emblem of the Nazi Germany, was used by Iranians in pottery and elsewhere very early in their arts. Per Professor Girshman, it was used in profusion in Susa and other sites in Iran dating back to the 4th millennium B.C.

The Unicorn used as a part of the British Royal Emblem, according to Professor Girshman, was used in Sialk pottery of Necropolis.

Cuisine

According to Ferdosi's Shahnameh, it was during the reign of Zahhak, the tyrant king, that Satan appeared to him in the form of an able cook and prepared for him various types of dishes of various kinds of animals. Based on this myth, prior to this time people did not kill animals to make dishes; they made use mainly of fruits and wheat in the form of bread. This shows how old the art of cooking has been in Iran.

Based on reports from Cultural Heritage News, excavations in the 5000-year-old Burnt City (Shahr-e Sookhteh) in the southeastern province of Sistan-Balouchestan have revealed that the ancient residents of this area enjoyed a rich diverse variety of food including a piece of bread and a dish that is a combination of lentil, fish and coriander. Another food of theirs was something like today's pottage (or Aash in Persian), which to this date is enjoyed by Iranians.

According to Professor Lorenzo Costantini, researcher with the Oriental Museum of Rome, Italy:

> The discovery of this small porous piece of bread was one of the most significant achievements of our work on the site. The bread had changed a lot during time and we could only find out about its true nature with microscopic examinations. We studied the piece under microscope and compared it with the wheat grains taken from tomb no. 1400 which was well preserved; we found traces of flour that had not yet lost its quality. We are now sure that the piece is bread

Xenophon the Greek states that Persians in the Achaemenid period "have given up none of the cooked dishes invented in former days, on the contrary, they are always devising new ones, and condiments to boot; in fact they keep men for the very purpose" and "the Persians have butlers and cooks, and confectioners and cupbearers...to serve at table or remove dishes...."

According to Tha'labi's *History of the Kings of Iran*, Khosro Parviz had a young page who was very skillful in preparing delicious dishes. In a number of questions asked by the king regarding various foods, he provided the following opinion:

The best meat of quadrupeds is the meat of a lamb which has sucked two ewes and has grazed for two months, and which is boiled and then roasted in an oven...or the breast of a young fat cow cooked in vinegar...the best meat of fowl is that of a fat pheasant, that of the winter partridge, that of fattened young pigeons and that of the chicken brought up on the grains of wheat, on hemp seeds and on olive oil. The best cold hors-d'oeuvr is veal, tender and succulent, prepared with very strong vinegar, and very piquant mustard. The best jelly is the meat of a young gazelle, tender, cut in long thin slices, marinated with vinegar, mustard, brine, dill, garlic, caraway, and cumin.

The best pastry is that made of rice flour, with very fresh milk, and the fat of the gazelle and sugar candy; and also the cake made of the dough of walnuts, prepared with the oil of almonds and syrup; the cake made of the dough of almonds prepared with crystal sugar and rose-water The most delicious wine is the grape wine which is at the same time of good color and absolutely limpid, a little thick, of an agreeable bouquet and of an excellent taste, and which makes one tipsy rapidly. The best dessert is the peeled cores of almonds crushed and mixed with sugar, the grains of sweet pomegranate and of sour pomegranate with rose-water....

Early forks, spoons, knives, and table manners: According to the Journal of British Institute of Iranian Studies, Volume III published in 1965 in Iran, two very beautifully proportioned silver spoons were found in 1964 in Iran belonging to the second half of the 5th century B.C. One spoon has a duck or swan's head handle. The other, a zoomorphic handle ending in a cloven hoof. The same publication noted that among Achaemenian works of art, other spoons or ladles terminating in swan's handles had been recovered.

Also according to Byzantine and Christian sources, the Iranian nobility in Sassanian times, had special knives to serve fruit with, and used gold forks and spoons and special gold cups at their dinner tables.

The sharp contrast between Iranians and Moslem Arabs who invaded Iran over 1,300 years ago, is evident in Ebn-e Gotaibeh (Ibn Qutaiba), the Arab writer's statement when he writes:

Iranians are proud of their table manners and boast that they eat their food with knife and fork and spoon while the Arabs eat with their hands...But this question that the Persians eat with spoon and knife and fork and they consider it as a part of their good table manners and boast about it, is vain because eating with the hands is far more delicious and utensils the Persians use for eating are not only harmful for the food they consume, but also they decrease the pleasure one gets from the taste of the food. The hand is for eating food and these ' hard –to-please' attitudes and lack of conformity with natural instincts are unwarranted.

Perfumes

The art of obtaining the essence of various flowers and preserving them in small containers was for the first time invented by the Zoroastrians in Iran as perfume played a great role in Zoroastrian religious ceremonies.

From the Old Testament we learn how the ancient Persians considered perfume of utmost importance. It is stated in Esther that the virgins who were being prepared to be presented to Ahasuerus, the King of Persia, were obliged to be purified with oil of myrrh and for the next six months with sweet scents and other things.

Xenophon writes that Iranians in the time of Artaxerxes II had servants responsible for perfuming their masters. Also, Plutarch provides an account of how Alexander enjoyed the Bath of Darius with all the perfumes they rubbed on his body after he took the bath.

In *Ardai-Viarf-Nameh*, which was the earliest precursor of Dante's *Divine Comedy*, we read that a Zoroastrian priest called Ardai Viraf taking a bath and perfuming himself with fine perfumes wearing a white robe goes into a trance and thus visits the heaven and hell and when he wakens, recounts his experience.

The province of Fars and especially the ancient town of Firoozabad or Jur/Gur during the Eslamic period were the center of perfume-making industry and were well-known throughout the world. At all times Fars has been celebrated for the so-called attar of roses (Attar or itr in Arabic signifies perfume or essence), which was especially made from the red roses that grew in the plain of Jur . The rose water was exported to all parts of the world namely India, China, Syria, Egypt and Maghreb (Morocco) in Northwest Africa. According to 'The Lands of Eastern Caliphate' by Le Strange, ten different kinds of perfumed oils, or unguents, made from violets, water-lily (Nenufar- modern Persian Niloofar), narcissus, palm-flower, common lily, jasmine, myrtle, sweet marjoram, lemon and orange flowers were produced in the city of Shapour and its surroundings, and these oils were exported far and wide over the eastern world.

The perfume industry was established in the city of Kufa by the people of Shapour , and from there it found its way to other Eslamic lands and finally it reached Europe.

Baths: According to Persian mythical stories, bath was invented by Jamsheed, the ancient Pishdadi King of Iran. In excavations headed by Professor Girshman in Shoosh (Susa), in a layer attributed to 2,000 years B.C., bath-rooms were found in the houses of the richer classes in the Susian community. Also the book of Esther provides a description of the way the country girls who were being prepared to meet the King of Persia, had to be bathed in hot baths for the period of a year.

World's First Orchestra

Excavations in Chogha Mish, about 15 miles south-east of Dezful in the province of Khoozestan have provided evidence that it was a city of considerable size in the Protoliterate period (about 5,500 years ago) when writing was probably first invented. Most significant of the items found are the cylinder seal impressions on clay. Per Sylvia Matheson in *Persia: An Archeological Guide*, "one of these gives the earliest known evidence of music as an organized art-form, showing an orchestra and a vocalist."

Early Dog Trainers

An observant visitor can find a masterfully cut statue of a dog in Tehran Archeological Museum. This 2,500 year old statue of a guard dog which was found in the ruins of Persepolis, has a characteristic that is not discussed much. There is a collar around its neck that proves Persians had not only domesticated dogs, but had trained them and utilized them in their daily life. According to Will Durant, in old Persia the animal- above all others the dog- was an integral part of the family. The nearest family was enjoined to take in and care for any homeless pregnant beast. Severe penalties were prescribed for those who fed unfit food to dogs, or served them their food too hot. It was only after the advent of Eslam that dogs lost their popularity.

Literature

The renowned French scholar and Iranologist, R. Grousset, writes about Persian Poetry: "...All these apparently diverse tendencies- mystic exaltation, sensuality, skepticism, melancholy- were molded by Persian poetry into a classic harmony of an unimitable beauty and tenderness.... Barbier de Meynard shows it to us 'fond of beauty and combining in the same sentiment, lasting beauty and ideal perfection'. Is not this the definition of classic arts?"

The American writer-philosopher, Ralph Waldo Emerson considered the *Golestan* of Mosleheddin **Sa'di** to rank with the Bible and other sacred texts. Benjamin Franklin was so impressed by some parts of the *Golestan* that he used to say that they no doubt were parts of the lost verses of the Holy Book. H. Massé in his book on Sa'di puts him in the class of the small number of those who have enriched not only their own but world literature. He provides a ling list of European writers including Goethe, Victor Hugo and Balzac, who have been influenced by Sa'di.

Professor A.J. Arberry in his introduction to a partial translation of Jalal-Eddin **Rumi** writes: "In Rumi the Persian mystical genius found its supreme expression. The influence of his example, his thought and his language is powerfully felt through all the succeeding centuries.... To the West now slowly realizing the magnitude of his genius...he is truly able to prove a source of inspiration and delight not surpassed by any other poet in the world's literature." E. G. Browne opines that Rumi "is without doubt the most eminent Sufi poet whom Persia has produced, while his mystical *Mathnavi* deserves to rank amongst the great poems of all time."

When Goethe, the great German philosopher and poet, read the poetry of Shams-eddin Mohammad **Hafez**, remarked in his *West-Ostlicher Diwan*: "Suddenly I came face to face with the celestial perfume of the East and invigorating breeze of eternity that was being blown from the plains and wastelands of Persia, and I came to know an extraordinary man whose personality completely fascinated me." He later wrote: " I am getting mad. If I do not immediately start composing poetry, I will not be able to bear the amazing influence of this extraordinary personality who has suddenly entered into my life." Freidrich Nietzche, the famous philosopher wrote: "O Hafez thou hast built a tavern of philosophy which is mightier than any other place in the world, and it, thou hast prepared a wine full of sweet words that surpasses the power of a world to drink."

Mathematics, Science & Medicine
Ancient Ruler

Based on reports from Iran's Cultural Heritage News, recent excavations in the archeological site of the Burnt City (Shahr-e Sookhteh) have led to the discovery of a ruler with millimeter measurement units. The ruler — believed to be some 5000 years old- is a 10-centimeter-long piece of ebony wood with some cuts which have evidently been made with a sharp tool. Experts believe now that the ancient residents of the city used precise units for measurements and was skilled in areas of mathematics and geometry.

Durant writes in *The Age of Faith* that Mohammad ebn Moosa, known as **Kharazmi** (Khwarazmi), contributed effectively to five sciences: he wrote on the Hindu numerals; completed astronomical tables which as revised in Moslem Spain, were for centuries standard among astronomers from Cordova to Chang-an; formulated the oldest trigonometrical tables known, collaborated with sixty-nine other scholars in drawing up for al-Mamun, a geographical encyclopedia, and in his 'Calculation of Integration and Equation gave analytical and geometrical solutions of quadratic equations'.

This work was translated in the twelfth century and used as a textbook in European universities until the sixteenth century. It was through this translation that the word Algebra was introduced to the West.

In his *History of Science*, G. Sarton calls the first half of the ninth century the Time of Kharazmi and considers him as one of the greatest mathematicians of all time.

B.L. Gordon, M.D. writes in Medieval and Renaissance Medicine that Abu Bakr Mohammad ebn Zakariya **Razi** "was the first physician to apply the science of chemistry to the treatment of disease and he thus may be considered the founder of iatrochemistry." Razi was a pioneer in the use of empirical method through which he made important discoveries relating to the diagnosis and treatment of various illnesses. He discovered several new medicines and was the first person to prepare alcohol which he called alKahl (yellow).

Abu Ali Hossain **ebn Sina** (**Avicenna**) was a true genius whose 99 books and papers in medicine, philosophy, geometry, astronomy, the principles of religion, poetry and art earned him the title of *Stupor Mundi* or the *Marvel of the World*. His *Ghanoon fel Teb* (*Canon of Medicine*) investigates in detail the structure of body, health and illnesses and their cure, and provides an unprecedented manner of dealing with nervous and mental disorders. Dr. W. Osler writes in The Evolution of Modern Medicine that Canon served for a longer period than any other work as the medical Bible. It was a textbook at Oxford University in the 17th. century. Dr. B. L. Gordon writes, "From the twelfth to the seventeenth centuries, his (Avicenna's) Canon was accepted in European universities as the most authoritative medical work." His other work, *Ketab al Shafa* (*Book of Healing*), consists of eighteen books dealing with metaphysics, mathematics, natural sciences, religion, economics, politics and poetry. W. Durant writes in The Age of Faith, "Avicenna's Shifa and Qanun mark the apex of medieval thought, and constitute one of the major synthesis in the history of the mind."

World's first Cesarean Section

There have been references in the ancient Hindu, Greek, Egyptian, Roman and other folklore in regards to childbirth through what is known as "Cesarean Section". Many scholars believe the word originates from the word "Caesarea", or cut, in Latin. According to the American College of Obstetricians and Gynecologists, the earliest documented case of a cesarean section was in 1505 illustrated in Suetonius' *Lives of the Twelve Caesars* woodcut of 1506. However, Dr. Masood Khatamee writes in a later issue of the same journal that the world-renowned Iranian epic poet A.G. Ferdosi (940-1020 AD) had explicitly described this procedure in Shahnameh or Book of Kings in about 500 years earlier. He thus contends that the first cesarean section was performed in Iran. Dr. Khatamee writes that based on Ferdosi's poem, Roodabeh had a very troubled pregnancy and developed Jaundice. "Further into her pregnancy, her condition deteriorated and, near the birth of Rostam (the mythological Persian hero), she became comatose." Zal, Roodabeh's husband, thought of a solution. "In his desperation, he seized a piece of a feather of Simorgh, a legendary bird, and glasses of wine to anesthetize Roodabeh. He also brought a physician with a dagger and Roodabeh's abdomen was opened and Rostam was delivered." A loose translation of Ferdosi's description is as follows:

He slit the flank of the goddess of beauty and the head of a boy came into view.

The boy, "Rostam," was brought out of the womb magnificently without harm;

No one had seen this wonder up to that time.

ENDNOTES

1. Girshman, Iran, pp.29-35.

2. Ibid., 239p.

3. As narrated by A.A. Hekmat in Iranshahr, Vol. II, p.1567.

4. Frye, Heritage of Persia, p.151.

5. Vladimir Loukonine & Anatoli Ivanov, *Lost Treasures of Persia* (Washington, DC,1996), p.75.

6. William O. Douglas, *Strange Lands and Friendly People* (New York: Harper and Brothers, 1951), p. xiv.

CHAPTER ELEVEN

CONTRIBUTION OF IRANIANS TO THE UNITED STATES

The ever-rejuvenating Persian culture has never ceased its contribution to the world. It seems that Iranians have strived to confirm the truth of the Prophet of Eslam's words quoted in Donald Wilber's *Iran: Past and Present* who said: "If scholarship hung suspended in the highest parts of heaven, the people of Fars (Persia) would reach to take it." This type of mentality coupled with the fertile ground that the Iranians found in the United States after their exodus in 1979- no philosophical, societal, political, religious, or technological restraints or limitations- provided them the opportunity to once again flourish in ingenuity in all aspects of human life. Describing the contributions of these outstanding architects, bankers, businesspeople, computer wizards, engineers, fashion designers, filmmakers, physicians, professors, scientists, sculptors, sportspeople, writers would be an enormous task with encyclopedic proportions. Due to time, budgetary and personnel constraints only a very concise sample is provided here — based on the author's limited personal knowledge- with the hope that it would be considered as an infant step and a stimulus for publication of a Who's Who of Outstanding Iranians:

Arts

Siah Armajani has been recognized for more than two decades for his pioneering efforts to reunite people and art via environmental projects that convey meaning without fanfare, intelligence without pretension. Armajani's art embraces the democratic ideals of American society and

American literature. He passionately embodies the spirit of writers like Walt Whitman, Ralph Waldo Emerson and John Dewy in art. In April 1992, the Los Angeles Times wrote: "he has influenced a generation (or two) of environmental artists who, like himself, marry art and architecture without diluting the spirit and function of either one." In the same year, the American Institute of Architects honored Armajani "for achievements in the allied arts and sciences." The cauldron structure of the 1996 Olympic Games in Atlanta was designed and built in its entirety by Armajani.

Shirin Bazleh is a producer, director, editor, and film maker whose works have been shown on TBS/CNN, PBS, CBS, A&E and Fox. She has won many awards including 1997 Gracie Award for producing, directing and editing "Mother Teresa" series, Cable Ace Award, Best Documentary Series 1996 for a six part series called "The Revolutionary War", New York International Film and Video Festival's gold medal for directing and editing 'Iran, Behind the Veil". She is also the recipient of the Best Australian Documentary award for directing and editing "Paradise of Martyrs."

Lotfi Mansouri has been the General Director of San Francisco Opera since 1976. He has brought many innovations to the opera including simultaneous translation- a process called Supertitles which is now being used in opera houses all over the world. This process has truly broken the barrier to the opera. Under his leadership, the San Francisco Opera has been exposing more than 20,000 children every year to opera and other forms of art. He was recently described by the New York Times as *a revolutionary in the world of opera*.

Business

Faramarz Salek is the President and CEO of CleanNet U.S.A., Inc. America's 10th largest franchise of any kind.

Kosti Shirvanian emigrated to the U.S. in 1950 and attended Atlantic Union College in Massachusetts. Mistakenly drafted into the Army, he served as a front line medic in the Korean War. In 1955, he bought a trash hauling company for $1,500 and put $800 down on a used truck. In the early years, he drove the truck and hauled trash while his sister, Savey, handled the administrative matters. Concentrating initially in southern California, Western Waste expanded into Colorado, Arkansas, Louisiana, Texas and Florida. The company went public in 1983 and began trading on the New York Stock Exchange in 1991. Prior to its merger with USA Waste Services, Western Waste exceeded $270 million in annual revenue with over 1,800 employees. Shirvanian has been extensively involved in humanitarian efforts including helping earthquake victims in Armenia, Iran and Mexico. He is an active supporter of civic and philanthropic organizations such as Centinella Hospital Children's Foundation, Athletes and Entertainers for Kids, Wings Foundation, and Ronald Reagan Presidential Foundation. In 1990, Shirvanian received an honorary doctorate degree in Commerce from Atlantic union College. He is a member of the Hall of Fame of the National Solid Waste Management Association.

Computer

Kamran Elahian received a BS in Computer Science and BS in Mathematics concurrently at the age 20 in 1975 followed by a Masters degree in Engineering, Computer Graphics in 1977. In 1981 co-founded CAE Systems, Inc. and sold it for $75 million within three years. In 1984 he co-founded Cirrus Logic, Inc. with a revenue of over $1 billion in ten years. In 1989 he co-founded Momenta Corporation, lost $40 million and went bankrupt within three years. In 1993 he co-founded NeoMagic Corporation, IPO valuation over $300 million within three years of founding. Neo-Magic was the first semiconductor company to combine memory, graphics and logic functions on one chip for the portables market. Its products won a place in 18 of the 20 notebook computers on the market. In 1996 he co-founded PlanetWeb, Inc., an internet appliance software company. In 1996 he also co-founded Projectneat, Inc., a non-profit public charity organization to endow the world's poorest schools with a window to the internet. In 1996, Projectneat spent nearly $1 million ($200,000 of which came from Elahian's own wallet), donating one 27-inch TV set and the Net-capable Sega Saturn to each of 1,000 disadvantaged schools in the United States. Elahian's goal for 1998 is to connect 10,000 schools. Kamran Elahian who has been featured in Forbes, Businessweek, Entrepreneurial Edge, etc., remarks, " I have this belief that if you develop the right technology that brings the world together, you've done something good with your life."

Mory Ejabat is the President/CEO of Ascend Communications, Inc. Ascend, founded in 1989, is a leading provider of technology and equipment solutions for telecommunications carriers, Internet service providers

(ISPs), and corporate customers worldwide. Prior to joining Ascend, Ejabat was vice president for wide area communications products at Micom Systems, Inc., where he improved pretax profits by more than eight points, establishing Micom as the leader in the low-end market segment by introducing and positioning the X.25 networking product line, and a marketing campaign and cost-reduction program for the most effective price/performance 9.6 low bit rate digital voice product in the market.

In its May 20, 1996 issue, Forbes magazine called Ejabat 537th most powerful man in America.

Hossein Eslambolchi serves as the Vice President of Network operations at AT&T. Eslambolchi is in charge of the entire AT&T Network and has an organization of 10,000 people.

Sina Tamaddon serves as the Vice President of Apple Computers.

Fashion

AMIR- According to April 1998 issue of Los Angeles Magazine: "When President Clinton gave his 1998 State of the Union address, he knew the nation was really curious about his behavior when in a state of undress. Looking proper was no doubt Clinton's goal when he called on designer Amir...." And per Leaders Magazine of 1997: "Amir, whose company is based in Beverly Hills, California, and operates worldwide, is one of the world's premier fashion designers. For more than 20 years he has advised a select clientele that includes President Clinton, Tony Bennett, Lee Iacocca, Julio Iglesias, Larry King, President Ronald Reagan, Prince Charles, the King of Malaysia, former U.S. Senate Majority Leader George Mitchell, former Soviet Union President Mikhail Gorbachev, Liza Minnelli, and Sophia Loren , among many others."

This successful designer who takes pride in his Persian heritage , has designed for six Kings, five Presidents, twelve Prime Ministers, sixty-eight Princes, twenty-eight Diplomats....

Bijan is the head of one of the most exclusive and prestigious menswear and fragrance businesses in America. Bijan has been at the couture game for over twenty-eight years. Time Magazine in Apri 1995 wrote,

Bijan is arguably peerless in his menswear designs. With a worldwide enterprise encompassing more than 82 countries and based in Beverly Hills, Bijan has set the standard in luxury from menswear, jewelry, fragrances, and denim casualwear to his provocative image advertising.... Capturing the hearts of all those who experience it, the designer's award-winning Bijan Perfume for Women boasts a plethora of stars who indulge in its floral oriental notes. From Annette Bening, Julia Ormond and Whitney Houston to Oprah Winfrey, Princess Diana, Hillary Rodham Clinton...the essence of quality has become legend at the House of Bijan.

In February 1994, Woman's Journal U.K. quoted Bijan saying, "I get calls from the most powerful men in the world in the middle of the night, asking me what they should wear.... On one occasion, I had three Prime Ministers in my New York showroom at once."

Dineh & Pooneh Mohajer- A former U.S.C. bio-chemistry student, Dineh created the line of Hard Candy nail-polish in 1995 when she was unable to find a pale-blue polish to match her pumps and resorted alchemizing her own. When Pooneh-her sister- saw it, she spotted a business opportunity. After the runaway success of an initial 200-bottle delivery to L.A.'s fashionable clothing store Fred Segal, the Hard Candy line caught the attention of many other retailers and became a favorite accouterment among young celebrities. Within a year of launching, Hard Candy had sold $10 million worth of nail polish, expanding its palette from four colors to 43. Knockoffs soon appeared from big-league competitors Estee Lauder and Revlon, while Mohajer struck back by expanding into matching lipsticks and eye shadows. Inspired by Hard Candy's growing popularity among rock stars and surfers, the company launched its male counterpart, Candy Man, in 1997. Today, Hard Candy's nail, lip and eye makeup can be found on cosmetic counters around the world. In March 2000, Forbes magazine wrote: "With a brilliant sense of style and a knack for mixing colors, Dineh Mohajer shook up the staid nail polish industry."

Finance

Afsaneh Mashayekhi Beschloss is the director of the World Bank's investment management department and chief officer responsible for pension investments, managing World bank and affiliated institution assets of about $35 billion and pension assets and other benefits of about $10 billion. She joined the Bank in 1981 and has served in various capacities, including economist and division chief in energy operations, special assistant to the Senior Vice President for finance, investment officer responsible for management and trading of the Bank's fixed income portfolio, and senior manager for derivative products and liability for the Bank's borrowing operations.

Mrs. Mashayekhi serves on the New York Stock Exchange Pension Managers Advisory Board, as well as on investment fund advisory boards, and provides advice to a number of pension investment funds and central banks in emerging markets. Before joining the Bank, she taught international trade and development economics at Oxford University, worked with Shell international on scenario analysis and strategic planning, and as a financial adviser with J.P. Morgan. She is the author of two books on natural gas economics.

At the time of this print Ms. Mashayekhi was with the Carlyle Group where former U.S. President George Bush, former U.S. Secretary of State James Baker, former Prime Minister of Great Britain John Major may be considered as her colleagues.

Javad Khalilzadeh-Shirazi is responsible for the World Bank's East Asia development strategy and relationship-building with major financial partners and other stockholders. He is a key spokesperson on the Bank's approach to the financial crisis in east Asia. Prior to his appointment in 1977, he directed World Bank programs in Cambodia, Korea, Lao PDR, Malaysia, Mekong Committee, Myanmar, Philippines, Thailand, and Vietnam, managing an annual lending program worth about $1.5 billion, and a portfolio of 96 development projects in eight countries. Earlier bank positions include director of resident staff in India, chief of India Country operations (industry and finance), chief of public economics, and chief of resource mobilization in the country policy department.

Media

Christiane Amanpour- CNN Chief International Correspondent Christiane Amanpour has worked in most of the hot spots of the 1990's. Her reputation as a world-class correspondent began with her reporting of the dramatic changes occurring in central Europe during 1989 and 1990. During her assignment in the Persian Gulf, she covered the Gulf War from Iraq's invasion of Kuwait in 1990 to the Kurdish refugee crisis on the

Iran/Iraq border that persisted after the cease-fire. She also covered the break-up of the Soviet Union in 1991 and subsequent war in Tblisi.

Amanpour's reports from former Yugoslavia have received a News and Documentary Emmy, George Foster Peabody Award, George Polk Award, courage in Journalism Award, Worldfest-Houston International Film Festival Gold Award and the Livingston Award for Young Journalists. She was named the "1994 Woman of the Year" by the New York Chapter of Women in Cable and Telecommunications and "1996 Person of the Year" by the national organization of The Iranian-American Republican Council. In addition, she helped CNN win a DuPont Award for its Bosnia coverage and a Golden Cable Ace for its Persian Gulf War coverage. Her contribution to the 1985 four-week series, "Iran: In the Name of God," helped CNN earn its first DuPont award.

Asieh Namdar is Asieh Namdar is an anchor and segment producer for CNN Headline News. She also provides in-depth reports and analysis on developing and breaking international stories. During her tenure at CNN, Namdar has reported on numerous stories and events, including the Middle East conflict, the war in Afghanistan, Iraq and relations between the United States and Iran. Namdar has also interviewed various world leaders and newsmakers, including former U.S. President Jimmy Carter, Jordan's Queen Rania and former Pakistani Prime Minister Benazir Bhutto.

Rudabeh (Rudi) Bakhtiar is a news anchor for CNN Headline News. Bakhtiar was on the air live when the Sept. 11 terrorist attacks began. She reported throughout that day. She has provided multiple reports for the network while on assignment from numerous countries including South Africa, Israel, Rwanda, Ethiopia and Indonesia.

Medicine

Mina Bissell is a cell biologist and director of Life Sciences Research at the Lawrence Berkeley national laboratory. She is one of the seven researchers to receive the Ernest Orlando Lawrence Award from the U.S. Department of Energy for her work in breast cancer research. Dr. Bissell, a graduate from Harvard University, discovered a direct link between breast cancer and the extracellular breast cells. She was elected to the Institute of Medicine, National Academy of Sciences, was Chair, NASA Committee on the Role of Animal Research in Space, was member Secretary of energy's Advisory Committee, President of American Society of Cell Biology, and elected fellow of American Association for Advancement of Science. Dr. Mina Bisselle has extensive publications and has received numerous awards.

Habib Fakhrai, Ph.D. is a cancer scientist at the University of California in Los Angeles who has developed a vaccine that has completely eliminated brain tumors in all laboratory rats tested. The study, published in the proceedings of the National Academy of Science, appear so promising that they have caused a wave of reaction from news media around the world. The anti-cancer vaccine uses advanced genetic engineering, called antisense technology, to prevent cancer cells from secreting a protein that would otherwise shield them from the body's immune system and allow them to spread unchecked.

Dr. Jamshid G. Ghajar, called "Life Saver" by The New Yorker Magazine- is a neurosurgeon with a M.D. and a Ph.D. who has ten medical-device patents to his name. At age 17, as a resident of New York Hospital, Ghajar invented a device that made the cover of the Journal of Neurosurgery.

According to The New Yorker, Dr. Ghajar is one of the country's leading neuro-trauma specialists. In 1993, Dr. Ghajar, along with Dr. Randall Chestnut and Dr. Donald W. Marion, in conjunction with the Brain Trauma Foundation gathered some of the world's top brain injury specialists together for eleven meetings between the winter of 1994 and summer of 1995. Four thousand scientific papers covering fourteen aspects of brain-injury management were reviewed. In March of 1996, the group produced a book laying out the scientific evidence and state-of-the-art treatment in every phase of brain-trauma care.

The New Yorker states: "The guidelines represent the first successful attempt by the neurosurgey community to come up with a standard treatment protocol, and if they are adopted by anything close to a majority of the country's trauma centers, they could save more than 10,000 lives a year. A copy has now been sent to every neurosurgeon in the country."

Dr. Camran Nezhat is the Director of the Stanford Endoscopy Center for Training and Technology, clinical professor of surgery and clinical professor of OB/GYN at Stanford University. Best known for his groundbreaking innovations in laparoscopy, Dr. Nezhat has made significant contributions to the field of minimally invasive surgery. The benefits of the introduction and adoption of the new techniques he created are seen world-wide by thousands of patients who are able to enjoy fast recovery time and improved outcome as a result of these procedures.

Dr. Farhang Soroosh was the first neurosurgeon ever to practice in Casper, Wyoming. Dr Soroosh saved the lives of so many people and had such an impact on the citizens of that state that a Bill (F.F. 204 or the Soroosh Bill) was passed by the state legislature in 1969 extending the time, from five to eight years, in which a physician or surgeon could practice medicine in Wyoming on a temporary license before becoming a U.S. citizen. A former mayor of Casper was quoted in the local papers as stating: " the people aren't thinking about the mineral tax or the possible raise in property tax, but about what the legislature will do to keep Dr. Farhang Soroosh in Casper."

Politics

Shireen Hunter Tahmasebi is the director of the Islamic Studies program at Center for Strategic & International Studies. She previously served as director of the Mediterranean Studies program with the Center for European Policy Studies in Brussels. Dr. Hunter is the author of many books, including *The Future of Islam and the West: Clash of Civilizations or Peaceful coexistence?* (CSIS/Praeger, 1998), *Central Asia Since Independence* (CSIS/Praeger, 1996), and *The Transcaucasus in Transition: Nation-Building and Conflict* (CSIS, 1994). Her articles have appeared in leading journals such as Foreign Affairs, Foreign Policy, Current History, the Middle East Journal, Security Dialogue, the International Spectator, Relazioni Internazionali, the Third World Quarterly, and SAIS review, as well as prominent newspapers including the Los Angeles Times and the Christian Science Monitor. She holds a Ph.D. in political science from the Institute Universitaire des Hautes autudes Internationales in Geneva and an M.A. from London School of Economics and Political Science.

Science

Dr. Firouz Naderi became the manager of the Mars Program Office at NASA's Jet Propulsion Laboratory in April 2000. Prior to that, Naderi was the manager of NASA's Origins Program since 1996. He joined JPL in

1979 and has served as program manager for space science flight experiments and project manager for the NASA Scatterometer project. In addition, he was program manager at NASA Headquarters for the Advanced Communications Technology Satellite program and at JPL for the Mobile Satellite program. The new Mars Program Office will serve as the single point- of-contact for NASA Headquarters at JPL for all Mars exploration efforts. The office will work closely with the NASA Headquarters Mars Directorate Office for the development and implementation of the long-term strategy for the robotic exploration of Mars, as well as for the program's architecture and management of related funding. Born March 25, 1946, in Shiraz, Iran, Naderi holds three degrees in electrical engineering: a bachelor's from Iowa State University, Ames, IA, and a master's and doctorate from the University of Southern California.

Jaleh Daie, Ph.D. was inducted into the International Network of Women in technology (WITI) Hall of Fame in June 1996. She is a professor at the University of Wisconsin-Madison and senior advisor to the System Vice President for Academic Affairs. She is also president of the Association for Women in Science (AWIS) in Washington, D.C.

Daie is a member of the Executive Board of the Council of Scientific Society Presidents (CSSP). She also serves in various capacities at the national level for agencies including National Science Foundation, National Institute of Health, and the National Research Council. She was an invited participant at the White House /OSTP-sponsored Forums in 1994 and 1995, and the White House Women's Leadership Briefing in 1995. She has authored or co-authored more than eighty scholarly papers and articles. She holds a Ph.D. in plant physiology. Mrs. Daie is listed in several Who's Whos including America, Science & Engineering, and World.

Professor Faghri, Distinguished Professor of Mechanical Engineering at University of Ohio, Dayton, has been closely working with NASA in space programs on Thermal & Heat Transfer matters involved in space missions.

Professor Abol-ghasem Ghaffary is a retired professor of Mechanical and Aeronautical Engineering who was one of the major scientists and researchers at NASA in the 1960's just after it was renamed from NACA to include space programs into its agenda. As a leading aerodynamicist, he was responsible for research in the area of supersonic flight and gas dynamics in super and hypersonic conditions.

Najmedin Meshkati, Ph.D. is the Director of the School of Engineering Continuing Education programs of University of Southern California which include the 47-year old USC Aviation Safety, Transportation Safety, and Process Safety Management. He is also an Adjunct Scholar at the Department of Human Work Sciences and the Center for Ergonomics of Developing Countries, Luela University of Technology in Sweden.

Dr. Meshkati was a member of the Committee on Human Performance, Organizational Systems and Maritime Safety. The committee was organized by the National Research Council (NRC), the NRC's Commission on Engineering and Technical Systems, and the NRC's Marine Board. He is also a member of the Review Panel for the NRC, which is the principal operating agency of the National Academy of Sciences and the National Academy of Engineering. He has been either the principal investigator or co-investigator for several funded research projects, including two by the U.S. Nuclear Regulatory Commission.

Meshkati's articles are published in numerous scholarly journals. He is the co-editor and a primary author of the book Human Workload, North Holland, 1988. His technical reports and articles on safety, health and environment; the risk management, ergonomics and safety of petrochemical plants and nuclear power stations; and aviation safety have been published, disseminated and cited by different United Nations specialized agencies such as the U.N. Industrial Development Organization (UNIDO), the U.N. Educational, Scientific and Cultural Organization (UNESCO), the International Labor Office (ILO), and the International Civil Aviation organization (ICAO).

Dr. Meshkati is a fellow of the Human factors and Ergonomics Society and a recipient of the Presidential Young Investigator Award from the National Science foundation in 1989. His analysis of the Bhopal (India) disaster earned him the 1988 American Society for Training and Development International Research Award. He is also the recipient of the 1985 Cooperation and Appreciation Award from the Ministry of Manpower, Government of Indonesia. He was the organizer and the first chairman of the Human factors and Ergonomics Society's Technical Group on International Technology transfer. He was the chairman of the International Ergonomics Association (IEA) Committee on Technology Transfer and Developing Countries from 1985 to 1995. As the Chair of the "Group of Experts," Meshkati coordinated international efforts which culminated in the publication of the ILO Ergonomic Checkpoints book in 1996, and he received the 1997 International Ergonomics Association Award for his role and contribution. The book is published in 11 languages.

Parviz Moin, Ph.D. is the professor of Mechanical Engineering and Director of Center of Turbulence Research at Stanford University. Dr. Moin is the youngest member of the prestigious National Academy of Engineering.

Manijeh Razeghi, Ph.D. is one of the leading researchers in the field of optolectronics. She was responsible for the design and implementation of epitaxial growth techniques such as metalorganic chemical vapor deposition (MOCVD), VPE, MBE, and metalorganic molecular beam epitaxy (MOMBE). She has developed a number of semiconductors, advanced photonic and electronic devices such as lasers, photodetectors, and transistors which are in turn used in fiber optics communication.

Dr. Razeghi received Ph.D. degrees in both Physics and Materials Science from the University of Paris. She is the Walter P. Murphy Professor of Electrical Engineering and Computer Science, and Director, center for Quantum Devices at Northwestern University. She holds 50 patents, is the author of The MOCVD Challenge: Vol. 1 (1989) and Vol. 2 (1995), and the author and co-author of more than 700 papers. Dr. Razeghi is the co-editor of the Journal of Applied Physics, associate editor of Opto-Electronics Review (Poland), and a member of the editorial board of Semiconductor Science and technology, the Journal of Opto-electronics, and the SPIE Press Editorial Advisory Board. She was awarded the prestigious IBM Europe Science and technology Prize in 1987 and received the 1995 Achievement Award from the Society of Women Engineers (SWE). Dr. Razeghi has chaired several international conferences on Physical Concepts of Materials for Opto-electronics Device Applications.

Professor Cumrun Vafa is a world-renowned theoretician of physics in string theory. He is nicknamed as the "Ace of Harvard". The Presidential Young Investigator Award is among many awards that this member of National Science Foundation has received.

Professor Lotfi A. Zadeh is the creator of the concept of "Fuzzy Logic", an unorthodox theory which has had a great impact on computer technology.

His original paper on Fuzzy Logic was first published in 1965 and encountered skepticism and, in his words "occasional downright hostility". Three decades later, people are studying this field in every country which offers advanced education. Twelve journals are now published which include the word "Fuzzy" in their title. An estimated 15,000 articles have been published. An estimated 3,000 patents have been applied for and 1,000 granted. The Japanese, with 2,000 scientists involved in Fuzzy Logic, have been very quick to incorporate this concept in the design of consumer products, such as household appliances and electronic equipment. Panasonic/Quasar acknowledged that in 1991-1992 alone, they had $1 billion worth of equipment that used Fuzzy Logic.

The "father of Fuzzy Logic" finished high school at Alborz in Tehran in 1938, received his B.S. degree in engineering from University of Tehran in 1942, his M.S. from M.I.T. in 1946, and his Ph.D. from Columbia University in 1949, where he began teaching Systems Theory. From 1959 trough 1990, Zadeh taught at Berkeley. He is now Director of U.C.-Berkeley Initiative on Soft Computing.

He is affiliated with 30 journals, including Automation and Soft Computing, where he is the honorary editor. He received the IEEE Education Medal in 1973, the IEEE Centennial Medal in 1984, Japan's Honda Award in 1989, the IEEE Richard W. Hamming Medal in 1992, ASME's Rufus Oldenburger Award in 1993, and the IEEE Medal of Honor in 1994.

IRAN AS A SUPERPOWER

Much has been documented about the role and contributions of the Persians in the history of civilization. Indeed history and those familiar with Persia of yesterday and Iran of today have often referred to the Persian Empire as a nation of superpower in every sense of the word. Comte de Gobineau very aptly observes:

The Persians...are a very old nation, and, as they say themselves, perhaps the most ancient of the world which has had a regular government and has played the role of a great people. This reality is present in the mind of the whole Iranian family. It is not only the educated class that knows it and expresses it; people of the lowest level believe in it, come back to it readily, and make of it the subject of their ordinary conversations. This is the basis of the firm feeling of superiority which constitutes one of their common ideas and forms an important portion of their moral patrimony.

For some seven thousand years, the Persians were recognized and praised for their rich cultural history and their persistence in offering these qualities to humankind. The determination by the Persians to excel was often tested and interrupted by those who waged war and wreaked havoc on their empire. Although Alexander of Macedonia did defeat the Persians in battle, he became exposed to and was influenced by this "super" culture.

The interruption was short-lived. The Sassanians revived the empire and for the next four hundred years extended the Persian influence throughout the Old World.

Next the Arabs invaded the region. But here too the superiority of the Persian culture and mentality prevailed. The Arabs were so influenced by this rich culture that they became the vehicle for disseminating it throughout the world, from China to Spain.

Later, the barbaric Mongols imposed their destructive presence on China, India, Persia and Russia as far as Kiev. Not surprisingly, these invaders were also exposed to and affected by the Persians' devotion to culture. The impression was so great that the Mongols were transformed and became a constructive force in promoting and patronizing Persian literature, science and art.

In the fourteenth century, Tamerlane, yet another obsessive and brutal conqueror, so admired Persian literature and poetry that he broke off military campaigning to visit and pay homage to the renowned Persian poet, Hafez.

In the mid twentieth century, Iran's military did not have the sort of sophistication and might to repel the Russian occupation of its Northwestern province. It was Ghavam, Iran's brilliant prime minister, who won the battle of wits against Joseph Stalin.

In the 1970s, for the first time in world military history, a regular army— the formidable Iranian armed forces—won the war against leftist guerilla insurgents in the Sultanate of Oman.

Today, Iranians continue their historical commitment to humanitarianism and time honored hospitality. Despite its own socio-economic plight, the country, according to The Christian Science Monitor, provided refuge to more than 4.5 million displaced Afghani and Iraqi Kurdish victims of war in the 1990s. This humane gesture was acknowledged and applauded by the U.S. Secretary of State in her statement of June 14, 1998.

Today, there are some one million Iranians who live and work in the United States. The U.S. Census data reveal the following about this contingent:

- 46% have a bachelor degree or higher (This academic achievement ranks higher than any other group- whether Americans or other recently-arrived immigrant groups);
- 43% are in professional and managerial positions;
- 35% are in technical and administrative services;
- 10% are in various other vocations;
- 48% are dual income earners;
- 22% own their own businesses.

...And they have a median annual income of $55,501—substantially higher than the national average of $35,492 a year.

It can be said, therefore, that Iranians as individuals continue the tradition of being a people of substance and achievement. As Professor A.U. Pope asserts: "How often has Persia disproved the gloomy prophecies that her day was done. Evidently, Persia is immortal, and her destiny promises to ride with humanity itself." The desire to contribute and the will to excel and make a positive impact are qualities that are necessary to the propagation of progress in partnership. There is much to be gained by all involved.

Should Relations be Resumed?

Throughout the past years compelling arguments have been made in leading U.S. media to encourage the normalization of relations and the resumption of trade with Iran. To this end, it has been widely reasoned that the return to normalcy would be of immense benefit to both nations.

Edward Shirley, a former CIA agent who knows Iran and Iranians well, quietly entered the country in 1994. In his book subtitled "A Spy's Journey into Revolutionary Iran", Mr. Shirley quotes an Iranian as saying: "I love America. All Iranians do. You shouldn't believe all that mollah-shouting. All those people who yelled 'Death to America! Death to America!' really liked America. The akhunds did all that. Iranians have always loved America. We have had problems with the American government, but we love the American people. Personally, I like the American government, too...America saved us from Russia. We will never forget that."[1]

Norie Quintos Danyliw in the News & Views section of U.S. News On Line writes, "What undoubtedly surprises visitors the most is the overwhelming friendliness of the Iranians toward Americans. Strangers we met invited us into their homes, and students engaged us in conversation.... Even in the ultra-religious city of Qum- the one place American tour groups have been barred from entering a mosque- someone in our group found a willing mullah to pose for photos."

Mark Litke, the ABC News correspondent, recently reported from Tehran that Iranians were delighted to have Americans in Iran. "The Americans in the Tajrish Bazaar were almost breathless in describing the goodwill they felt", he added.

And finally and perhaps the most poignant, Bruce Laingen, the last U.S. Charge d'Affaires who was taken hostage by militants, recently remarked, "Iranians are among the most hospitable people in the world. What happened to us was out of character for them. I look forward to going back myself someday."[2]

Other positive signs are: Iran was invited to lend its good offices to solve disputes between Azarbaijan and Armenia, in Sudan, and in Uganda; and Iranian envoys have mediated between ethnic factions in Bosnia, Tajikestan and Afghanestan. Moreover, Iran has muted its opposition to the Middle East peace process and has stepped up its war on drugs. Furthermore, Iran's humanitarian aid to the victims of ethnic cleansing in Kosovo is parallel to U.S. foreign policy regarding this crisis.

Iran deserves a fresh look, and events there are evidence of a proud nation anxious to be restored to its rightful place in the world. These facts require us to develop a future-oriented policy. In fact, according to Gary Sick- who served on the National Security Council staff under Presidents Ford, Carter and Reagan,

The last comprehensive review of U.S. Persian Gulf policy occurred under President Nixon in 1969. Since then the Cold War has ended, the Soviet Union has disintegrated, the United States has replaced Britain as the region's predominant military power, the Iranian monarchy has vanished, Iraq has invaded two of its neighbors, the Asian subcontinent has gone nuclear and oil has evolved from a strategic weapon to a routinely traded commodity.

The need for a policy of positive engagement with Iran makes even more sense when one remembers the speech by congressman Lee Hamilton (D-IN) before the Council on Foreign Relations who stated:

The importance of Iran cannot be denied. Iranians are a proud people, with a long and distinguished history and a rich culture. With over 65 million people, Iran is the most populous country in a region of vital importance to the U.S. national interest, the Persian Gulf. Iran has some of the world's largest oil and natural gas reserves, and it is the second-largest oil producer in the region after Saudi Arabia. Iran controls half the coastline of the Persian Gulf and one side of the Straits of Hormuz, through which half of the world's traded oil moves. Iran borders the Caspian Sea, the Caucasus, and Central Asia, where huge reserves of oil and gas are now being tapped. Poor U.S. ties with Iran harm the competitive position of U.S. companies in Central Asia and make it more difficult to bring new energy supplies to world markets. Iran has a 900 mile border with Iraq.... Improved relations with Iran could lead to comparable benefit. An Iran that rejoins the family of nations and follows its rules could make a major contribution to regional prosperity and stability. A better relationship with

Iran would...improve the climate for the Middle East peace process.

It should be emphasized that the breakup of the Soviet Union in 1991 which resulted in the Caspian area suddenly becoming a region unto itself, filled with newly independent states with their own history, problems, resources and ambitions- to borrow a phrase from Ambassador John J. Maresca- has made Iran's position even more unique. Iran is the only country linking the Caspian with the Persian Gulf and the Indian Ocean.

Moreover, many major issues for the U.S. in the new millennium such as drugs trafficking, international terrorism and proliferation of weapons of mass destruction will require cooperation between Iran and America in order to come to an effective fruition.

On January 31, 2005, during a town hall meeting in the Dean Acheson Auditorium, Secretary of State Dr. Condoleezza Rice stated: "We face a world in which we recognize after September 11th that we have to have change in the Middle East, change based on democratic values, change based on the spread of liberty...." She further remarked: "the Department of State is going to be leading a tremendous effort to use our diplomacy literally to change the world." It is clear that after twenty-six years of trading insults between once close friends and partners, and over two and a half decades of hot rhetoric and mutual recriminations accompanied with an unprecedented lack of dialogue, the path of change may contain bumps, detours and possible setbacks. But patience and mutual goodwill can and should lead both nations to the desired destiny. It is interesting to note that a clergy in the highest echelon of the Islamic government recently remarked in a confidential conversation that the problems between the two countries are like the marital discord between a couple. In spite of all the fights that they may have during the day, they end up making up at night, he added. The same thought was conveyed by former U.S. Secretary of State Cyrus R. Vance when he stated that the two countries' "destinies are intertwined."

A road map leading to normal relations should contain the following:

Encouraging People to People Dialogue - Intellectuals, artists, writers, professors, scientists, journalists and members of humanitarian and non-governmental organizations should have a dialogue on subjects of mutual interest. This will enhance understanding between the two nations which will lead to resumption of friendship and cooperation.

Addressing the Roots of Discord and Resentment - The grievances by both sides should be addressed directly in a neutral setting and corrective measures be taken so that a solid foundation can be laid for a mutually beneficial relationship. These grievances include American interference in internal affairs of Iran as far back as the 1940's. An example of direct intervention can be found in the State Department's archives showing that on October 14, 1946 Ambassador Allen told the shah that he had "finally reached the conclusion that he [the shah] should force [Prime Minister] Ghavam (Qavam) out and should make him leave the country or put him in jail if he caused trouble." This was considered by some as a coup d'etat against Ghavam. This was followed by the infamous 1953 coup against Dr. Mohammad Mosaddegh.

Another thorny issue is what is known in the U.S. as the Status of Forces Agreement (SFA) and in Iran as the Capitulation Agreement which finally came into existence in 1964 under tremendous and continued pressure from the United States. Based on this agreement Americans serving in Iran could no longer be held accountable in Iranian courts for any crimes that they may have committed. This caused an explosive anti-American sentiment among Iranians who considered it an assault on their national sovereignty. The U.S. role in the revolution of 1978-79 and later in the Iran-Iraq war should also be addressed as sources of pain.

Americans have their own reasons for discord, the most important of which is the hostage crisis.

It is heartwarming to note that President Khatami, in addressing the American people on CNN, expressed regret about the hostages. So are Cyrus Vance's remarks addressing American-Iranian Council on January 13, 1999 when he mentioned "America's regrettable role in the 1953 coup...."

Establishing Minimal Diplomatic Relations - By clearly declaring that we have no intention of using an authoritative dialogue to denigrate Iran and that we support the sovereignty and territorial integrity of this ancient country, we should offer to establish a fresh diplomatic relationship on a minimal level. This should be followed by efforts from both sides to establish sufficient mutual respect, confidence and trust. Once this step is accomplished, the U.S. should begin a constructive dialogue with Iran regarding issues of importance to us such as human rights, Middle East peace process, international terrorism, etc. To be most effective, the proverbial economic and recognition "carrot" and positive reinforcement should be made an essential and integral part of the discussions on various issues. The importance of this becomes evident when one takes into consideration Iran's need for foreign direct investment, capital infusion for infrastructure and development projects, and desire for recognition within the international community.

Human Rights - This is probably the most sensitive and the most difficult issue. While it is absolutely necessary to be firm on the issue, the

U.S. should make it clear to the Iranian government that it should not be considered as interference in their internal affairs. Human rights is and should be a universal concern and for all people regardless of their religion, type of government, culture and customs.

Middle East Peace Process - It may sound strange, but the best way to neutralize Iran's opposition to the peace process is perhaps to get this country involved in the negotiations and publicly seek their input. This may well become the point of convergence- a trilateral thaw- where fear and distrust can be alleviated. Iran has had Jewish people as part of its population as far back as 2,500 years. There is no substantive reason as to why Iran and Israel should not have amicable relations. Persian wisdom, pragmatism and goodwill can be utilized in a positive fashion to help the new road map declared by President George W. Bush reach the desired destination.

International Terrorism- It appears that officials in Iran are abandoning previous policies in this regard, as Iran, too has paid a price for terrorism. President Khatami's policy which was echoed in the declaration of the Organization of Islamic Conference should be used as a foundation for a universal comprehensive anti-terrorism accord.

Nuclear Concerns - Once the U.S. reaches out to Iran for the use of its good offices for the fruition of the Middle East Peace process, and the animosity between Iran and Israel is over, nuclear concerns and fears will substantially diminish on all sides. Moreover, the U.S. should work to revive the Middle East multilateral arms control talks, and gain Iran's participation in them.

President Bush's recent statement that "We are working with European allies...." is very encouraging. It appears that a truly fruitful outcome should include a closely contained and monitored enrichment program as well as economic and political integration of a representative (freely elected) government of Iran with the West. Perhaps the best way of ensuring the implementation of a true and actual monitoring program would be the establishment of a partnership between the U.S. and Iran in the Iranian nuclear industry.

If for nothing else, for the sake of world protection against a Chernobyl-type nuclear disaster, there needs to be a resumption of diplomatic and scientific relations between the United States and Iran. In order to relate the urgency and the needed awareness of potential consequences of such disasters, it is both appropriate and starkly relevant to quote the entire March 1998 article by Najmedin Meshkati, Ph.D., CPE and Guive Mirfendereski, J.D., Ph.D. The authors respectively are professor of engineering at the University of Southern California and professor of International Law at Brandeis

University. The Russian Academy of Sciences has translated Meshkati's research on the safety of nuclear power plants into Russia, and most recently published in a book form. Moreover, Meshkati was a member of the U.S. nuclear inspection team that visited the Chernobyl site.

Dual Engagement:
Nuclear Diplomacy with Russia and Iran

The United States foreign policy with Ukraine has killed two birds with one stone. First, Ukraine has agreed to forgo the manufacture of turbines destined for the Iranian nuclear reactor in Bushehr on the Persian Gulf, which is under-construction with Russian assistance. Second, the U.S. Administration would permit American companies, such as Westinghouse electric, to bid on the $1.2 billion Ukrainian project to complete two unfinished Soviet-ear nuclear reactors. Miffed by all this, Russia countered immediately by offering to have the Iranian turbines manufactured at a factory near St. Petersburg and to sell several more nuclear reactors to Iran, all to be installed in Bushehr. The U.S. has reacted in turn by promising Russia more satellite launch accounts if Russia would forgo its nuclear cooperation with Iran. Russia ignored U.S. requests and has reiterated its commitment to Iran. Russia's aggressive push for selling more reactors to Iran is either intended to amortize the high cost of retooling that factory over making more turbines, or it is the personal initiative of the newly appointed Minister of Atomic Energy, Mr. Yevgeny Adamov, who has a passion for civilian power reactors, and reportedly, is "an active supporter of the Chernobyl-type RBMK reactors" (NYT, 3/17/98). If not dealt with systematically and proactively by the Bush Administration, this contentious nuclear reactors issue would have dire, unintended consequences and could further strain Ruso-American relations.

The Russian reaction points once again to the futility of attempts by the U.S. to isolate Iran. In a porous world, sanctions are really ineffective and coercion cannot control the flow of nuclear technology. The dismal fate of Washington's policy of "dual containment" in the Middle East is proof positive that restriction or containment through foreign economic relations do not work.

Both the U.S. and Israel are concerned about Iran's development of nuclear weapons and their delivery mechanisms, and the U.S. insists that Iran must refrain from seeking nuclear weapons, as a precondition for normalization of relations. As far as nuclear technology is concerned, the issue of nuclear weapons must be de-coupled from development of nuclear energy. On the issue of nuclear weapons, it would be unrealistic to expect Iraq or Iran to forgo the nuclear option when nearby countries like India, Israel, Kazakhestan, Pakistan, and Russia pursue or possess nuclear weapons. The solution to this issue will not come about in any bilateral dialogue, but rather in a comprehensive regional approach based on universal principles of non-proliferation, safeguards, test bans, and international inspections.

By pressuring Russia to cancel its $850 million contract to finish the nuclear reactor in Bushehr, and by providing no viable alternative, the United States unintentionally is taking a major risk, which could have dire consequences for the whole Middle East region. Iran, determined to develop her nuclear energy option, will acquire components for nuclear reactor systems, through various means, from many sources that are scattered around the world. Technically, this effort could result in a piecemeal assemblage of potentially incompatible parts of dubious reliability in an untested reactor of questionable Soviet-designed technology with no operational track record and obsolete safety systems, and virtually no human factors considerations. The radioactive fallout from the April 1986 accident at the Chernobyl nuclear power plant near Kiev in Ukraine spread around the world, including Europe and the United States. Chernobyl taught us that *a nuclear accident anywhere is a nuclear accident everywhere.* A hastily or secretly-designed and untested Iranian nuclear reactor, in the long run, will pose a much greater risk to the region's health and environment than a well-designed, tested and safely operating reactor.

The "cooperative threat reduction program," which was initiated by Senator Sam Nunn (D-GA) and Richard Lugar (R-IN) in November 1991 and targeted the risk and security of nuclear weapons and missile material in Russia, Belarus, Kazakhestan, and Ukraine, is a relevant precedent for the U.S. to pursue in the case of Iran. Furthermore, there is another precedent for the process of cooperation among even discordant countries concerning nuclear weapon and reactor technologies, as has been analyzed masterfully in a recent book by Leon V. Sigal, *Disarming Strangers: Nuclear Diplomacy with North Korea.* (Princeton University Press, 1998). In June 1994, the U.S. went to the brink of war with North Korea about its nuclear weapon programs, but in October 1994 North Korea signed the Agreed Framework, which diffused the crisis. North Korea agreed to forgo nuclear weapons in return for two modern Western (U.S./Japan) light-water nuclear power reactors. Nuclear cooperation would have been almost inconceivable just a few years ago, but it has worked in the case of North

Korea. According to a 1997 study by the General Accounting Office, "nuclear diplomacy" has resulted also in "modest improvements" in the normalization of economic and political relations between the United States and North Korea. That American businesses stand to reap the benefits of nuclear diplomacy is also self-evident.

The premise of nuclear diplomacy or *cooperative threat and hazard reduction* approach toward nuclear technology, is that the most efficient control on technological matters is obtained through the systemic integration of one of the country's technology with that of other countries, such that no one component of the system could operate independently of the total system. Tight integration, inter-dependency and correlation among technologies of different countries provide much more oversight, control, and assurance than does a policy of restrictions and economic or technological embargo. This approach, based on dual engagement with Russia and Iran, constitutes a paradigm shift in foreign policy. It not only will reduce the risk of nuclear accidents, but also it will provide a much more assured and effective control, and accurate verification of nuclear technologies in the receiving countries.

The U.S. agreement with Ukraine will help Ukraine complete the two reactors with the help of safe and superior American nuclear reactor technology. In contrast, by not engaging in nuclear diplomacy with Iran, the U.S. is pushing Iran further into the lap of Russian and Chinese nuclear technology and inadvertently converting Bushehr into a dumping ground for different models of unsafe (and in cases of VVER 440 or Chernobyl-type RBMK, inherently unstable) Soviet-designed reactors. This would subject the Middle East, including Turkey, Israel, Saudi Arabia, Iraq, friend and foe, to the risk of a Chernobyl-type catastrophe radiating from Iran.

Similarities Between the Two Nations

The Persian Empire during the time of Dariush the Great was comparable to today's United States. It was an empire of 29 interdependent provinces of 29 separate peoples enjoying equity under the law. Like the U. S. today, the armed forces were under command and control of the Emperor and independent of the governors.

Persians, like Americans, have always advocated justice and fairness. This is best documented on Dariush' mausoleum: "It is not my desire that the weak man should have wrong done to him by the mighty; nor it is my desire that the mighty man should have wrong done to him by the weak. What is *right*, that is my desire."

Also, former Supreme Court Justice William O. Douglas said: "Persians are spiritually close kin to Americans." According to Will Durant in The Story of Civilization, in the Persian Empire there was a High Court of Justice with seven members (like the U.S. Supreme Court), and below this were local courts with laymen and laywomen sitting as judges. Bail was accepted in all but the most important cases, and a regular procedure of trial was followed. All disputants were proposed an arbitrator of their own choice who might bring them to a settlement. As the law gathered precedents and complexity, there appeared a class of people called "speakers of the law," whose job was to explain the law to litigants and help them conduct their cases (like today's attorneys). The law forbade any one, even the king, to sentence a man to death for a simple crime.

Respect for the environment, love for trees and flowers, and love for animals are other common characteristics between the two nations.

Perhaps the best testament in support of the spiritual closeness between Americans and Iranians is a 2,500 year old bas relief at Persepolis depicting the emblem of the Persian kings which was an eagle with outstretched wings- one that is astonishingly similar to today's official U.S. emblem.

In order to utilize these similarities in a positive way, we need to explore ways to build mutual trust and confidence and avoid taking stances that would generate misunderstanding. Skeptical Iranians seek assurance that the U.S. genuinely desires friendship and will lend support to the cause of Iran's independence and freedom.

A U.S. policy of positive reinforcement is not without significant benefit. As an important oil-producing nation with considerable oil and gas reserves, Iran has a major impact on the availability and the price of these natural resources. Iran's ability to have *positive* political impact in the entire Middle East and its unique geophysical presence in the Caspian region as well as in the Persian Gulf- both from an economical and a military standpoint- are positive factors in the pursuit of equitable relations.

While traditional methods in re-establishing a mutually rewarding relationship are, of course, important, America has in its Persian-American community a readily available reservoir of capable scientists, scholars, statesmen, sociologists and business professionals who have a profound understanding of the subtleties of both cultures. This group, in the United States along with their post revolutionary Iranian counterparts can be considered basic and vital ingredients to create the solid foundation upon which to bridge the interests of the two nations.

When it comes to the resumption of diplomatic relations, both governments must be prepared to observe international protocol and adhere to political and social expediencies.

Six centuries have passed since Hafez, Persia's great poet reflected and represented the deep-rooted ideologies of the people...then and now:

Lasting peace in this world and the next,

Is found in the interpretation of this text:

Always with selfless generosity dealing with friends,

And find, that tolerantly treated enemies will make amends.

The learned and much admired American diplomat in Iran, Luis Dreyfus' advice to his own government was—and this remains true today—: "Our policy should be firm, but kind, forceful, but friendly, insistent, but considerate."

ENDNOTES

1. Shirley, Edward- Know Thine Enemy: A Spy's Journey into

2. Revolutionary Iran (New York: Farrar, Straus and Giroux, 1997), p.74.

3. As quoted in U.S. News On Line, March 22, 1998.

* This author's father taught in that institute for several years.

SELECTED BIBLIOGRAPHY

Abrahamian, Ervand. *Iran Between Two Revolutions*. Princeton, N.J.: Princeton University Press, 1982.

Acheson, Dean. *Present at the Creation*. New York: W.W. Norton, 1969.

Adamiyat, Fereydoon. *Fekr-e Azadi (The Thought of Freedom)*. Tehran: Sokhan, 1961.

Alexander, Yonah, and Allan Nanes, eds. *The United States and Iran*. Frederick, MD.: Aletheia Books, 1980.

Amirie, Abbas, and Hamilton A. Twitchell, eds. *Iran in the 1980s*. Tehran: Institute for International Political and Economic Studies, 1978.

Armajani, Yahya. *Iran* N.J. : Princeton-Hall, Inc., 1972.

_____. *Modernization in Historical Perspective*, 1972.

_____. Personal notes.

Avery, Peter. *Modern Iran*. New York: Praeger, 1965.

_____. *The Cambridge History of Iran*. eds. New York: Cambridge University Press, 1991.

Bahar, Mohammad Taghi. *Tarikh-e-Mokhtasar-e Ahzab-e Siasi-e Iran: Engheraz-e Ghajarieh (A Short History of Political Parties in Iran:The Fall of the Ghajar dynasty)*. Tehran,1321/1942.

Banani, Amin. *The Modernization of Iran, 1921-1941*. Stanford, Calif.: Stanford University Press, 1961.

Behruz, Zabih. *Khat va Farhang (Alphabet and Culture)*, Iran-Kudeh no.8

ed. Mohammad Moghadam. Tehran, 1950.

————.*Taghveem va Tarikh dar Iran (Calendar and History in Iran)*, Iran-Kudeh no.15 .Tehran 1952.

Benjamin, S.G.W., *Famous Nations, the Stories of People Which have Attained Prominence in History*. Vol. II, Part II, the Story of Persia. New York and London, 1892.

————. *The Nations of the World, Persia*. 1889.

Berzezinski, Zbigniew. *Power and Principle: Memoirs of the National Security Advisor, 1977-1981*. New York: Farrar, Straus, and Gitoux, 1983.

Bina, Ali Akbar. *Tarikh-e Siyasi va Diplomasi-ye Iran (Political and Diplomatic History of Iran)* Tehran: University of Tehran Press, 1959.

Bonnie, Michael E., and Nikki R. Keddie, eds. *Modern Iran: The Dialectics of Continuity and Change*. Albany, N.Y.: State University of New York Press, 1981.

Bozeman, Adda B. *Politics and Culture in International History*. Princeton, N.J.: Princeton university Press, 1960.

Browne, Edward Granville.-"*The Press and Poetry of Modern Persia*", Cambridge, 1914.

Cameron, George G. ed., *Persepolis Treasury Tablets*. Chicago: University of Chicago Press, 1948.

Chubin, Shahram, and Sepehr Zabih. *The Foreign Relations of Iran*. Berkeley, Calif.: University of California Press, 1974.

Cottam, Richard. *Nationalism in Iran*. Pittsburgh, PA.: University of Pittsburgh Press, 1979.

Cullican, William. *The Medes and the Persians*. New York: Praeger, 1965.

Dawes, R.R. A *History of the Establishment of Diplomatic Relations with Persia*. Marietta, Ohio: Aldeeman and Sons, Printers,1887.

Entner, Marvin L. *Russo-Persian Commercial Relations, 1828-1914*. Gainesville, Florida: University of Florida Press 1965.

Falsafi, Nasrollah. *Chand Maghale-ye Tarikhi, (A Few historical Essays)*. Tehran: The University of Tehran Press, l962.

Farmayan, Hafez F. *The Foreign Policy of Iran, A History Analysis 559 B.C.-*

A.D.197. Salt Lake City: University of Utah Press 1971.

_____. "The Forces of Modernization in Nineteenth Century Iran," William Polk and Richard Chambers, eds., *Beginnings of Modernization in the Middle East, The Nineteenth Century*. University of Chicago Press, 1968.

Diba, Farhad. *Mohammad Mosaddegh: A Political Biography*. London and Dover, N.H.: Croom Helm, 1986.

Douglas, William O. *Strange Lands and Friendly People*. New York: Harper and Row, 1951.

Eden, Anthony, *Full Circle*. Boston: Houghton Mifflin, 1960.

Fateh, Mostafa. *Panjah Sal Naft-e Iran (Fifty Years of Iranian Oil)*.Tehran, 1335/1956.

Fatemi, N.S. *Diplomatic History of Persia, 1917-1923*. New York: Russle F. Moore, 1952.

Ferrier, R.W. *The History of the British Petroleum Company: The Developing Years, 1901-1932*. Vol. 1. Cambridge: Cambridge University Press, 1982.

Fesharaki, Fereidun, *Development of the Iranian Oil industry: International and Domestic Aspects*. New York: Preager, 1976.

_____. *Zendegani-ye Shah Abbas* (*Life of Shah Abbas*), III .Tehran: Ebn Sina.

_____. *Tarikh-e Ravabet-e Iran va Oroopa dar Doreh-ye Safaviyyeh* (*A history of Irano-European Relations During the Safavid period*) Tehran: Ebn Sina,1939.

Frye, Richard N. *Heritage of Iran*, London: Cambridge University Press, 1975.

_____. *Persia*, New York: Schocken Books, 1960.

Ghirshman, R. *Iran*. Baltimore, MD.: Penguin Books, 1965.

Grant, Asahel, M.D., *Account of the Nestorian Christians Settled in Oroomieh.*, 1840.

Grayson, Benson Lee. *United States- Iran Relations*. Washington, D.C. :University Press of America, 1981.

Hendershot, Clarence. *Politics, Polemics, and Pedagogues*. New York: Vintage Press, 1975.

Heravi, Mehdi. *Iranian-American Diplomacy*. Brooklyn, N.Y.: Theo Gaus' Sons, 1969.

Heuser, Frederick J. Jr., *A Guide To Foreign Missionary Manuscripts in the Presbyterian Historical Society*. New York, 1988.

Hinnells, John R. *Persian Mythology*. New York: Peter Bedrick Books, 1973.

Huyser, Robert E. *Mission to Tehran*. New York: Haroer and Row, 1986.

Irving, Clive. *Crossroads of Civilization: 3,000 years of Persian History*. New York: Barnes and Noble Books, 1979.

Katouzian, Homa. *The Political Economy of Modern Iran: Despotism and Pseudo-Modernism, 1926-1979*. New York: New York University Press, 1981.

Kai-Ostovan, Hossain. *Siasat-e Movazeneh-e Manfi dar Majless-e Chaharda-hom*(The Policy of Negative Equilibrium in the Fourteenth Majless).Vol.1. Tehran, 1327/1949.

Kasravi, Ahmad. *Tarikh-e Mashrooteh-e Iran* (History of Iran's Constitutional Movement). Tehran: Amir Kabir, 1940.

_____. *Tarikh-e Hijdah Saleh-e Azarbaijan* (Azarbaijan's Eighteen Year History). Tehran: Amir Kabir, 1967.

Kazemzadeh, Firooz. *Russia and Britain in Persia, 1864-1914*. New Haven: Yale University Press, 1968.

Keddie, Nikki R. *Religion and Rebellion in Iran, the Iranian Tobacco Protest of 1891-1892*. London: Frank Cass, 1966.

_____. *An Eslamic Response to Imperialism: Political and Religious Writings of Sayyed Jamal al-Din "al-Afghani"*. Berkeley: University of California 1968.

Kermani, Nezam ol-Eslam. *Tarikh-e-Bidari-ye Iranian (History of Persian Awakening)*. Tehran: Bonyad-e Farhang, 1966.

Kirk, George. *The Middle East in the War*, Survey of International Affairs, 1939-1946 series, ed. Arnold Toynbee. London: Oxford University Press, 1952.

Lenczowski, George. *Russia and the West in Iran, 1918-1948*. Ithaca: Cornell University Press, 1948.

Lilienthal, David E. The Journals of David E. Lilienthal. *The Road to Change, 1955-1959*. Volume 4. New York; Harper and Row, 1969.

Louis, Wm. Roger, and James A. Bill, eds. *Mussadiq, Iranian Nationalism and Oil*. London: I.B. Taurisand Co.,1988.

Loukonine, Vladimir & Anatoli Ivanov, *Lost Treasures of Persia*. Washington, DC. 1996.

Lytle, Mark H. *The Origins of Iranian-American Alliance, 1941-1953*. New York: Holmes and Meier, 1987.

McLellan, David S. Dean Acheson: *The State Department Years*. New York: Dodd, Mead, 1976.

Mackey, Sandra. *The Iranians: Persia, Islam and the Soul of a Nation*. New York: The Penguin Group, 1996.

Mahmood, Mahmood. *Tarikh-e Ravabet-e Siasi-e Iran va Inglis dar Gharn-e Noozdahom* (The History of Anglo-Iranian Relations in the nineteenth Century).8 Vols. Tehran, 1336-41/1957-62.

Matheson, Sylvia A. *Persia: An Archeological Guide*. London, 1976.

Millspaugh, Arthur C. *The American Task in Persia* . New York: Century, 1925.

_____. *Americans in Persia*. Washington, D.C.: Brookings Institution, 1946.

Moghaddam, Mohammad. *Mehrabeh ya Parasteshgah-e Deen-e Mehr* (Mithraism or the Temple of the Religion of Mithra).Tehran: Iran-e Bastan, 1965.

_____. *Jostar Dar Bareh-e Mehr va Naheed (Research About Mithraism and Naheed)*. Tehran: Markaz-e Irani-e Motale-e Farhangha, 1958.

Noldeke, Theodor. *Aufsatze zur Persischen Geschichte*. Leipzig, 1884.

Pahlavi, Ashraf. *Faces in a Mirror : Memories from Exile*. Englewood Cliffs, N.J.: Prentice-Hall, 1980.

Pahlavi, Mohammad Reza. *Answer to History*. New York: Stein and Day, 1980.

INDEX